Rev. Gregory J. Pike
213 Millstone Road
PO Box 474
Perrineville, NJ 08535

CALVIN, GENEVA
AND THE REFORMATION

CALVIN, GENEVA
AND THE REFORMATION

A Study of Calvin as Social Reformer,
Churchman, Pastor and Theologian

RONALD S. WALLACE

WIPF & STOCK
PUBLISHERS
790 East 11th Avenue • Eugene OR 97401

1998

Calvin, Geneva and the Reformation
by Ronald S. Wallace
Copyright© 1998 by Ronald S. Wallace

ISBN: 1-57910-099-6

Printed by ⟨WS WIPF & STOCK PUBLISHERS⟩ 1998
790 East 11th Avenue • Eugene OR 97401

CONTENTS

To Mary
with thankfulness
on our
Golden Wedding Anniversary
1937–1987

FOREWORD

For several years I read and collected material for a biographical work on Calvin. I discovered eventually, however, that I was engaged too much in parish work, and in other studies, to be able to master the complicated details of affairs in Geneva to the extent necessary for such a task.

Since I was in the ministry myself, I was especially interested both in the kind of ministry which Calvin set himself to fulfil in his city Church (or Church-city), and in the way in which he actually succeeded in fulfilling it. This book therefore is an account, chiefly drawn from the material I collected, of Calvin's ministry as a social reformer, churchman and pastor in the sixteenth century. It cannot be called a "Life of Calvin", but is, rather, a series of essays on his work and on the thought and devotion which he put into it. Nevertheless, I have tried to give as full and accurate an account as possible, within such limitations of structure, of the early preparation and setting of Calvin's life, and of all the important events of his struggle and triumph in Geneva, so that the reader can have all the necessary facts on hand, without requiring at the same time to consult a biography.

Calvin's work — and his approach to it — can be fully understood only when we comprehend also the constraint in which he found himself under the Word of God; for it was his experience of the Word, and his interpretation of it, which determined what he attempted and achieved. I have tried, therefore, throughout the book, to show how his thought determined his aim and policy. Indeed, I found that his practice helped to direct my attention to aspects of his teaching in the *Institutes* which I had not noticed during my former studies of his writings. Since his chief contribution to the Reformed Church was in the realm of theology, I felt that to justify my title, I owed the reader some distinct account of his teaching on central theological issues, and on doctrines most closely associated with his name.

Calvin's attitude in some matters is difficult for us to understand today, and certain aspects of his policy and activity are partly responsible for a tradition which has persistently circulated amongst those not fully informed — or otherwise unsympathetic — of his harshness and tyranny as a leader, and his inhumanity as a man: this is a tradition that has recently been called "the Calvin Legend". I have attempted to face these problems and accusations, yet it will be obvious to the reader that as I began to understand his thought and aims better, I found myself growing in admiration for his achievement. I have endeavoured to record this appreciation, especially at the end of the book where I try to evaluate him personally.

In the dedication of the book I have expressed something of my gratitude to my wife for her unfailing help and constant encouragement in the writing of it. I am grateful for the excellent library facilities at Columbia Theological Seminary, and for a Sabbatical leave which gave me some time to concentrate directly on the work of writing it. At various stages in the development of the final manuscript, I can remember being indebted to Dr Duncan Shaw, the Rev. A. Ian Dunlop, Dr Peter Toon, Mr Tony Lane, and latterly my son-in-law Professor George Newlands who has given me wise advice and encouragement. Dr Douglas Grant, as always, has been immensely helpful and patient as a publisher. My sister, Miss Mary Wallace, and one of my neighbours, Mrs Fiona Kelly, both gave me invaluable help in the preparation of manuscripts.

Postscript: On the day the page proofs arrived at my home, my dear wife passed away. Although herself extremely ill, she was expecting them as keenly as myself. Thankfully, I have felt no need to alter the present tense implied in the above foreword and dedication.

ABBREVIATIONS USED IN FOOTNOTES

C.L.   *Letters of John Calvin* Vols I–IV, edited by Dr Jules Bonnet,
        English Translation of Vols. I and II, Edinburgh 1835–7,
        of Vols. III and IV, Philadelphia 1858.

C.Tr.   Calvin's *Tracts and Treatises*, Calvin Translation Society
        Edition, Edinburgh.

Inst.   *The Institutes of the Christian Religion.* I have in the text
        adhered mainly to the translation by Henry Beveridge
        (Edinburgh edition, 1879), checking it against the original.
        I have found it helpful to refer at times to that by Ford
        Lewis Battles (Westminster Press, Philadelphia, 1960).

I.C.P. Calvin's Introduction to his *Commentary on the Book of Psalms*,
        as in the Calvin Translation Society Edition, Edinburgh.

R.C.P. *Register of the Company of Pastors in Geneva at the time of Calvin*
        (containing the Ecclesiastical Ordinances of 1541). Trans-
        lated, with Introduction by Philip E. Hughes, Grand
        Rapids 1966.

L.W.   The American Edition of Luther's Works — Concordia.

        Calvin's commentaries when referred to (e.g. *Comm. on
        Gen.*, etc) have been consulted in The Edition of the Calvin
        Translation Society, Edinburgh, and of his New Testament
        commentaries, eds. T. F. and D. W. Torrance, Edinburgh.

        References to his Sermons (e.g. Serm. on) may be
        followed up in, e.g. *John Calvin's Sermons on Ephesians*, The
        Banner of Truth Trust, Edinburgh and London 1973. In
        Sermons of Master John Calvin upon the Book of Job, London
        1574.

C.O.   Refers to the *Ioannis Calvini Opera* in the *Corpus Reformatorum*,
        Brunswick 1863–1900.

CHAPTER I

A SIXTEENTH CENTURY PILGRIMAGE

IN a rare autobiographical passage in the introduction to
his commentary on the Psalms, Calvin briefly reviews
some of the important influences and turning-points in his
early career:

> When I was as yet a very little boy, my father had
> destined me for the study of theology. But afterwards,
> when he considered that the legal profession commonly
> raised those who followed it to wealth, this prospect
> induced him suddenly to change his purpose. Thus it
> came to pass that I was withdrawn from the study of
> philosophy, and was put to the study of the law. To this
> pursuit I endeavoured faithfully to apply myself, in
> obedience to the will of my father: but God, by the secret
> guidance of His providence, at length gave different
> direction to my course. And first, since I was too
> obstinately addicted to the superstitions of papacy to be
> easily extricated from so profound an abyss of mire, God
> by a sudden conversion subdued and brought my mind
> to a teachable frame, which was more burdened in such
> matters than might have been expected from one at my
> early period of life. Having thus received some taste and
> knowledge of true godliness, I was immediately inflamed
> with so intense a desire to make progress therein, that
> though I did not altogether leave off other studies, I yet
> pursued them with less ardour.[1]

The Mediaeval Background

In his boyhood, therefore, he was deeply devoted to the
Roman Church which he was later to renounce: "too

[1] I.C.P., p. xl.

obstinately addicted ... to be easily extricated from so
profound an abyss and mire"!

He was born at Noyon in Picardy, France, on July 10,
1509. His father had worked his way up in the legal
department of the Church to become a secretary to the
Bishop and procurator of the Cathedral. His mother, who
died when he was young, was pious. She is said to have taken
her infant Jean on devotional pilgrimages to local shrines and
altars to reverence the relics and pray to God and the saints.
Described by Beza as being "remarkably religious" in his
youth, Calvin was then sensitive enough to catch something
of the deep yearning for God that lay behind the superstition,
as men and women put out their hands to touch, as they
believed, the hem of Christ's garment. He later criticised such
blind piety in his book *"on Relics"*. It was, however, the
blindness he criticised and not the piety itself. He recognised
that the human soul has implanted deeply within it an
"instinct for religion".[2] He never despised anything that was
truly human.

His father at first thought that he would do well in the
priesthood. "Destined ... for the study of theology" at the age
of twelve he was sent to Paris for his schooling. For this
purpose his father procured for him a cathedral benefice. This
means that throughout his whole student life, Calvin lived on
money originally given for the fulfilment of religious services,
and diverted it for his own use by the payment of a mere
pittance to a local substitute in the cathedral. In Paris, he was
sent for a short period to the *Collège de la Marche* where, he
later confessed, he conceived a great admiration for one of the
leading humanist educators of the age — Mathurin Cordier.
He was soon transferred, however, to the *Collège de Montaigu*.

Descriptions of this latter place speak of foul odours, dirt,
whippings, starvings, iron discipline, rotten food, outmoded
educational methods and obscurantism. Erasmus and
Rabelais both had been pupils of the college and later wrote
grimly about the experience. But because Calvin himself has
left no record of such personal disgust we need not assume, as
his enemies have done, that he found the place exactly to his

[2] Cf. *Inst.*, 1:3:1.

taste. Beza mentions that Calvin was inspired to make remarkable progress in philosophy there by a master who was a Spaniard, "a man of considerable attainments".[3] This was Antonio Coronel. John Major, a famous Scotsman, was also on the staff, and one of its former heads had been connected with the Brethren of the Common Life. It was possibly through this lingering influence that Calvin gained his familiarity with Thomas à Kempis' *Imitation of Christ*. He is certain to have been taught a good deal of Augustine and Bernard, whose writings were to mark his later outlook so deeply.[4]

Before young Calvin went to Paris, the Reformation had broken out elsewhere in Europe. Martin Luther nailed his 95 Theses to the door of the Castle church in Wittenberg in 1517. Huldreich Zwingli began to preach, and to bring about radical reform in Zurich in 1519. The movement was growing and spreading. Its teachings must have been discussed at Montaigu even if to be condemned. Calvin no doubt also later heard contemporary accounts of the meeting between Luther, Zwingli and their followers at Marburg in 1529 when they failed to agree on the doctrine of the Lord's Supper.

We have to regard it as providential that while the Reformation spread vigorously in Germany and Switzerland, he himself, destined to play a decisive part in its later development, and to work for its unity, was being quietly brought up and thoroughly trained within the mediaeval scholastic tradition. He was to throw off much of it when he was delivered from "the superstitions of the papacy". He renounced the Pope, the priestcraft, the mass as it then was, the authority that had been given to church tradition alongside the Scriptures, the pastoral tyranny of the confessional, the erroneous views of grace distributed through institutionally controlled sacraments, and the idea of a monastic vocation superior to those in the secular world. But there was much in his early training which, remaining with

---

[3] Theodore Beza, *The Life of John Calvin*, C.Tr., vol. I, p. xxi.
[4] See A. N. S. Lane: "Calvin's Use of the Fathers and the Medievals", in *Calvin Theological Journal*, 16, 1981, pp. 149-205; and "Calvin's Sources of St Bernard" in *Archiv für Reformationsgeschichte*, 67, 1967, pp. 253ff.

him all his days, helped to shape his later thought, aims, and life-style.

For instance, much of what he later wrote about our need for deliverance from self-love, and of the Christian life as one of stern self-denial and cross-bearing, in conformity to the dying and risen Lord, is closely aligned to the thought and practice of the great mediaeval and monastic devotional writers. The piety with which he fulfilled his earthly vocation controlled in every detail by prayer and the personally discerned will of God, his wonder at the mystery of our union with Christ, and his intense longing for its final perfection in the heavenly life and in beatific vision, were no doubt the developments of attitudes fostered within him even while he was becoming "addicted" to other habits of mind and devotion which he had later to reject. Though he approved of the break-up of the too-close union of civil and ecclesiastical power which had been a central feature of the Christendom of the Middle Ages, his attempt in his own day to find a new basis for the closest possible cooperation of Church and State within a renewed Christian commonwealth shows that he always had a great respect for this aspect of the mediaeval synthesis.

We could, of course, argue cogently that the whole of his later teaching and outlook developed from the Bible. He insisted always that tradition must be constantly corrected by, and subordinated to, the teaching of Holy Scripture. But he was always careful and judicious in sifting within past tradition what was to be rejected from what was to be accepted. No one was more tenacious in holding on to what he had experienced as good, whatever its origin, as long as its retention did not hinder his total subjection of his mind and his life to the Word of God or divert him from following Christ.

Humanism

A rift occurred between the Cathedral chapter and his father, who became alienated from the Church, and changed his mind about his now obviously brilliant son: "my father . . .

afterwards ... considered that the legal profession raised those who follow it to wealth ... Thus it came to pass that I was withdrawn from the study of philosophy and was put to the study of law." Calvin, unlike Luther, in similar circumstances, was obedient. "To this pursuit I endeavoured faithfully to apply myself, in obedience to the will of my father."

He went to study law under the supervision of Pierre de L'Estoile at Orleans, where, during a second formative period, he came strongly under the influence of the humanism that was then affecting the outlook of many teachers in the universities of France and of certain leaders of the Church. He began to seek enlightened and up-to-date teaching, and he went for a time to study under André Alciat at Bourges. After his father's death in 1531, he resided at the *Collège Fortet* in Paris where teaching was sometimes given by the Royal Readers, an illustrious body of humanist scholars recently instituted by Francis I. The place had a flexible curriculum and academic freedom. One of its leading lights was Guillaume Budé who had achieved European fame, along with Erasmus, for humanistic learning. Calvin had already begun to study Greek under Melchior Wolmar at Bourges. He was able to continue it here under Pierre Danés. He was also able to learn the rudiments of Hebrew under François Vatable.

Eventually, in April 1532, he published his Commentary on Seneca's *De Clementia*. Seneca's book is a plea for merciful rule by those who have power. This first work proves that Calvin had a good deal of natural sympathy with the sensible and sober outlook of Seneca; that he was an immensely capable scholar; and that he now was ambitious to be recognised by the learned men of his day as a contemporary of notable stature and original judgment.

Beza asserts that even when he was at Orleans Calvin made "astonishing progress", often "officiated for the professors and was considered rather a teacher than a pupil". He quotes reports from "persons still alive" who knew Calvin at this period to the effect that his habit was to sup frugally, study till midnight, to rise in the morning to meditate for the purpose

of "digesting what he had read in bed". Beza attributes to
such habits the weakness of stomach which was later the cause
of his innumerable sicknesses and "untimely" death.[5]

The young student seems to have opened his mind, and his
life too, to what such humanism could give him. Some of his
biographers associate this time with a portrait of him
fashionably groomed and looking well pleased with life. Can
we take this also as a sign that his "addiction to Rome" was
tending to become undermined? After all, humanism was a
movement of protest against everything that restricted
human thought, cramped the human spirit and narrowed
human experience.

Calvin's sympathies at this time seem to have been moving
towards reform of some kind within the Church. The need for
such reform had been discussed by a group of men who had
been much influenced by the great French humanist Lefèvre
d'Étaples. They were Guillaume Budé, Guillaume Briçonnet
(the Bishop of Meaux) and Gerard Roussel. To these men
humanism was in harmony with true Christianity. What was
best in humanism, they affirmed, had helped them to
rediscover what was best in the Gospel itself. They carefully
studied Holy Scripture as they had studied the other
documents of the past. They were excited with what they
found, and with the comparisons they could now make. The
Gospel itself was seen as a Christian philosophy relevant now
to the new age of enlightenment in which they were living.
They made Bible translations and encouraged people to
study the Word of God for themselves. They sought to bring
gradual change within the present structure of the Church.
They were convinced that the Gospel had not been properly
understood by those in France who were seeking to defend
every aspect of the distorted form and life of the Church from
the attacks of Luther. They did not wish to provoke division
but they said bold things. Their influence spread. The
response within the diocese of Meaux was such that in 1525
the Bishop, Guillaume Briçonnet, had been forced by the
authorities finally to clamp down on the developments that
were taking place under his charge. Marguerite of

[5] *Op. cit.*, pp. xxii–xxiii.

Angoulême, the king's sister, however, gave the whole movement her patronage and even sheltered its adherents in her court when things were dangerous for them.

In 1533, Calvin found himself in trouble in Paris. On November 1st, his friend Nicolas Cop gave the inaugural address as Rector of the University in the church of the Mathurins. The address interpreted part of the Sermon on the Mount as Erasmus might have done, and if it had a flavour of Lutheranism it was a very mild one. But it was based on a contrast between the Old religion and the New. It had a certain amount of passion and it was felt to constitute a serious challenge to the conservative establishment in the State and University. The authorities had heard too much of this kind of thing, and now moved to suppress it. There was an immediate search for Cop and for Calvin. It is obvious that they had both underestimated what might happen, and they had to take flight. Some scholars think that Calvin himself actually wrote this address, for there is extant a copy of it in his own writing. But this need not imply actual authorship.

Calvin fled to Angoulême where he stayed in seclusion with his friend Louis du Tillet and studied in his library. He visited the court of Queen Marguerite and met Lefèvre d'Étaples himself. Perhaps the stir made by the address helped Calvin to realise that even a programme of quiet and steady reform was not going to win over the forces of reaction in France. Perhaps he asked himself whether bolder thinking might not lead him nearer to the truth, and a bolder witness might not have more effect on the situation around him. It was probably not long after this period of retreat that there occurred the "sudden conversion" to which he refers in the preface to his *Commentary on the Psalms*.

Sudden or Gradual?

Calvin's biographers disagree over both the date and the nature of the "sudden conversion" which he refers to as an episode of some significance in his early life. The fact that he mentions it only once in his writings and that alongside his account he speaks of achieving only a "taste of true godliness" has led a number of historians to consider it simply as the initial stage of a long period, lasting possibly for seven years, in which he gradually made progress in seeing things differently; came to a fuller experience of the new life; and gradually came to see how false and empty the Roman Church teaching really was. Beza, who was his closest associate in Geneva for many years, gave currency to this view. It allows us to date the initial experience as early as 1527, at the very beginning of his excursion into the new world of humanistic study. It suggests that the Reformer lived with his religion as an increasingly uncomfortable burden on his mind all through the years of his study for the legal profession and for his doctorate.

Several important considerations make us reject this account. It seems unlikely that Calvin would rank as a "sudden conversion" any inward experience which did not visibly bring about an acknowledgeable change in outward ways and professed loyalties. The fact that he was now greatly "inflamed with an intense desire to make progress" in what he had encountered suggests rather an introductory experience with a good deal of warmth, breadth and illumination.

Moreover, the strong "addiction", which Calvin confesses he had to Rome, indicates one of his natural characteristics. He was the type of man to hold his life-patterns and views closely bound together in one coherent whole, and so deeply based that any great change could come only through a violent, and therefore sudden, psychological upheaval. In a defence of the Reformation which he wrote later, his *Reply to Sadoleto*, there is a passage in which he tries to show how rational and deliberate were the decisions of his contemporaries when they left Rome to join the Reformation. He describes a convert as at first lending "an unwilling ear" to the new teaching, as "strenuously and passionately" resisting it, and as having the "greatest difficulty"[6] in admitting past

---

[6] *Reply to Cardinal Sadoleto's Letter*, C.Tr., vol. I, p. 62. For a full discussion of this matter cf. F. Büsser, *Calvin's Urteil uber sich selbst*, Zurich, 1950, pp. 26ff; also John T. McNeill, *History and Character of Calvinism*, N.Y., 1954, pp. 109ff.

error. No doubt there is something autobiographical in this account.

Calvin, finally, at the time we suggest for his conversion, was openly committed to loyalty to the Roman Church and was now living off the endowment of benefices. It would be quite uncharacteristic for him secretly to be one thing and publicly another. He despised such conduct. Later he always advised those in France who accepted the Reformed faith to break outwardly with the Roman Church, and there is no trace of any confession that he himself had ever been involved in such hypocrisy. But Calvin had visited Noyon in 1533 to make arrangements for certain prayer services, without showing any sign of change of mind or heart. It was not till 1534 that he went back and resigned his benefices. His sudden conversion, we may asume, had taken place during this interval.

Of course it had been prepared for. He had studied Holy Scripture. He had been influenced to some extent by his cousin Olivetan, who had translated the New Testament into French. He at least had had information about Luther's writings and had been interested in reports of the colloquy at Marburg. He had been in Paris when Protestants had suffered martyrdom and had had lodgings at one time in the house of one of these — Étienne de la Forge. An avalanche can be prepared for in that the circumstances that bring it about gradually build up. It can be, nevertheless, a sudden and cataclysmic affair when it occurs.

The "Peculiar Power" of Holy Scripture

We relate Calvin's "intense desire to make progress" and his lessening ardour in pursuing his "former studies" to the fact that from this time on the whole corpus of humanistic literature to which he had ardently devoted himself began to suffer neglect, as his time and attention were taken up with the study of Holy Scripture.

At the heart of all the experience and inspiration that lay behind the Reformation we always find this one book. It was through the Bible that Luther heard it said "Christ is your own, with his life, teaching, works, death, resurrection, and all that he is, has, does, and can do",[7] and was able to know himself justified. It was through the Bible that the Reformers found themselves brought continually to the cradle at Bethlehem, and to the cross at Calvary, and thus to the place where they knew at last they could see God as he truly is. Moreover in all their reading of it and in their listening at its door, they heard continually the living voice of Christ himself, and thus experienced communion with the power of his resurrection. When they made Holy Scripture their sole authority they were not simply seeking to replace the old Pope by a new one; they were, rather, paying tribute to the most joyful and liberating element in their new Christian experience. Whenever they spoke about that experience they were inevitably forced to acknowledge the part played in it by the Word of God.

We are therefore simply placing Calvin's experience alongside that of all who were caught up into support of the Reformation, if we think of it as an experience of the power of the Word of God to thrust itself into the centre of a man's life and affections, and to transform all things. In a passage in the *Institutes* he describes this power:

Now this power which is peculiar to Scripture is clear from the fact that of human writings, however artfully polished, there is none capable of affecting us at all comparably. Read Demosthenes or Cicero: read Plato, Aristotle or any other of that class. You will, I admit, feel wonderfully allured, delighted, moved, enchanted. But turn from them to the reading of the sacred volume and whether you will it or not, it will so powerfully affect you, so pierce your heart, so work its way into your very marrow, that compared with the impression so produced, the power of the orators and philosophers will almost disappear; making it clear that the Holy Scriptures breathe something divine, which lifts them far above all the gifts and graces of human industry.[8]

[7] L.W., vol. 35, p. 361.
[8] *Inst.*, 1:8:1.

We are justified in regarding this passage as an account of his own personal experience. It is a confession by Calvin himself that after years of searching for enlightenment where it should most naturally be found — amongst the world's greatest thinkers and observers of nature and human life — he had found himself still ignorant of a whole new realm which the human soul must enter in order to find God and final truth. Holy Scripture alone had enabled him to hear the living divine voice addressing him personally, had thus introduced him to the true God who presents himself in his grace to be known and grasped by the humble and believing.

Here was now opened up to him a vast new world of knowledge standing over against and infinitely surpassing everything he had hitherto seen and understood. Through the Bible he had come to know his creator and redeemer. It was the course his experience took in this matter which made Calvin's theology finally always centre on Christ and the Scriptures.

Augustine somewhere confesses that had he known Christ before he threw himself with all his natural ardour into the pursuit of philosophy and the religious cults of his day, he would have come to the conclusion that these things had something of Christ in them. Only the fact that during his years of devotion at their altars, they had nonetheless still left him Christless, had convinced him now that in themselves they were devoid of the truth. Calvin's conversion, like that of Augustine, took place after some years of intense study within humanism which had been presented to him as a close ally of the Gospel, and he had accepted it at the time as having Christian content. But when it took place, it must have made him conscious of how little, if any, of the new light of the Gospel had trickled through to him in the midst of what he now called "my former studies".

CHAPTER 2

CALL AND EARLY MINISTRY

1534-1536 — A Doctor of the Church

PARIS, Poitiers, Orleans, Strasbourg, Basel, Italy — these
are the main points in the itinerary of Calvin during these
two years or more. He confesses himself "somewhat
unpolished and bashful". His timidity made him seek "some
secluded corner" to find peace for study. But his retreats
became "like public schools" for "before a year had elapsed,
all who had any desire for pure doctrine were continually
coming to me to learn, although I myself were as yet a mere
novice and tyro".[1] His stay at Orleans is to be connected with
the writing of his first theological work *Psychopannychia* — a
book against one aspect of current Anabaptist teaching. The
subtitle explains it: "A refutation of the error entertained by
some unskilful persons who ignorantly imagine that in the
interval between death and judgment the soul sleeps,
together with an explanation of the condition and life of the
soul after this present life." The book was later printed in
1542.

He passed through Strasbourg on his way to Basel where he
arrived early in 1535. There he worked in partial seclusion
publishing, in March 1536, the first edition of the *Institutes of
the Christian Religion*. This was then a comparatively short
work of compact size. The Reformed faith was, in France,
being confused both with the wild teachings of the
Anabaptists and with revolutionary and seditious doctrines.
Its followers were being persecuted indiscriminately, as if
their beliefs were to be identified with such "perverse ravings
and false opinions". Calvin wanted therefore to give a fair
account of it. He introduced his book with a letter to the King

[1] I.C.P., p. xli.

of France appealing for fairness in judgment and clemency. "Had the monarch read it" says Beza, "I am much mistaken if a severe wound would not even then have been inflicted on the Babylonish harlot." The letter reveals that Calvin's aim in writing was also pastoral. He had found many of his fellow countrymen in various places "hungering and thirsting for Christ" yet completely uninstructed. He therefore gave them a handbook to help them to understand.

In the spring of 1536 he set out again on his travels, this time journeying to Italy under the assumed name of Charles d'Espeville (a name which he frequently used in later correspondence). He undertook this journey in order to see Renée, the Duchess of Ferrara, a daughter of Louis XII who had given shelter in her court to a number of important refugees of the Reformed faith. Calvin "confirmed her in her zeal for true religion", says Beza. She later sought his help and advice through correspondence. The future Reformer met Clement Marot the French poet and hymn writer under her roof.

There can be little doubt that by this time the publication of the *Institutes* had given him some reputation among the Reformers, and he had thrown himself decisively into the Church struggle on their side. Indeed, his life-work within the Church had already begun. He believed that, of the two chief offices appointed by Christ for a permanent place in the Church, the nearest to that of pastor or bishop was to become a doctor — i.e. a theological professor — who had the responsibility for the maintenance of "sound doctrine" generally throughout the Church.[2] He regarded himself at this time as fulfilling such an office even though the unsettledness of the times did not allow him to enjoy a regular ordination to such a ministry.

The Call to Geneva

Though Calvin's father had died in 1531, his affairs had not yet been settled. Calvin therefore had made a journey to France after his return from Italy to wind up the estate. After

[2] *Inst.*, 4:3:4.

this, in June 1536 he met his brother Antoine and his sister
Marie in Paris and persuaded them to follow him abroad. He
had set out intending to go to Strasbourg or Basel but a war
that had broken out made the way impossible, and he had
had to make a diversion which led him into Geneva. There
Guillaume Farel met him. Farel, a fellow Frenchman, twenty
years older than Calvin, had been largely responsible for
bringing about the Reformation of the Church in Geneva;
and he now felt he desperately needed Calvin's help.

Farel had taken part in the Reformist movement at Meaux
to which we have already referred. He had fled from the
persecution to Switzerland, and had preached in many areas
round about Bern, remaining courageous and undaunted in
face of bitter opposition, and effectively spread the influence
of the Reformation. He first entered Geneva in October 1532
with Antoine Saunier and Pierre Robert Olivetan. He made
a deep impression in conference with some leading citizens,
but the Roman authorities reacted with extreme violence,
attempting to throw him into the Rhine, and wounding him.
A month later he sent in his place Antoine Froment to take a
fresh approach. Froment opened up a language school,
offering at the same time some instruction in religion.

The interest in the Reformation had meanwhile grown
great enough to attract a crowd, and soon preaching began in
the open air. There was determined and rowdy resistance
from the Roman party. The local council, now inclined to
protect the incomers, tried to keep order. People took sides
and tension mounted. The Reforming party consolidated
and during Easter of 1533 they celebrated the Lord's Supper.
In opposition, the local clergy seemed able only to resort to
violence and verbal abuse, and the Bishop fled from the city.
Farel was able to return in December 1533, and he was
followed by Pierre Viret a young Swiss preacher milder in his
approach to people, but no less effective in winning their
support. At the request of the Bernese authorities a church
was occupied by the preachers on March 1, 1534.

The Roman clergy and the monastic communities
throughout the whole conflict when challenged to public
discussion were unable to respond, and could give no

reasonable defence for their theological positions or their superstitions, and gradually other religious houses and churches became vacant. A plot to poison the preachers which involved Viret in a severe illness was discovered, and it brought more discredit to the Roman side. By the end of 1535 mass was abolished. On May 21, 1536 the citizens assembled as a General Council of the city accepted the Reformation, and swore to live and worship according to the Word of God.

It has to be conceded that political forces also had a part in bringing about change in Geneva. During the religious conflict some of the tension within the city was due to a clash of interests between the authorities of Fribourg the neighbouring Roman Catholic stronghold, and Bern the neighbouring Protestant stronghold. Moreover, the Duke of Savoy himself tried to gain control over Geneva and in cooperation with the Bishop he conducted military operations, harassing the city and damaging communications, until finally Bern declared war on him and rescued Geneva from his grasp.

It must also be admitted that Geneva had reformed in name but not entirely in heart, many of its citizens having wanted rather freedom from the restraints of the old regime than the guidance of the Word of God. In the years of struggle law and order had suffered badly. By the end of July 1536 when Calvin appeared on the scene Farel seems to have felt that the situation was slipping from his grasp.

The story of the first encounter between those two men has been told dramatically by Calvin himself. He had intended to stay in Geneva for only one night, but Farel discovered his whereabouts and went to his lodgings. Might not God have sent Calvin to him at this very moment, because he was the man for the job he himself was unable to complete? He unburdened his mind to his fellow-countryman with a challenge that had the force of blackmail. He warned him that a curse would fall on him if he dared to reject his call from God to stay and work in the very place where he arrived so providentially.

Calvin confessed that he was detained in Geneva "not so

much by counsel and exhortation as by dreadful impreca-
tion". "Stricken with terror", it seemed to him that the
"hand of God from heaven" was there arresting him. Perhaps
we are meant to notice a touch of divine irony in the fact that
God used the very shyness which had made Calvin previously
shrink from people, now to force him into their service. But
some timidity still remained: "sensible of my natural
bashfulness ... I would not bring myself under obligation to
discharge any particular office".[3]

Pastor and Preacher

The first arrangement made, therefore, was that he should
start work in Geneva simply as a teacher. "In that Church
...", he later explained, "I held the office first of doctor."[4]
They soon discovered, however, that none could equal him as
a preacher, and at some point he was called to become pastor
or bishop of the local congregation. This, in his mind, was the
highest and most comprehensive office which God could give
to anyone within the Church. It involved responsibility for
the care and discipline of the flock, for keeping the members
together in unity, as well as for teaching and preaching.
Calvin always believed that no one could ever hold or retain
the pastoral title without having a people of his own to preach
to regularly. This is why, in his view, a pope who merely
attended to general Church administration had no right to
call himself a bishop.

Possibly he found, too, that for the sake of his effectiveness
as a teacher or theologian he needed the parish fellowship.
Only in the active leadership of the people of God, and in
close relationship to them could he test the faithfulness of his
teaching to the Word of God, and its practicability, as he
tried to work out the implications of the Reformation for the
Christian life and for the Christian good of the community.
His teaching would have lost its soul if he had diverted himself
into entirely academic secluded scholarship. Having a

³ I.C.P., p. xli.
⁴ *Reply to Sadoleto*, C.Tr., vol. I, p. 26.

particular job near the front line saved him from becoming merely a talkative aristocratic church bureaucrat with inevitably partial insights, able to feed the press better than the flock.

The task of regularly preaching the word brought him at last into the heart of the Reformation movement in its battle for the soul of Europe, for it was more through his preaching than through any other aspect of his work that he exercised the extraordinary influence everyone has acknowledged him to have had.

It has been by no means unusual in the history of the Church for preaching to become a powerful factor in converting individuals and communities, in changing social customs and moving men to political action. We can think, for example, of Augustine's remarkable account of how his preaching at Caesarea in Mauritania subdued the men of the wild community there and moved them permanently to abandon their customary annual periods of intra-family murder.[5] Moreover, the Middle Ages was not lacking in preachers of exceptional power and influence. But at the time of the Reformation what had before been occasional, and even rare, seemed to become for a time a common experience within the normal life of the Church.

Often the preacher's influence in his community was a deeply pervasive force difficult to trace in its precise workings. But, often too, preaching was the obvious immediate cause of important changes in attitudes and temperatures at critical periods in the whole struggle — as, for example, in Luther's sermons at Wittenberg in 1522, or John Knox's sermon at Perth at a critical time in the Scottish Reformation. The Reformers themselves were conscious of the powerful and widespread influence they exerted through their preaching. Luther was quite confident that he could resist and overcome the "ungracious lords and angry nobles" as he had resisted and overcome "their idol, the pope", with words alone.[6] John

---

[5] Cf. Augustine, *On Christian Doctrine*, IV.53.

[6] *Temporal Authority: To what Extent it Should be Obeyed*, L.W., 45: 84-5; cf. also second sermon at Wittenberg, L.W., 51: 75ff. "Christian love should not employ harshness nor force matters. However, it should be preached with the tongue and

Knox writes in a letter dated June 23, 1559 of how "for forty days and more hath my God used my tongue in my native countrie to the manifestation of his glorie",[7] and he was confident enough to tell Cecil in the same year that "Christ Jesus crucified, now begun heir to be preached", could join the hearts of those long dissevered by Satan and bring "perpetual concord" between the two realms of Scotland and England.[8]

The accounts of the time moreover indicate that there was an unusual hunger on the part of the common people to hear the preaching of the Word of God. We have noted already Calvin's early experience of finding himself surrounded constantly by those who had a "thirst for sound teaching", and in spite of all their differences and tensions the people and authorities of Geneva wanted Calvin as much as Calvin wanted them. The demand for pastors who could preach the Word was intense all over the Reformed world. When we read that in Geneva in 1549 the council ordered the preachers to give a sermon every morning of the week instead of every other morning,[9] and that the first book of discipline in Scotland in 1560 ordered that "in every notable town, one day besides Sundays be appointed for sermon and prayer", we need not imagine that behind such ordinances we have an aggressive, self-important clergy insuring for themselves and their views a dominating position of influence in the community. The initiative came from a laity who wanted even more than many of their pastors could give. The "multitude of people" who were recorded by the Council in Geneva to be attending the sermons of Viret and Calvin were not there as victims of an iron discipline. They wanted to hear the Word. John Knox's letter from St. Andrews, June 23, 1559, may be quoted: "The thirst of the poore people als weill as of the nobilitie heir, is wonderous great, which putteth me

pen that to hold mass in such a manner is sinful, yet no one should be dragged away from it by the hair; for it should be left to God, and his Word should be allowed to work alone without our work and interference."

[7] To Mrs. Anna Lock from St. Andrews, June 23, 1559. *Works* (ed. Laing, Edinburgh, 1895), vol. VI, p. 26.

[8] *Works*, VI, pp. 31-2.

[9] *Register of the Council*, June 19, 1559.

in comfort, that Christ Jesus shall triumphe for a space heir in the North and extreme parts of the earth."[10]

Failure

In 1 Timothy 3:6 Paul advises his younger colleague never to make any "novice" a bishop. Calvin makes the comment: "What Paul says here we can confirm from our own experience." He explains that when men of "outstanding ability and learning" are brought to the faith they often think they can "fly beyond the clouds". "There is good reason", he adds, "to debar them from episcopal office, till, with the passing of time, their high flown notions are subdued."[11] When he spoke about his "own experience" of this kind of thing, Calvin had reason not only to think of young pastors of his time who had behaved unwisely in their first charge, but also to remember his own disastrous start in his first months in Geneva, when he came up against more difficulties than he could deal with and a strength of opposition he had not taken into his reckoning. Of course the Genevan authorities with whom he and his colleagues had to deal with were foolish and provocative. But they often acted the same way later on, and he had by then learned how to put up with it.

Tension was allowed to mount. Farel, Viret and Courault (who was blind) obviously expected too much too fast in the way of subscription to creed and improvement in morals. They underestimated local reaction and failed to remember that they were merely foreigners from France trying to bring order within a Swiss commune! They failed to realise that having only recently delivered themselves from Rome, the people of Geneva were going to be unusually suspicious of everything that seemed to suggest any new tyranny. Perhaps Farel was not a wise colleague for Calvin to work with in such a situation.

The crisis came through an unnecessary confrontation over

[10] Cf. letter from Hooper to William Cecil: "You and I if we shall kneel all the days of our life could not give condign thanks to God, that he hath mercifully inclined the people to wish and hunger for the Word of God." Quoted A. G. Dickens, *The Reformation in England*, London, 1965, p. 243.

[11] *Comm. on 1 Tim.*, 3:6.

worship and discipline. The ministers were ordered by the council of Geneva to adopt the Bernese custom of using unleavened bread at the Supper, of observing the traditional Church festivals, and of using the stone fonts in the church for their baptisms. These orders involved very trivial alterations in the customs already adopted. But Calvin and his colleagues had already publicly committed themselves to rigid positions. They declared that they could not celebrate the Supper on the forthcoming Easter Sunday because of the dissension and strife prevailing in the city. They were then forbidden to preach, but they defied the order. In the resulting disturbances within the cathedral swords were even drawn. But things calmed down and they were ordered to leave the city within three days. This was Easter 1538. Calvin himself went into exile in Strasbourg till September 1541 when Geneva called him back.

The Strasbourg Interlude

The Church and city life of Strasbourg had an effect on Calvin's thinking and attitude, the extent of which is only now being appreciated by scholars. Martin Bucer was its leading theologian. It is only in recent years that historians have discovered the importance of his insights into both doctrine and organisation. "He embodied in his thinking what was best in Luther, and foreshadowed what was best in Calvin."[12] The city seems to have become a meeting point for the various traditions — Lutheran, Zwinglian, Anabaptist — to encounter each other and make exchanges in an atmosphere of more generous toleration than was found elsewhere. The strong, wise guiding hand of a great statesman Jacques Sturm had helped to create a healthy and stable state of affairs generally in the life of the town. A year before Calvin, there had arrived also Jean Sturm with a wide experience of what was being done in the field of youth education. He started a college in the city, and Calvin was involved in teaching there. There had also been some very important development of Reformed liturgical usages in the

[12] J. D. Benoit in *Calvin à Strasbourg 1538-1541*, Strasbourg, 1938, p. 17.

Strasbourg churches. Bucer had organized the poor relief so well that beggars had disappeared from the streets.

Calvin would discover that others, facing situations like that of Geneva and moving towards goals similar to those he also had set himself, had managed to take their people further with them by more careful and moderate dealing. It is one of the sad events of history that what was developing in Strasbourg to be such a noble and powerful model of a truly Reformed Christian commonwealth was denied its full fruition when the city reverted to Roman domination. It is some compensation to know that what Calvin saw and experienced there helped decisively to shape his later programme and his strategy in Geneva, and contributed in no small way to his success there.

In Strasbourg Calvin was given an opportunity to develop his pastoral understanding and his preaching in the midst of the life of the comparatively small French congregation which he was called to serve. The attitude of the congregation can often be decisive in shaping the ministry a pastor seeks to give. This congregation seems to have accepted Calvin's ministry as from God, and to have had towards him an openness of mind and heart that enabled him to give his best to them. He was able to put some of his convictions about discipline to the test in an atmosphere free from the intense tension that had spoiled things in Geneva. He tried the custom of inviting each member of his congregation to have a personal interview with the pastor before each communion, so that those who had been poorly instructed in the faith might be better prepared, and those who were troubled in conscience might be assured. It is obvious here that his dominant concern in such discipline was not moral improvement but pastoral care for the individual.

His Strasbourg congregation cooperated with him in developing a French liturgy into which he incorporated much that came from Martin Bucer's own work in this field. He was also able to have printed for his people a small collection of *Psalms and Canticles* for use in worship. Some were translations of his own, some were by Clement Marot. They were set to tunes written by one of the Strasbourg organists.

Calvin had wished for such a book in Geneva but his proposal had not been taken up there.

Calvin was at Strasbourg during the period in which the Emperor Charles V was attempting to bring about unity between the opposing sections of the Church. He attended all the three conferences arranged for this purpose — at Hagenau in June 1540, at Worms in November of the same year, and finally at Ratisbon on April 5, 1541. There he was able to meet the world's leading theologians and churchmen, to learn their views at first hand, to assess their ability and observe their methods. He made his own important contribution to the debates, though in the end the colloquies proved to be in vain. Philip Melanchthon came to know and admire Calvin at these meetings, and the two became life-long friends.

An important event in Calvin's life in Strasbourg was his marriage to the widow of a former Anabaptist, Idelette de Bure, who brought him much happiness and comfort. He wrote there his first New Testament commentary, that on Paul's Epistle to the Romans. He produced a new and much enlarged edition of the *Institutes* in 1539, and a *Short Treatise on the Lord's Supper*.

During Calvin's absence from Geneva, Cardinal Sadoleto wrote a letter to "The Syndics, the Senate and the citizens" of the town, flattering them, calling in question the motives of the Reformers, and inviting them to return to the Roman fold. A copy of the letter was sent to Calvin. Within a few days he produced one of his finest short works — his *Reply to Sadoleto*. It is a notable defence of the Reformation and of his own part in it, written in a dignified and restrained style with great sincerity and depth of feeling, especially as he reveals to his readers his reasons for repudiating the Roman Church.

He mentions only in passing the "cruelty, avarice, intemperance, arrogance, insolence, lust, and all sorts of wickedness" which had prevailed throughout that Church, marked even some of Sadoleto's rank, and alienated the minds of the common people.[13] The prevalence of such things in themselves would not have justified the drastic action

[13] *Reply to Cardinal Sadoleto's Letter*, C.Tr., vol. I, p. 49, cf. p. 55.

taken by the Reformers. Rome's chief sin, however, had been to deny the common man any place of security before God whose face had been made stern and whose presence had been made dreadful. They had placed man "on ground so slippery, nay, so precipitous that he can scarcely stand a moment if even the slightest push is given him". In the midst of man's desperate battle for assurance and peace, they had deprived him of the sword of the Word of God and given him up "unarmed to the devil for destruction".[14] Calvin pleads with Sadoleto to admit the futility of the theology he had been taught as a candidate for the ministry:

> you yourself know that it was mere sophistry, and sophistry so twisted, involved, tortuous, and puzzling . . . might well be described as a species of secret magic. The denser the darkness in which anyone shrouded a subject, the more he puzzled himself and others with preposterous riddles, the greater his fame for acumen and learning.[15]

He refers again and again to the gross deformity of the Church and the overthrow of the true ministry by "the Roman pontiff with his whole herd of pseudo-bishops" who had encouraged the fears that drove people on pilgrimage from shrine to shrine and from altar to altar feeding them with superstitions instead of with bread of life, like "ravening wolves" exploiting their tragic ignorance for financial gain by the sale of indulgences.[16]

Calvin had repudiated the Roman Church because of its refusal to reform itself under the Word of God. It had for centuries allowed traditions and practices alien to the Word to grow unchecked, and had regarded the development as sacred — indeed, as of greater authority than Holy Scripture. It had convinced itself, moreover, that Christ had ordained for his Church a chief place within the power-structures of this world, and had meant it to glorify his name by the exercise of such power and by an accompanying display of pomp, wealth and circumstance. One of its central dogmas had been that the Church was as great in the eyes of heaven

[14] *Ibid.*, pp. 52-3.   [15] *Ibid.*, p. 40.   [16] *Ibid.*, p. 50.

c

as it tried to be in the world, that it had God's grace at its disposal to grant to whomever it willed to save, and to withhold from whomever it willed to damn. It had given to the Pope in the chief seat of authority over all this the place and power of God.

The fact that he had written the *Reply to Sadoleto* implied that Calvin still cared enough to seek to defend his former flock.

They had begun to want him back, and gradually they put more pressure on him to return. In October 1540 they sent a deputation to him while he was in conference at Worms with a definite invitation from the Seigneury to return and take up office among them.

Seldom can an invitation to a pastorate have been received with so much reluctance. He was convinced that Geneva was largely to blame for what had happened previously and his memories of it brought fear: "Not a day passed in which I did not ten times over wish for death." He had regarded it as a singular act of the kindness of God when he was forcibly thrown out, for only the sanctity of his call had kept him at his post so long.[17] Set free through such a merciful deliverance by God, who could blame him for not wanting to replunge himself "into the gulf and whirlpool" which he had already found to be so dangerous and destructive.[18] His letters show feelings of abhorrence and despondency. But he recognised that the will of God often goes contrary to our own inclinations and self-interest. He consulted others, and when he found he had to go back expressed himself vividly:

> As to my intended course of proceeding, this is my present feeling; had I the choice at my own disposal, nothing would be less agreeable to me than to follow your advice. But when I remember that I am not my own, I offer up my heart, a slain victim for a sacrifice to the Lord ... I submit my will and my affections subdued and held fast to the obedience of God.[19]

He returned to Geneva on September 13, 1541.

[17] Cf. C.L. to Pastors of Zurich, May 31, 1541; I.C.P., xliv.
[18] C.L. to Farel, October 27, 1540.
[19] C.L. to Farel, August 1541.

PART I

THE REFORMER AND HIS CITY

CHAPTER 3

THE AIM AND THE PLAN

Growing Involvement

WILHELM PAUCK has pointed out that the Gospel always requires liturgical, ecclesiastical and theological forms to enable its followers as Christians to participate in the ongoing common life of the Church, and in the movements of history which it is intended to initiate and promote. Yet, at the same time, no form of Christianity can adequately express the content of the faith, and a stage is sometimes reached at which traditional and established forms prove inadequate for the Church's continuing health and mission in the world.[1]

Such a stage had arrived in the Church's life at the end of the fifteenth century, but the powerful impact of the Word of God on the Church at the Reformation enabled it, and indeed, forced it to break through the old forms which had restricted and hindered its life for so long.

It was, of course, under Luther that the work of breaking through the old forms and structures took place and the Word was given freedom to work again creatively. But it was Calvin who took the lead in defining the new forms of Christian service and Christian living, of Church and community life, that under the newly discovered teaching of the Bible, and the power of the Spirit, were now possible and adequate for the task and witness of God's people in the sixteenth century.

Calvin had such reconstruction in mind when he returned to Geneva, and no doubt, he had a vision of the whole community in its secular life as well as in its Church life being transformed into what can be called a Christian common-wealth, in which those responsible for civil government obeyed the Word of God and served Christ in their own secular sphere no less responsively than those who had the

[1] W. Pauck, *The Heritage of the Reformation*, Beacon Press, 1950, pp. 135-6, 142-3.

task of Church government. He was convinced that the
challenge and power of the Gospel must be allowed to
cleanse, regenerate and direct not only the human heart but
every aspect of social life on earth — family affairs, education,
economics and politics. Christ sought not only an altar in the
human heart for his priestly ministry, but a throne at the
centre of all human life for his kingly ministry. "Holy writ",
as John Bright once expressed it, had to be "put into act of
Parliament".

In spite of such firmly held convictions about the social
implications of the Gospel, when he returned to Geneva he
did not intend or wish himself to become engaged in civil
affairs. His own first concern then, as at all times, was the
reconstruction and health of the Church. He once spoke
about the "zeal with which every true pastor should burn" so
that the purity of the Church might be protected, and its
welfare advanced. "Love and anxiety for the church", he
said, "carry me away into a sort of ecstasy so that I care for
nothing else."[2]

These comments reflect his mind on the matter in 1541. In
a letter in that year about the difficulties which he knew he
would have to face, he referred to his future task simply as
"the superintendance of a church".[3] He first of all
concentrated on producing his *Ecclesiastical Ordinances* of 1541
in which he outlined what was needed so that there could
be a true and healthy Church within the city.   In these
ordinances he defined the new kind of ministry required
within a truly reformed Church. Along with the *Ordinances* he
produced a *Catechism of the Church of Geneva* to replace one he
had already written for Geneva in 1537. In 1542 he issued his
Form of Ecclesiastical Prayers and Hymns.

It was always his strongly held view that the office of Pastor
disqualifies its holder from any public office, and he believed
that under normal circumstances social and political affairs
should be left to laymen. Christ decreed "not only that the
office of pastor be distinct from that of the prince, but also
that the things are so different that they cannot come together
in one man".[4]

<hr />

[2] *Comm. on Gal.*, 5:12.   [3] C.L. to Viret, March 1, 1541.   [4] *Inst.*, 4:8:11.

By 1555, however, describing his own calling he could write: "Life is not dearer to me than the holy bond to which is annexed the public welfare of our city."[5] God had now enlarged the scope of his ministry. As well as to the Church he felt himself also bound by God to the "city". To teaching and pastoral care there had been added "public welfare". He could justify such a development from Biblical precedent, for Moses, by "a rare miracle of God's power and grace had combined both secular and sacred offices in his own person".[6] Calvin himself, however, had taught that though private persons should normally restrain themselves from any interference in governmental affairs such activity could be readily undertaken by them when under exceptional conditions it was ordered by the magistrates themselves.[7]

Therefore, even though the magistrates had already called him to be theologian and pastor, he was also ordered by them, in their exceptional circumstances, to take an active part in their political and civil affairs. He had come to believe this call, too, to be of God.

His involvement in the secular business of the city began immediately after he had put their ecclesiastical laws in order. It seemed also good that they should codify and tidy up their civil legislation, and he was obviously one of the best qualified men in Europe for such a task. They put him on the committee, and he took over most of the work, showing his intense practical interest in the details of the day-to-day working of the city administration. Those who have examined Calvin's work in this field have been impressed by the memoirs in his own handwriting, revealing his knowledge of police affairs, fire-fighting, building inspection, guard duty, the care of artillery, marketing processes, etc. He was responsible for the final drafting of the edicts. Geneva's statute book was thus given a new orderliness and greater simplicity. Legal processes were shortened. The council tried to relieve him of other tasks to encourage him on.

They were soon using his gift as a lawyer and negotiator to settle a long-standing boundary dispute between their city

---

[5] C.L. to Nicholas Zerkinden, February 21, 1556.
[6] *Inst.*, 4:8:11.   [7] *Inst.*, 4:20:23.

and Bern. Later we find him heavily involved in further complicated negotiations with the Bernese over the renewal of an important treaty.

That they greatly valued his work is obvious not simply from the gifts of old wine which they occasionally sent him, but from an extract from the Register of the Council on August 20, 1556: "M Calvin being entreated to repair to Frankfort, to try to appease great trouble which has arisen in the Church in the said city, demands leave of absence from the council in order to go there, which is granted to him with a request that he will return as soon as possible, and according him if he desires, a seigneur of the council to keep him company, and a servant of the town for his service."[8]

Calvin, however, realised that over-involvement in politics could damage his influence as a minister of the Gospel. As if he had a twinge of conscience about the entire secularity of the business in hand when he was revising the treaty with Bern, he wrote to Farel admitting that: "There is no opportunity for religion being mixed up with this question", but he expressed the hope that "some chink or other will be opened up through which it will pass".[9]

In 1556 when rumours were being spread that as a churchman he was too much involved in such affairs he explained his position and his fears in a letter to Nicholas Zerkinden written on February 21 of that year:

You will ask why I should mix myself up with those affairs which do not become my profession, and engender great animosity against me among many — Though I rarely meddle with these political matters, and am dragged on to them against my inclination, yet I sometimes allow myself to take part in them when necessity requires it ... I wish I had been at liberty to demand my exemption. But since I returned here fourteen years ago, when God held out his hand to me, men importunately solicited me, and I myself had no decent pretext for refusal. I have preferred to bestow my

[8] Cf. C.L. vol. III, p. 291 (footnote).
[9] C.L. to Farel, December 7, 1555.

pains in pacifying troubles to remaining an idle spectator of them.

Discussing Calvin's involvement in civil affairs Owen Chadwick has observed that, "One of the consuming passions of his life was a hatred of public mess".[10]

Discipline

It is to be noted, however, that his methods of "pacifying troubles" in Geneva were those of a churchman rather than of a politician. In his *Ordinances* he had suggested to the council some practical improvements in their system of poor relief and in their care of the city hospital. But he did not try to produce a blue-print for social reconstruction within the city. He never suggested any changes, for example in the very complicated set-up of councils in the political structure of the town.[11]

His programme could be described as one of social sanctification rather . than of social reconstruction. A transformation first had to be brought about in the personal lives of Geneva's citizens. This was to be achieved chiefly by two means: through social discipline, and through the sacramental power of the Word of God.

Discipline, for Calvin, was essential if people were to live together in love. "No society", he wrote, "indeed no house with even a moderate family, can be kept in a healthy condition without discipline."[12]

Discipline within any social group — family, church, city or nation — means that certain basic, high standards of morality and, indeed, of virtue are set for and expected of everyone. Those standards need not always be clearly defined or written down. They are embodied in the educational system, in the current ideals for family and home life. They

[10] O. Chadwick, *The Reformation*, Penguin, 1964, p. 82.
[11] The "General Assembly" was a gathering of all the citizens. The heads of families regularly elected four "Syndics", and other members to form a "council of 25", which cared for executive and routine matters. A "council of sixty" was also elected by the people, and met with the little council. There was also an important "council of 200" which mediated between the other councils and the Assembly.
[12] *Inst.*, 4:12:1.

are upheld strictly by enlightened public opinion. When the
basic standard fails to be attained the erring individual is
urged on by encouragement or reproof or by more
progressively severe sanctions administered by those in
authority who are themselves expected to prove exemplary.
Thus we have what Erich Fromm describes as a "learned
system of feeling and acting" which prevails within the
majority of a community and produces a "social character".[13] To Calvin himself we owe the phrase: the "formation
of social behaviour".[14]

Calvin's anxiety to ensure the prevalence of a strong
tradition of discipline within the Geneva community arose as
much from his concern for the welfare of the individual as
from his desire to produce a model society. His own
experience and reading had taught him that within the
Church life itself the warmth of the zeal of the individual and
the strength of his resolution depend almost invariably on the
help and encouragement that can come to him from the
Christian community. Each one in the Christian race must be
made by God to "feel the spur" through being "stirred up by
others" even while he tries to "push himself on".[15] What held
good on this matter within Church life, Calvin believed, held
good in civil society.

The force of the discipline prevalent within the community, of course has its maximum impact and influence on the
individual growing within the life of the family. Habits of
mind, heart and will that are learned within the home
produce a bias to healthy social behaviour.

Calvin admitted that such enforced restraint imposed
upon the outward behaviour of people by family tradition
and social sanctions could sometimes produce a "goodness"
that concealed hidden hypocrisy. "Some", he conceded, will
be "restrained merely by shame from breaking out into all
kinds of foulness, and others would simply conceal their

---

[13] Cf. Raymond Williams, *The Long Revolution*, Penguin Books, 1965, pp. 63-5,
96-7.   [14] *Inst.*, 4:20:2.

[15] C.L. To the Brethren of France, November, 1559. Calvin in this letter strikes
exactly the note sounded in "Onward Christian Soldiers": "Nothing is more
opposed to Christianity than where the Son of God calls us to the combat, we should
be cold-hearted."

impiety because they fear the law".[16] But at the same time he believed that virtue could actually be created and increased by such imposed discipline. Under such discipline "some, because they consider an honest manner of life profitable, in some measure aspire to it". In the long run, as Erich Fromm points out, through an inward "shaping process" the individual's social activity becomes one with his personal desires.[17]

The Sacramental Power of the Word of God

Alongside social discipline Calvin laid stress on the sanctifying power of the Word and Sacraments within the life of the city. The Genevan authorities, when they invited him back, had indicated that they wanted the Word of God to have now a central place within the civic life. This meant that they shared with him the belief that all attempts at social improvement must find their chief inspiration, and the source of their power in the Gospel itself.

Yet, to bring the power of the Gospel to bear fully on the life of the city, Calvin believed, would require the sacraments as well as preaching. Certainly the power of the preached word even without the sacrament could bring people to faith and repentance, and change human life, but the Lord's Supper was also given to us by God, along with the Word to give the power of the Word support and to make the secret of its working visible to us.

What he wrote in his *Institutes* and elsewhere about the power of the sacraments makes it clear to us that when Calvin looked on the people of his church-city seated around the Holy Table in St. Peter's Cathedral, and receiving the supper, he saw in that action the source of Geneva's true life. Bread and wine, the signs of Christ's body and blood, were given and received by his people. It was a visible enactment of the mystery that Christ was theirs, and they were his. What was made visible by Christ at the Lord's table did not mock those present. The forgiveness, new life and power which each person present, therefore, received by faith through the sacrament could become the most powerful force for the

---

[16] *Inst.*, 2:3:3.   [17] Cf. Williams, *op. cit.*, p. 97.

transformation of individual character, of social and family life within the city.

Calvin tried to help everyone else in the town to see this "mystery" of the Supper, as he himself saw it, to understand its meaning and to accept the love and power it brought into their lives and to work out its moral implications. In his preaching he often referred to the union of the believer with Christ which was made visible at the Supper in the eating of the bread and the drinking of the wine and he urged people to accept its implications and work out in their lives its consequences. In the first articles on the nature of the Church's ministry which he delivered to the council in 1537 he pointed out that if the citizens partook of this mystery they were "pledged to live in a Christian manner". He thus enforced his moral and social Gospel from the Lord's table.

The Consistory

If the Lord's Supper was to be given such a prominent and lasting place within his new Geneva, Calvin saw that some way must be found for guarding its sanctity and thus the health of the Church. The Supper would be profaned, even mocked, if people were allowed to indulge freely and openly in un-Christian ways of behaviour and at the same time to partake freely and openly of the Lord's Supper.[18] The Supper, while it offered the grace of God, inspired and demanded true evangelical repentance and holiness of life. It must not be made to seem that Christ fed and supported those who insisted on living contrary to his teaching. In the New Testament people who lived lives "in open sin accompanied by public scandal" were solemnly admonished, and those whose way of life was in complete contradiction to the Word of God were excommunicated till they repented.[19]

To avoid such public scandal, and the defilement of the sacrament, it had been the custom of the Church from the earliest times that in giving the elements to the people, the priest should utter the words both of exhortation and of warning, "holy things for the holy". When mass was

[18] *Inst.*, 4:6:12ff.   [19] *Inst.*, 4:12:3-4.

abolished and the new form of the Lord's Supper had
appeared, the custom had been frequently observed by which
the minister gave warnings from the table that those who
were not prepared to reform their way of living must not partake of so holy a mystery. Farel had already introduced this
practice in Geneva and Calvin had cooperated with him.[20]

Calvin now proposed, in his 1541 *Ecclesiastical Ordinances*
that there should be set up in Geneva a court which could
have authority and make judgment on such matters of
Church discipline. It was to be called a Consistory. Its
function was to exercise a "spiritual supervision . . . of the kind
which our Lord demonstrated and instituted by His
Word".[21] Thus there was now to be formed in the city the
"twofold government" which Calvin referred to in his
Institutes.[22] His thought on the subject had developed while in
Strasbourg. In 1537 he had suggested that the supervision of
the Church be undertaken by "certain persons of good life"
appointed by the Council. By 1541, he had discovered that by
the ordination and appointment of Christ there were meant
to be four distinct ministries within the Church — pastors,
teachers, elders and deacons,[23] and the task of "spiritual
oversight" was now to be undertaken by the elders who hold
the authority to do this within the Church from Christ, in the
same way as the pastors hold the authority for their task from
Christ.

The Consistory therefore was to be made up of pastors and
elders. The elders were to be twelve laymen nominated by the
Council to act along with the ministers. The duty of the
Consistory was to summon, admonish or excommunicate
those whose lives were regarded as incurring such censures. It

[20] Cf. John T. McNeill's account of Farel's 1525 and 1533 liturgies in *The History
and Character of Calvinism*, New York, 1962, p. 151.

[21] Cf. *Inst.*, 4:20:2 and Calvin's *Ecclesiastical Ordinances*, 1541. Cf. R.C.P. p. 35.
Calvin previously (in 1537) had asked that such supervision be carried out by
"Certain persons of good life and reputation from among the body of the faithful".
By 1541 he believed there was sufficient Biblical evidence for regarding such
supervision as fulfilling an office sanctioned by Christ. For a full account of the
important part played by Oecolampadius in Reformed thinking on this matter see
Gordon Rupp, *Patterns of Reformation*, London, 1969, pp. 38-42.

[22] Cf. *Inst.*, 4:20:1.

[23] Cf. *Inst.*, 4:3:6-9, *Ecclesiastical Ordinances*, 1541, R.C.P., pp. 35-6.

was to be a Church Court acting on the authority of Christ within the Church. Oecolampadius the Basel reformer had outlined such an ideal in a memoir he wrote to the Synod of Basel in 1530. He had stated that while the civil authority had the duty to seek to produce good-living and orderly citizens, the Church had the further task of making men Christians, and that it must not be deprived of the powers it required for this task.[24] Here is Calvin seeking exactly such a set-up in his Geneva, "as no city or village can exist without a magistrate and government, so the Church of God ... needs a kind of spiritual government".[25]

The function of the elders was "to watch over the life of each person, to admonish in a friendly manner those whom they see to be at fault and leading a disorderly life", and when necessary to report them to "the Company" (i.e. the ministers) who were authorised to "administer fraternal correction and discipline and to do so in association with the elders". The elders at that time were elected from the several town councils, "men without reproach and beyond all suspicion, above all who fear God and possess the gift of spiritual prudence, and their election shall be such that there will be some of them in each quarter of the city".[26]

Calvin was emphatic that ecclesiastical discipline was not enough by itself to produce the healthy society. Social discipline for moral and religious ends enforced by the civil magistrate with civil legal sanctions was also required and had to be distinguished from Church discipline. "These two things are widely different, therefore neither does the Church assume anything which is proper to the magistrate, nor is the magistrate competent to what is done by the Church."[27]

The introduction of this additional court, and especially Calvin's association of its discipline with fitness for admission to the communion was, as John T. McNeill has pointed out, without precedent in the cities which had accepted the Reformation.[28]

---

[24] G. Rupp, *Patterns of Reformation*, London, 1969, p. 40; cf. also Jacques Courvoisier (*Bucer et Calvin*), in *Calvin à Strasbourg 1538-41*, pp. 50-1.

[25] *Inst.*, 4:11:1.   [26] Cf. R.C.P., pp. 41-4.

[27] *Inst.*, 4:11:3.   [28] *Op. cit.*, p. 140.

CHAPTER 4

DECISIVE ISSUES IN A MUNDANE SETTING

Calvin's View of his Times

CALVIN believed that by the power of the Word of God, the reformation movement in which he was called to be a leader would have success. Yet he never underestimated the power of evil.

He was convinced, as many of his contemporaries were, that in human affairs the countdown of the last days had begun. All round him in history the stage was being set for the appearance of signs which would lead up to the second coming of Christ. The initial events of the Reformation were a prelude to that great final event.

He was certain, too, that the final Anti-Christ whose appearance would immediately precede the return of the Lord, was the Pope. Previous Anti-Christs, such as certain Roman Emperors, had had their little day, and time had still gone on till a worse one appeared. But it was impossible to imagine any future monster of evil who could surpass in iniquity and strength this Papal one. Therefore he believed that in the times in which he himself was called to work, the powers of evil would be specially active all around him to thwart success.

We find a clue to some of his thoughts in the tone and phraseology of a letter he sent to Farel on October 24, 1538. Calvin had learned about Corauld. When he and Farel had been expelled from Geneva, Corauld their fellow pastor had . suffered with them. He had been put in prison in the city before his banishment. He had then become pastor at Orbe, and had suddenly died. It was rumoured that his death was due to poisoning by his enemies when he was in Geneva. Calvin was tempted to believe the story and was horrified at "that atrocious deed": "The death of Corauld has so overwhelmed me that I can set no bounds to my grief. None of my daily occupations can so avail to engage my mind so that they do not seem to turn upon that one thought."

He complains of distress and wretchedness all day, and melancholy thoughts harassing and exhausting him all night long and destroying his health. He meditated on the times they were living in: "to what degree of wickedness must our posterity at length arrive when in the very commencement such monstrosities rise up before our eyes?" He is sure God is a witness and avenger of the villany, and that it will all be put right at the judgment seat. But he expresses his belief that in all this darkness there is light all round him ready to "shine forth" — there is the hidden kingdom of Christ — even though he and Farel may have to "stand resolutely upon the watchtower even to the end" to see it.[1]

Throughout his whole life he was to think much about a gradually intensifying final struggle between light and darkness, between the Kingdom of Christ and the powers of evil, which he believed to be a feature especially of the last days of human history. The dispersion of the English Protestants at the time of the accession of Mary made him feel that a permissive age was at hand when anything would be tolerated except the faith of "those who sought to honour God in purity". God would be forced then to bring the world itself to an end because even he would be able to find no place for refuge on earth for his children.[2]

The astonishing success which the Reformation had had in many places, however, was the sign and effect of the triumph of the Word of God over such spiritual powers of darkness. Indeed the preaching of the Gospel in his day was to Calvin like a second coming of Christ himself to the Church. He regarded it as an event linked directly with the final coming. As the sun scattered the darkness of night so Christ was by this

[1] C.L. to Farel October 24, 1538.
[2] C.L. to Coligny, September 4, 1558; to Valeran Poulain, August 27, 1554.

means "scattering the darkness" of Anti-Christ "by the rays which he will emit before his coming".[3]

Before he finally manifested his presence fully, however, Christ wanted the Church rebuilt and restored in order that the work of the Reformation might come to its climax and full fruition. At the time of the first advent of Christ, the influence of the kingdom of God had manifested itself in a "general diffusion of the doctrine of piety in every direction" throughout the world, in spite of the imperial anti-Christs. Calvin expected the Church, even in these last days to receive "some degree of honour after emerging from obscurity".[4]

In his interpretation of many Old Testament prophecies he reveals the way he thought about the meaning of his own times and this task of rebuilding the Church. When he came across passages which spoke of how God was going to do great things to restore his people to glory, freedom, and new life, he tried first of all to find circumstances in Israel's own history which would fit the text. Then he would try to show how the same prophecy was fulfilled in the early Christian centuries when, after the death and resurrection of Jesus, the infant church was launched out in vigour and beauty into the new Christian era. After he said all this, he would then take a further step and would assert that the events of his own time indeed "those last thirty years" had also produced another and final fulfilment of these great promises spoken centuries before.[5] Even with eternity now only a moment away, therefore God would hold back the end, to reveal within earthly affairs the power of His reign and to allow his people room and time to rebuild the Church, to make and fulfil programmes, to see progress, and to experience success.

In all the events of contemporary history Calvin saw God

[3] *Comm. on 2 Thess.*, 2:8-9; cf. *Comm. on 1 John*, 2:18-19. Calvin sees in the Reformation a kind of revelation of Christ destined to precede his final appearance; cf. H. Quistorp, *Calvin's Doctrine of the Last Things*, London, 1955, p. 122.

[4] *Comm. on Dan.*, 7:23-4.

[5] Cf., e.g., *Comm. on Isa.*, 66:8: "These things were fulfilled in some measure when the people returned from Babylon, but a far brighter testimony was given in the Gospel by the publication of which numerous and diversified offspring was immediately brought forth. In our own times have we not seen the fulfilment of this prophecy? How many children has the Church not brought forth these last thirty years?"

at work with one main purpose: the reformation of His whole Church and its restoration to the glory and unity it had lost. Everything was ready for the final advent. "We may look expectantly for the coming of Christ at any time."[6] The final day, however, "does not depend on the flow of present time, but on the eternal decree of God".[7] The evil power of the universe was creating such wild disturbance in social and international affairs because the kingdom of God was pressing in upon it to destroy it. Threatened with final extinction it was simply lashing out in desperate retreating fury.

He expected therefore to see the gospel triumphing, in the midst of all the wild disturbances of the times. He could accept compromise on many matters, but never with triumphant evil. In his *Institutes* the first of many attacks he launches against our human nature is against this tendency within us all to accept everything around us as being final and settled — to "confine our minds within the limits of human corruption", to be content with our "empty image of righteousness" instead of seeking the reality, to become delighted merely when things around us are not so bad as they could become.[8] He expected progress. He looked for results that would confound all human expectations, deserving only the comment: "This is the Lord's doing and it is marvellous in our eyes."[9]

The past history of the Church itself — its rise through its resurrection experience of Christ, the remarkable evidence of the miraculous working of divine providence in its affairs at critical periods — confirmed him in this faith. The time for such things to happen again — with greater intensity and on an even larger scale — had again appeared. He insists again and again in his correspondence that God was at work in such a way. Events "marvellous and beyond human conception" were going to take place. "It is proper that we should learn that it has been usual with God in all ages or preserve his own Church in a wonderful way and without human protection". "As he has done from the beginning of the world, he will

---

[6] *Comm. on 1 Pet.*, 3:9-10, *Comm. on 1 John*, 2:18.
[7] *Comm. on 1 Pet.*, 3:5-8.   [8] *Inst.*, 2:1:1.   [9] Ps. 118:23.

preserve in a miraculous manner and in a way unknown to us, the unity of faith." "The restoration of the Church is his own work."[10]

Geneva Makes History

The miracle "beyond human conception" took place in Geneva. When they called him back to be their pastor the Seigneury had written to him: "We pray you very earnestly that you would transfer yourself hitherward to us, and return to your old place and former ministry: and we hope, with the help of God, that this shall be a great benefit, and fruitful for the increase of the holy Evangel."[11] Most of them lived to see it happen. After less than twenty years of toil, planning, prayer, preaching, conflict, misunderstanding, suffering, cooperation, education, welfare work, political advice and help, Geneva became what J. S. Neale has described as "the godly society in actual working order",[12] and what John Knox echoing the opinion of many others called "the maist perfect school of Christ since the Apostles". G. D. Henderson describes what especially impressed the Scots Reformer during his stay there: "that while in other places the Word was indeed truly preached, nowhere else had behaviour and religion been so sincerely reformed. Calvinism held to Jesus Christ not only as the Truth but also as the Way and the Life: it involved not merely a set of principles but a manner of living, not only a city of hearers or even believers but a Christian city."[13]

Calvin's success in Geneva gave him a place from which he could exercise within the Reformation the kind of leadership which Luther in his great days had given. Such leadership was then urgently required. In Germany, towards the end of Luther's life the work seemed to be succumbing to what Butterfield calls the "gravitational pull of history" which

[10] Cf. C.L. to Somerset, October 22, 1548; to Musculus, April 21, 1547; to Cranmer, April 1552; to Edward VI, December 25, 1550.

[11] On October 22, 1540; cf. C.L., vol. I, p. 190 (footnote).

[12] J. E. Neale, *The Age of Catherine de Medici*, London, 1943, p. 22.

[13] G. D. Henderson, *Presbyterianism*, Aberdeen, 1954, p. 59; cf. Paul Henry, *The Life and Times of John Calvin*, vol. I, London, 1849, p. 364.

tends to bring down man's loftiest dreams.[14] The radical left, looking ugly and dangerous, was seeking to cash in on the breakdown of the authority which had always held it in check. The secular princes who had at first protected and sponsored the movement were thwarting its development at points at which they felt their own power was threatened. Zeal for reform had given way to conservatism and respectability. Theologians had become more important than pastors and evangelists, and were giving expression in their disagreements to that "fury" from which Melanchthon on his death-bed prayed to be delivered.

Yet the movement had still great potential and in lands beyond Germany its influence was still spreading with the same reforming and renewing vigour as it had shown in the early days in Germany. Scotland, France, the Netherlands and Poland had yet to come under its influence. Calvin through his ministry from Geneva was able to exercise a strong and inspiring leadership as this expansion took place.

From Geneva he influenced the wider Christian world in various ways. His writings were important. Three times he revised and expanded the *Institutes* till it began to be recognised even in his lifetime as one of the greatest text books on theology ever to be written. As the years passed he gradually produced his famous set of Biblical commentaries covering most of the Old and New Testaments. He normally preached continuously through various books of the Bible in series of sermons. Many of these expanded and practical commentaries on the text of Scripture were printed for wide circulation.

He attended ecumenical conferences and kept in touch with leading theologians by correspondence. He never seemed to be too tired or too afraid to enter any important current controversy, and whenever he knew that people

[14] H. Butterfield, *Christianity and History*, London, 1949, p. 38; cf. J. Atkinson, *Martin Luther and the Birth of Protestantism*, Pelican Books, 1968, p. 244. "The Reformation Movement was no longer a spiritual and religious movement led by a competent theologian and supported by men and women seeking God. It was slowly and certainly being submerged under the contemporary political, social and cultural movements of the period"; cf. p. 328; also G. R. Elton, *Reformation Europe, 1517-1559*, London, 1963, p. 173, and J. E. Neale, *op. cit.*, pp. 13-14.

anywhere were facing acute problems, tracts from his pen brought them comfort in their persecution, encouragement in their struggles, warnings in their dangers and temptations. He expressed his counsel and care personally for people in hundreds of letters which went all over the world to be read by others besides those to whom they were sent. People came to him in Geneva for counsel and the city became a haven for refugees from persecution elsewhere. Students finally came from all over the world to study and to be trained for the ministry of the Gospel.

Calvin's influence in the sixteenth century however was due not only to his writing, counsel and teaching but also to what Geneva itself became under his influence. The perplexed pastor of today finds much of what is written by experts, and given as advice even at heart-warming church conferences, does not really fit into his own actual situation in the parish ministry. Calvin, however, instead of writing a "Utopia", actually produced it in Geneva. He translated his ideas into ecclesiastical and even political institutions. He influenced the kind of individual people could meet as they went about the city. Geneva itself therefore became a fact of great importance. It attracted people. They sent their children so that they could come under the influence of the place. They came to believe it was possible for them to have something like it where they themselves lived and worked.

The Parochial Setting

It is a remarkable fact that an achievement that was to prove of such importance in world history was made within the confines of a small town of only a few thousand inhabitants by a man often fully immersed in a multitude of parochial and sometimes petty mundane affairs. Luther, as well as Calvin, it is true, worked on a comparatively small stage in his parish of Wittenberg. But he seemed to travel abroad much more than Calvin and at his decisive moment the local backdrop was lifted to show him making his dramatic decision in front of the Emperor, the princes and prelates of the world, with the Pope and the rest of his cardinals looking on with concern at what was about to happen. Calvin's corresponding great moments were witnessed only by his local congregation in a provincial church. His important decisions were made when he was summoned to attend the local council to answer their charges or give them some advice. "The story of the Genevan reform", wrote Mark Pattison, "may instruct us how the insignificant squabbles of a municipal council may be ennobled into one of the most important chapters in the history of civilisation."[15]

Calvin did at times feel himself cramped. There is an illuminating passage in a letter written when he found himself too completely immersed for his liking in the work of his congregation and in his home affairs. He expresses some vexation that he could not at the time fulfil his drive to do work more likely to be of ecumenical importance. "In regard to my commentary on the book of Genesis, if the Lord prolong my life, and I have sufficient leisure, I shall probably take the work in hand. My chief care, however, must be to fulfil my day and my present calling. If circumstances still prove favourable, I shall live for posterity. I would fain write more, but my wife is unwell and hence my thoughts are distracted."[16]

It is obvious where his priority lay: "To fulfil ... my present calling". He had marriages on his diary, baptisms to arrange, appointments with parishioners, visits to do, cases of discipline, some important but many petty, to be settled, meetings of the consistory and of the "honourable company" of pastors to attend. He had to do lobbying for the next local council meeting, and work on the revision of the law code of the city. He had to preach this coming Sunday and three times during the next week. He had to attend at the moment to his sick wife ... yet "I would fain write more".

We can, if we will, however, trace here the hand of Providence. Though he may not have realised it at the time, it was precisely because of the priority he gave to local needs of his own parish that he was ultimately so effective as a

[15] *Calvin at Geneva*, 1858. Reprinted in *Essays*, 1889; cf. pp. 27ff — quoted by R. Carew Hunt, *Calvin*, London, 1933.
[16] C.L. to Farel, July 1542.

Church leader and so important for "posterity". It was the impression his writings and commentaries gave of a teacher always close to life and always pastorally concerned that lifted him entirely above the level of the purely academic products that even then were being too commonly produced.

Elton has spoken of the "incalculably fruitful association of man and place".[17] Menzies has pointed out that it was in Geneva alone that Calvin's attempt to create a Christian society could have been made. In the other Swiss towns the magistrates had to an irrevocable extent taken the administration of religion into their own hands. Only in Geneva was there the possibility of a flexible open situation.[18]

Not only were things in Geneva flexible, they were also widely typical. The cultural, political and Church problems it presented were exactly those prevailing elsewhere in the life of the European community. Therefore though the stage was somewhat small, the decisions, plans and struggle of Calvin from start to finish had universal validity. We could indeed argue that Geneva was exactly the size required for the witness Calvin had to give and the kind of work he had to do. As a town it was large enough to contain people from different levels of society and extremely varied walks of life. The town aristocracy, middle classes and poor were all there, people in commerce, craftsmen, labourers, academics, shopkeepers, farmers, ex-noblemen, small businessmen, religious people and irreligious people, a large variety of the queer "with it" people produced by that particular age, criminals and prostitutes too. Geneva was large enough to be a microcosm in which the life of the whole world of Calvin's day was remarkably well reflected.

Geneva was also small enough to enable its leaders and pastors to be aware of the intensity and urgency of the needs of the time. They had all the ever-recurring world-problems of people of such variety living close together. Calvin having come from France must have been often depressed by the petty scale on which everything was conducted in his adopted home, and perhaps there is an unconscious echo of this in a

[17] *Op. cit.*, p. 222.
[18] A. Menzies, *A Study in Calvin and Other Papers*, London, 1918, p. 160.

reference he once made to his most powerful and influential Genevese opponent, Ami Perrin, as "our comic Caesar". But in fact this place enabled him to keep his mind and heart on the personal and intimate levels of life, while he was trying to think out Christian ways of meeting the human situation, and so prevented him from being content with the application of mechanical, monetary or merely legal solutions.

Geneva seemed therefore specially suited for the kind of work he was to accomplish. "The village or township", says de Tocqueville, "is the only association which is so perfectly natural, that wherever a number of men are collected it seems to establish itself. Local assemblies of citizens constitute the strength of free nations. Town meetings are to liberty what primary schools are to science: they bring it within the people's reach, they teach men how to use and enjoy it. A nation may establish a system of free government, but without the spirit of municipal institutions it cannot have the spirit of liberty." [19]

The Consistory Case-book — Thoroughness or Triviality?

Calvin refers to the affairs of Geneva in a letter written in February 1545 in which he expresses some frustration over the multitude and complexity of the problems that faced him: "Already I have broken ground upon the subject of the internal state of the city in ten sermons. Wherefore, however, should I enter into this labyrinth?"

The multitude of cases that were brought before the consistory itself with their often pathetic and sometimes intricate personal details must at times have presented to him a perplexing aspect of the Genevan "labyrinth" of bitterness and discontent, of official pettiness and untrustworthiness, in which he had tended to feel so lost.

The records of that body from 1542 onwards show that it

---

[19] *Democracy in America*, World Classics Edition, pp. 56-7. Walter Ullman (in *History of Political Thought: The Middle Ages*, Baltimore, 1965) has pointed out that it is more realistic to find the source of the development of the tradition of democractic freedom in England in the village assemblies of feudal times than in affairs like Magna Carta.

was concerned[20] to seek out, summon and warn many who were careless in church attendance. It dealt with misbehaviour in church such as laughing during sermons. It censured those who criticised the preaching, and who in conversation denied the accepted doctrines of the faith. It gave judgment in cases of blasphemy, cursing, lying and cheating, the possession of copies of books then considered to be unhealthy reading, and the singing of obscene songs. It reviewed cases of superstition: of people who went to have their fortune told, who wore superstitious amulets and offered to cure others by strange means, who reverted to Romish practices. It sought to prevent undesirable marriages.

People who played cards on Sunday, and dice on any day, who held improper dances in their homes, who were guilty of gluttony, drunkenness, fornication, adultery or unnatural vice, were brought before it. It sought to control the kind of names people gave to their children, forbidding those which had pagan and undesirable association, and it suggested Biblical substitutes. It intervened and gave advice on family quarrels which were beginning to cause public scandal. Under its supervision extravagances and improprieties were frowned on.

By its own authority it admonished, censured and excommunicated people. They were sent by it to the town council which executed the sentences it passed, such as imprisonment with bread and water.

We have to try to judge such proceedings in Geneva in the light of the customs of the day. In many of the communes of Europe the morals of citizens were controlled by detailed regulations. There were laws everywhere against swearing and blasphemy, against excess and extravagance in clothing, food and drink. You couldn't have a party in the privacy of your house without having to keep the rules, or you were in trouble. Public amusements, however, aroused special watchfulness. Dancing was completely forbidden by some

[20] For the proceedings of the Consistory see C.O., 21:289ff. A fair account is given, e.g., in H. Y. Reyburn, *John Calvin, His Life, Letters, and Work*, London, 1914, pp. 117ff, and Carew Hunt, *op. cit.*, pp. 149f.

authorities. By others it was controlled, and "decent" dances were clearly defined.

The records of Geneva show that the town was well used to such laws and practices. People were frequently banished for committing adultery and severe punishments were applied for what we today would not regard as crimes. The enforcement of the laws controlling pettier offences was sometimes slack and the regulations were rigidly applied only at intermittent periods. Sometimes the Church and civic authorities would unite in such a special moral crusade. In 1459 in a very unsettled period, the Cathedral Chapter issued fresh regulations relying on the City Syndics to help them to see that they were enforced. Prostitutes were segregated and controlled. Gambling was especially severely attacked because many other troubles were traced to cards and dice. Those who blasphemed God or the Virgin or the Saints were forced to kneel where they had sinned, uncover their heads, clasp their hands, ask pardon and kiss the ground as a sign of penitence.

When Farel arrived and the Reformation began to be established, affairs had again degenerated badly. Froment's contemporary account of the behaviour of the monks in Geneva shows that when they left the city "they left much moral filth behind them".[21] The council of Geneva simply reverted to the old practice of tightening things up. The women who dressed a bride over-luxuriously for her wedding with her "hair hanging lower down than is fitting" were put in prison. A card player was put in the pillory with his cards about his neck, and an adulterer was paraded through the streets with his mistress before being banished for a year. On February 28, 1536 the council posted up notices in taverns forbidding blasphemy and the sale of drink after 9 p.m. each day or during the sermons. Calvin had not yet come — and all these things were happening. We must not blame a man for the environment he is born into.[22]

Obviously the majority of responsible people in Geneva at

[21] Reyburn, *op. cit.*, pp. 122-3.

[22] For account of disciplinary cases in Geneva before Calvin arrived, and references to the *Registrar of the Council* see e.g. John T. McNeill, *op. cit.*, p. 135, and Carew Hunt, *op. cit.*, p. 67.

the time approved of what the consistory was doing. Calvin never presided over it. In the administration of discipline he was entirely dependent on certain members of the various city councils, and on leading citizens. He certainly could dictate nothing to anybody. T. M. Parker points out that those Swiss burghers around him were not used to being subjects of a monarch, but had had a great deal of "experience of self-determination".[23]

There is indeed evidence that sometimes Calvin perhaps too weakly allowed his policy to be dictated by the puritanical zeal of those who had narrower views than himself.

For example, in July, 1546 he supported the staging of a morality play entitled *The Acts of the Apostles* written by Abel Poupin, one of the ministers. Viret was invited to see it. But one of the ministers, Michael Cop, in a sermon said that "the women who should mount the theatre to act that farce would be shameless creatures". There was a tumult in which Calvin inevitably became involved. He protected Cop, though he judged him to have acted imprudently. Though the crowd said they respected Calvin, and wanted to have it out with Cop alone, Calvin insisted on a solid front by all the pastors until it was made plain that Cop had erred in his duty, for obviously Cop's freedom to preach his convictions was at stake. Abel Poupin with Calvin's help seems to have managed to quieten the actors. The play went on. Viret helped to pacify those whom Calvin significantly called "our furious friends". The Senate was coolly on the side of the ministers. The result of the affair was that the play, after a short run, was finally suspended "until the time was more favourable".[24] John McNeill comments on this incident. "Thus almost inadvertently Calvin lent himself to the suppression of drama."[25]

We can affirm that in the same way he lent himself even to what must at times have seemed to him to verge on the trivial and the legalistic in the disciplinary process. He did not try to modify its stringency even after his position in Geneva was

---

[23] *Christianity and The State in the Light of History*, London, 1955, p. 156.
[24] Cf. C.L. to Farel, July 4, 1546.   [25] *Op. cit.*, p. 167.

secure. We are told that in 1558-1559 there were 414 trials such as those above mentioned.[26]

Calvin normally avoided becoming lost in what he himself regarded as trivialities. In theology he always dwelt only on important central themes and refused to be sidetracked into the complicated discussions of side issues. In church ceremonies he hated the cluttering up of services by trifling ceremonies, and he refused to be drawn into too much controversy over such little things. Therefore we must conclude that in his mind such aspects of the discipline had some special significance.

We may find a clue in Calvin's concern for the personal sanctification of the individual. Where such is the concern, an individual conscience often refuses to regard as trivial what others would ignore. Moreover, following the general trend of Reformation thought, Calvin had reacted against distinguishing between venial and mortal sins. "In every little transgression of the divinely commanded law, God's authority is set aside", he wrote. "Let the children of God hold that all sin is mortal."[27] He criticised "the foolish distinction" that certain sins are more pardonable than others and therefore can be purged by easier remedies. "Those who rely on trifling satisfactions", he affirmed, "hold the judgment of God in contempt."[28]

He obviously believed that often, even in apparently insignificant decisions in matters of personal morality, human character is revealed for what it really is, and destiny is being worked out. Nothing that could register powerfully on the human conscience of his day was to him trivial. He believed that the health and happiness of a little town like Geneva depended on the putting right of a multitude of minor affairs.

Applying the Gospel to life meant applying it in detail. Social leaders and politicians today are often sheltered from the sobering contact with such details by the cover of a huge bureaucracy behind which they can hide comfortably and talk and plan grandly. Calvin had no such shelter. He had

[26] Henry, *op. cit.*, p. 448.
[27] *Inst.*, 2:8:59.   [28] *Inst.*, 3:4:27-8.

himself to go often with his deacons and elders to the point
where people lived and the trouble really was. His aim in
enforcing discipline was pastoral. It is easy to pillory the
district elders as they tried to the best of their ability to watch
over the flock. We can call them "informers", accuse them of
prying with vindictive or prurient motives into purely
domestic matters when they heard of scandal. But there was
a considerable amount of brutal wife-beating in Geneva, and
the same kind of cruelty to children, the consequences of
which often cause a public outcry when our social services
today are not sufficiently diligent. We have to remember, too,
that in this matter Calvin was as much concerned to find cases
of poverty to relieve as to find cases of moral lapsing, and in
these latter instances he was primarily concerned to give
pastoral help to the offenders face to face.

His aim was also positive. The minutes of the consistory
show only the negative side of the city discipline. Calvin's
programme involved the active promotion of the good life by
the exaltation of virtue.[29] He encouraged the city fathers of
Geneva not to become too absorbed with "law and order".
They were there to set up and maintain a good system of
public education, to encourage wholesome culture, and to
create, even by regulation, an environment for healthy social
attitudes. He believed that good morals can be produced by
good legislation and good social organisation. His experiment
proved in the long run that people who were carefully driven
into living virtuously began to prefer virtue to vice.

We have thought it best, in this book, first to review the
whole work of Calvin in his Reformation setting, and then to
estimate him as a man. It would be fair to him now, however,
if in reading through his ordinances on marriage we noted
how progressive and liberal were some of the views and
provisions he was trying to put across. For instance he insisted
that parents had no right to force their children into any
marriage, and he gave guidance to the young people on how
to stand up for their liberties when pressure was put on them
in this matter. He affirmed that (remembering Eph. 5:),

[29] The aim of discipline was to stimulate goodness by giving "due honour to
virtue", as well as to restrain wickedness by sanctions. Cf. *Inst.*, 4:20:9.

"although in ancient times it was otherwise", today in marriage "the wife is not more subject to the husband than the husband to the wife".[30]

[30] Cf. R.C.P., pp. 73, 77.

CHAPTER 5

THE STRUGGLE FOR
"SPIRITUAL GOVERNMENT"

Sources of Tension — "the Libertines"

GENEVA had an aristocracy consisting of some from the leading old families, and some from the ranks of the nouveaux riches. They were much inter-married. Many of them had been active early supporters of the Reformation and had taken part cordially in the recall of Calvin from exile. Possibly they thought that while he would effect many desirable improvements in city life generally he would leave them at peace. They had mistaken their man. Calvin treated everyone alike whatever their position or status. "Great kings", he wrote, "should not imagine it does them dishonour to prostrate themselves before the King of kings."[1]

This group of citizens and their followers were powerful as a political force because of the family status which the tradition of the city accorded to them, and the strength of their influence on the councils. It has become customary, in books about Geneva, to refer to them as the "Libertines".

What we read about them in the records of the time gives us a poor impression of them. Ami Perrin, their leader, the only son of merchant parents who had made a fortune, was a man of some ability and worth but he had too much bravado, and a basic instability that ultimately sealed his downfall. Perrin was married to the daughter of François Favre, the "elder statesman" of the group. Favre was over-fond of committing adultery in a way that led to public scandal. Doumergue's opinion is that they had all had very poor early education and that the atmosphere in which they lived had thwarted intellectual development. They had no viable

[1] *Inst.*, 4:12:7.

programme and they overdeveloped the protest mentality. The arrogance with which they conducted their demonstrations against the regulations, and their lack of self-control under their punishment, won for them disgust instead of sympathy.

Their womenfolk when summoned for their disorderly behaviour and their insistence on the right to dance, proved always more than a match even for Calvin, in spontaneous abusive eloquence, and of course, they had an even wider choice of picturesque vocabulary than he could dare to use. They quarrelled in public. Perrin's wife had to be jailed for an unruly brawl with her mother-in-law.

They did not mind being answerable to the city council, even to the extent of being rebuked and imprisoned under the old Genevan statutes for the sake of which their forbears had fought and sacrificed but they came to view Calvin as merely an upstart and a foreigner. His new court they regarded as being without authority. They became a determined opposition party against the supporters of the Reformer within the city.

Sources of Tension — the Council

Apart from the Libertines, the concern of many of the members of the Genevan council was to keep Calvin as long as they could, but to keep him in his place, and at a distance. Calvin soon rediscovered their temper, and he wisely restrained himself. When he faced the magistracy with his proposals for the Church in 1541 he found that they wanted to have control over the nomination of new pastors. They did not approve of ordination by the laying on of hands. They were suspicious of his proposals that the ministers should meet once a quarter for a mutual examination of their conduct. He had to give assurances that nothing done here would prejudice the right of the magistracy. Naturally they were watchful, for he was a foreigner as well as a pastor. It took them very many years before they changed the attitude expressed in their minute of March 1538: M. G. Farel and M. Calvinus are not to mix themselves in magistracy! Ten years later when they found that M. Calvin "with great choler preached that the magistracy permits many insolences", it was "ordered that he should be called before the council to know why he had so preached".[2] They did not want him to become too familiar with the workings of the power structure. "I am a stranger in this city", he wrote, even in 1556, "for every day I hear persons of lowest rank discussing matters which are entirely unknown to me."[3]

At first both Calvin and the council sought to avoid any clash over matters on which they basically disagreed. Very soon, however, the point became obvious over which the battle had eventually to be fought. Calvin's plan for the consistory, in the 1541 ordinances, involved, as Wendel points out, a spiritual jurisdiction trespassing on the political prerogative which the council felt to belong to itself. His outline of the scheme raised tense discussion as to whether the consistory could be allowed to excommunicate offenders. The Council was very willing to let them examine cases and admonish offenders but wanted to draw the line there. In the end there was a compromise. Calvin insisted on retaining power for the consistory to excommunicate if it so judged. But the magistrates added a significant stipulation that the "ministers have no civil jurisdiction and wield only the spiritual sword of the Word of God as St. Paul commands them, and that there is no derogation by the Consistory from the authority of the Seigneury and the Magistracy, but the civil power shall continue in its entirety".[4]

The jealousy of the Council to maintain their authority in Church affairs was understandable. Within the churches of the Reformation almost everywhere power had been taken over by laymen. In asserting their freedom from Papal authority, the civil rulers had tended to deny the Church effective control over any of its own important affairs. At the disputation of Zurich in 1523, it was the magistrates who convened the gathering. They stopped the proceedings when

---

[2] Register of Council, May 1548; cf. E. Doumergue, *Jean Calvin, Les hommes et les choses de son temps*, vol. VI, Neuilly, 1926, pp. 131ff.
[3] C.L. to Zerkinden, February 21, 1556.
[4] *Ecclesiastical Ordinances*, 1541. R.C.P., p. 49.

they judged that Zwingli had made his case, and then on their own authority they reappointed him to his charge. In Bern, from whom the Genevan authorities learned much, the council adopted a high tone towards their ministers. When they brought about the reformation of the Canton Vaud their edict read: "Let no one be appointed to preach the Word of God in the said country unless he be deputed by us for the work", and they chose for appointment four pastors who had had no previous examination by the other ministers already there.[5]

There is evidence that some of the local magistrates shared the feelings of King James I when he discovered in holy scriptures that "even by God himself the rulers are called Gods" with "power to exalt low things and abase high things, and make their subjects like men at a chess, a pawn to take a bishop". When Farel in Neuchâtel criticised the behaviour of the daughter of an important local figure the Sieur de Wattewille he was told in the name of the Bernese government that nowadays, one simply hired and fired the ministers like the domestics whenever one pleased.[6]

The leading reforming teachers and preachers had seemed to assent without reserve to the claims of the magistrates to such authority within the Church. Wolfgang Capito in Strasbourg believed that the secular prince was appointed by Christ to be the shepherd and father of the Church within his realm and he therefore approved of Henry VIII's assumption of rule within the Church of England. Zwingli appears to have expected the civil magistrate to rule the Church in almost all the details of its external life. Luther, at times against his better judgment, refused to present much resistance to the civil authorities in their control of Church

[5] Cf. J. L. Ainslie, *The Doctrines of Ministerial Order in the Reformed Churches*, Edinburgh, 1940, p. 126.

[6] Cf. A. Bouvier, *Henri Bullinger*, Neuchâtel, 1940, p. 96. Francis Drake once had his ship's chaplain chained and padlocked to the deck after what he thought was a disrespectful sermon, and summoning his crew around him, himself sitting "crosslegged on a sea chest with a pair of pantouffles in his hand", had told the clergyman, "Francis Fletcher, I do here excommunicate thee out of the Church of God and from all benefits and graces thereof, and denounce thee to the devil and all his angels." Garrett Mattingly, *The Defeat of a Spanish Armada*, p. 119.

affairs. Haller in Bern regarded himself as a servant of the State even in giving the Sacrament of the Lord's Supper, and he affirmed that even in cases where he felt reluctant, he would give it to those whom the State permitted to partake. As Owen Chadwick observes, "The Reformation did not take ecclesiastical power from a Church which grasped it. It afforded the opportunity for the cities and the princes finally to wrest power out of a hand from which it was already slipping."[7]

It is in this context that we have to understand and, indeed, to evaluate the struggle Calvin had to gain in Geneva even a small measure of the spiritual independence and freedom which he believed the Church and its ministry had had in New Testament times. Certainly when he returned to Geneva in 1541 the members of the town council had controlled all the events leading to and following upon, the Reformation. They had sacked the pastors when they were displeased with them. They had decided to recall Calvin when they felt they needed him.

It must not be imagined, however, that the lay authorities did not take their responsibility for the Church seriously. Many of them were God-fearing men deeply affected by the spiritual renewal that was taking place, and themselves students of the Bible. There was, for instance, Ami Porral one of the chief magistrates of Geneva who proved himself a more capable theologian than some of Calvin's colleagues in the ministry. He exposed the errors of two inexperienced young pastors, and with the approval of Calvin admonished them personally. This venerable old man, on his death-bed gave a sermon to those who had gathered around, revealing an insight into the meaning of the ministry and of the grace of God, which astonished Calvin.[8]

Such men no doubt sincerely believed that sitting on the bench in the town council they could very well discern by themselves what were the interests of their local church. Let the ministers cooperate, and they would certainly cooperate, but the ultimate responsibility for the spiritual welfare of their

[7] *Op. cit.*, p. 68; cf. Elton, *op. cit.*, p. 156; R. N. Carew Hunt, *op. cit.*, p. 254.
[8] C.L. to Farel June 16, 1542.

city, they believed rested on them. The Reformation had taught them the priesthood of all believers.

Compromise and Resistance

Calvin compromised while he temporised. Those who have had experience of the pastorate in congregations where the laity have enjoyed any real tradition of independence will be able to understand and sympathise with him. He accepted changes that he felt undesirable.

Against his better judgment, for example, the authorities in Geneva finally abolished all feast days. Calvin gives his own account of this matter in letters he sent to Bern defending himself from accusations that he was autocratic. The change, he affirmed, took place only because of public discussion and tension. When he and Farel were expelled from Geneva, the celebration of feast days was completely abolished by "the tumultuous violence of the ungodly". Under the circumstances since his return to Geneva he had followed a moderate course and had changed nothing except to try to introduce at least the celebration of Christmas. But things had moved quickly without any initiative on his part. On the old customary saints' days, to try to satisfy those who had desired some celebration, shops had been closed in the mornings and public prayers were held. This arrangement, however, had led "certain inflexible individuals who did not comply with common custom from some perverse malice or other" to upset everything, with the result that not a year had passed "without some quarrel and bickering because the people were divided, and to such a degree as to draw their swords".

Calvin had urged the Senate at least to remove the disagreement, and "with moderation". He had been astonished at the final result. The Senate solved the problem by abolishing altogether the weekday feasts — so that nothing was left to Geneva but the Sabbath. Calvin knew nothing about the decision till the debate was over.

Thus Geneva lost its feast-days. Calvin affirmed that if he had had his choice he would not have decided this way. But such things were "things indifferent" and could "be decided locally". The circulation of a pamphlet by Bolsec had spread the rumour that Calvin had wished to abolish Sunday in order to observe the Friday instead. Calvin's answer to this accusation was: "I have never shown the least sign of lusting after such innovations, but very much to the contrary." Referring to other charges about the radical changes he was supposed to have made he affirmed: "Before my arrival in Geneva, the manner of celebrating the Lord's Supper, baptism, marriage and the festivals, was such as it is at present, without my having changed anything."[9]

Even after Calvin's victory over the Libertines and the growth of confidence between him and the congregation, he did not insist on his own way in such matters. In 1558 he expressed his regret that the Lord's Supper was not administered to the sick, and also that those about to depart from this life should be deprived of this consolation. But he knew that the change would cause offence, "I have preferred to consult peace",[10] he wrote. He always wished to celebrate the Lord's Supper at least once a month or more often. He had to settle for it four times a year.

He accepted personal humiliation as well as political compromise. He was humiliated by the syndics even as late as 1554 when they insisted on sending one of his new books to be censored. Exasperated, he told them that if he lived a thousand years he would never publish anything again in Geneva.[11] When his brother's wife became unfaithful and his brother sought a divorce the whole Calvin household was spared no experience of shame in the local courts, and Calvin was deeply vexed about this. On one occasion he had to suffer reprimand and to make what was virtually a public apology to the council when a letter of his to Viret was intercepted — a letter in which he had let himself go and had accused the Senate of hypocrisy and of wanting to govern without God.[12]

Because he gave way so freely on the lesser issues, his rigid stand on other matters showed clearly where he drew the line,

[9] For above see C.L. to Haller, January 2, 1554; C.L. to Seigneurs of Bern, March 14, 1555.
[10] C.L. to Venceslas Zeuleger, August 1558.
[11] In 1554. This was after he himself had been appointed censor in 1542.
[12] C.L. to Viret, September 20, 1548.

and on what principles. He could, for example, accept personal insult but he never failed to show immediate and extreme sensitivity when he thought that an insult involved contempt for the ministry of the Word, or in any way tended to weaken its influence. One of the first cases which involved great public tension in Geneva in 1546 was that of Pierre Ameaux.

Ameaux had at first given Calvin loyal support. He manufactured playing cards and wax candles, and his business must have been badly affected by the reforms in the city. He attacked Calvin at a supper given to friends, saying he was a bad man and that his teaching was false. He was arrested. The Little Council wanted strong measures taken against him. He was ordered publicly to confess his guilt and fined heavily. When Ameaux was to be released after five weeks in prison Calvin was not content. Along with the other ministers he appeared before the council and insisted that an apology must be made in public, refusing even to accept one made before the Council of the Two Hundred and threatening to abstain from preaching if such an apology was not given. Calvin took up this stand even though he knew that a large section of the population were bitterly against him for what he was insisting on. There was a protest made in church when he was preaching. It was followed by a tumult the next day, to quieten which the council erected a warning gallows before the church. Calvin still insisted and Ameaux finally had to walk through the town bareheaded, in a shirt, with a torch in his hand, and to kneel at various points of his route to implore God's mercy.

The council was later to find Calvin equally sensitive when they themselves began to challenge him more acutely than before on the subject of who was to control admission to the Lord's Supper. Obviously, as we have seen, the wording of the final draft of the Ordinances on this point can be interpreted in many ways, and problems were bound to arise when its meaning had to be made clear.

The serious tension began in March 1543 when the council of sixty decreed that the consistory should have neither jurisdiction nor power to ban from the Supper. In a letter to

Viret on the day before Easter of that year Calvin expressed the shock with which the decree was received when the syndic announced it at a meeting of the consistory. "I immediately replied that such a decree could only be ratified by my death or banishment." He meant his words literally. The Senate held an extraordinary meeting at which Calvin gave "a large discourse upon the weighty argument". They assented but not willingly.[13]

The matter was again raised acutely in 1548 when the council asserted that the ministers possessed the right "only of admonition and not of excommunication" and in December of that year they authorised one Guichard Roux to receive the Sacrament against the wishes of the pastors. The decisive case was, however, that of Philibert Berthelier.

His father had been martyred for the cause of Geneva's freedom. He was gifted and comparatively well educated. He had married thinking his wife had money and when he discovered she had none he renounced the contract. In 1548 he is reported as being in trouble for insolence, drinking and assault. In 1551 he is reported in March as having an illicit affair with a widow in a labourer's house, and in October with two other persons he chased one of the pastors through the streets into St. Peter's. He was banned from communion.

In 1552 the council tried to restore him to communion but when they saw his rebellious attitude they, too, at first approved of the ban. They changed their minds later, however, only to receive a protest from the ministers who appealed to the ecclesiastical Ordinances and "unanimously declared that they could not admit this man, or other like him to the supper until the consistory had evidence of his repentance and absolved him". In September 1553, when the Servetus affair was creating added tension and Calvin's opponents had a good deal of power on the council, Berthelier was encouraged by one of the syndics, Ami Perrin, Calvin's arch-enemy, to bypass the consistory and to ask permission of the council to be readmitted to the Lord's Supper. It was

---

[13] C.L. to Viret "The day before Easter", 1543. For an excellent short account of the Berthelier affair, cf. R.C.P. Introduction, pp. 10ff.

granted. Calvin in a letter to Viret on September 4 describes another meeting he had with two of the councils when he endeavoured "partly by vehemence, and partly by moderation, to reduce them to a sound mind", repeating his oath that he would meet death rather than profane shamefully the Holy Supper of the Lord. The council upheld its decision, but revealed its uneasiness by secretly advising Berthelier not to challenge Calvin by trying to communicate.

On the following Sunday the Supper was due to be celebrated. Calvin, says Beza, "raised his voice and his hand in the course of his sermon, after he had spoken at some length of the despisers of sacred mysteries, and exclaimed, in the words of Chrysostom, 'I will die sooner than this hand shall stretch forth the sacred things of the Lord to those who have been judged despisers'. The sacrament was celebrated with extraordinary silence, not without some degree of trembling, as if the Deity himself were actually present."[14]

Calvin at this juncture realised that his whole future in Geneva was indeed at stake and in the afternoon of the same day he preached what could be interpreted as a farewell sermon, offering to stay if he was left "free to preach and serve", affirming his determination to leave if he was to be "burdened with intolerable restrictions".

It was the council who now gave way. Calvin therefore won a decisive moral and political victory, and many of Calvin's biographies make this incident a turning point in his struggle in Geneva. On December 21, 1553 the council itself ruled that Berthelier should not be admitted to the Supper, and on January 24, 1555 it resolved that "the Consistory should retain its statutes and exercise its accustomed authority in accordance with the Word of God and the Ordinances previously passed".

We can understand Calvin's sensitivity at this point. For the civil authority to decide who was to receive the Supper meant that they could ultimately decide what the content of the preached word should be. The pastor would now have to interpret certain New Testament texts in the way directed by the secular council. The issue in the case of Berthelier was the

[14] C.Tr., vol. I, pp. lxii-lxiii.

same as that in the case of Ameaux: the authority and independence of the ministry of the Word.

To Calvin, the preached Word of God was the Sceptre by which Christ continually established his unique and spiritual rule over the minds and hearts of his people. If such a word was to be heard with its full authority and power the pastors must be left entirely free to preach it in its fullness without interference. He believed that such unfettered preaching of the Word could change Geneva and indeed the whole world. But the Church had to maintain its independence over against all earthly authority in this one sphere of its activity. Therefore he had ensured that in Geneva though ministers on appointment had to vow to honour the magistrates of the city and to be subject to its polity and statutes, they nevertheless reserved the liberty to teach "in accordance with what God commands" and each made the vow: "I promise to be a servant to the magistracy and the people so far as by that I be not hindered in rendering to God the service I owe Him in my calling."[15]

The Issues in Longer Perspective

We have seen that after Calvin's conversion he did not renounce his love for humanism, though he pursued his former study of it "with less ardour". But he had begun to find that humanism is too complex and comprehensive a movement to be contained within any Christian mould. It was, after all, rooted far more deeply in pagan antiquity than in the Bible. It had apeared in the Middle Ages as a by-product of the revival of ancient learning, and the discovery of the greatness in classical ages. It sought to show how good life had been before the Christian Gospel ever dawned on the world. It could therefore show, too, how good life could be apart from anything the Gospel had to offer.

In its fuller development therefore humanism was bound to reveal features, and find its expression in attitudes, alien to

---

[15] Cf. Ainslie, *op. cit.*, p. 137 and R.C.P., pp. 36ff., for expressions of Calvin's sensitivity in such matters; cf. C.L. to Viret, August 23, 1542; to Dr. Marbach August 25, 1554.

the Christian faith. It encouraged immense pride in what made one simply human; and in its artistic expression it glorified man rather than God. It was a thoroughly secular movement for it refused to find the meaning of human life and destiny through reference to another world. Man did not need a heavenly dimension to give his life divine significance. His own form at its best was divine. Why look elsewhere? He could find eternity in his present human experience. He was meant simply to capture and enjoy that experience in its fullness.[16] Education rather than salvation was man's only need. His own ability could substitute for any law as a rule of ethics. Fully fledged humanists, such as Lorenzo Valla, had taught that man must never thwart his self-development or self-fulfilment, even when this might demand the uninhibited expression of his sensual desires. These in themselves were to be regarded as all basically good. Self-expression rather than self-denial was to be the rule of life.

Such views found expression in the teaching of those in Calvin's time who were commonly known in Europe as "libertines" or "spiritual libertines". Calvin had come up against these sects here and there, and in 1545 he wrote a tract *Against the Fantastical and Raging Sect of the Libertines*. Some of this sect were frankly anti-Christian. The Renaissance had given them a new vision of what they regarded as the fullness and health of men in paganism before life was spoiled by the Gospel. Christianity, they believed, had created a slave morality of conscience and restraint, from which indulgence in sensual desires would liberate men. Others liked to emphasise that they were spiritual and believed that this liberation should be linked up with the Gospel. Since Christ is the Spirit who is in us all, to yield to ourselves is to yield to the Spirit. The new birth is the power to suppress the fear of God. The children of God restored by Christ to the state of perfection and innocence need never now try to bridle the "flesh". It was the curse of the old Adam that brought about

[16] On the tension between humanism and the Gospel, see, e.g., Louis Bouyer, *Erasmus and his Times*, MD, 1959, pp. 22f; Van Gelder, *The Two Reformations of the Sixteenth Century*, The Hague, 1964, pp. 37ff; Herbert Grierson, *Cross Currents in English Literature in the Seventeenth Century*, London, 1929, pp. 31ff; J. Bronowsky and Bruce Mazlish, *The Western Intellectual Tradition*, Penguin, 1963, pp. 85f, 551ff.

the difference between honesty and dishonesty, fornication and chastity, integrity and cunning. But the power of the old Adam has been brought to an end in Christ and these differences are abolished.

Strangely combined with this libertarianism was a cast-iron moral determinism. How can one really sin, they asked, if it is God who moves the impulses within him? How can one pray when anyone who is enlightened and adult can see that such a practice is entirely superfluous? It was as if men gripped by some wild speculative fever simply could not resist trying to prove that everything in the Christian tradition tended to be perverse.[17]

We cannot call this teaching "humanism". It is rather something humanism can rot into. There is little doubt that Calvin saw this decadent humanism threatening to take possession of the prevailing culture in Geneva as a kind of spirit of the age which could eat its way into people's minds unconsciously, even subconsciously. He found such a spirit prevalent in the opposition of the Libertine party and in their jealousy for secular autonomy which he encountered from the council. His mission was to maintian the independence of the Word of God, over against such teachings and attitudes.

Sir Herbert Grierson in his *Cross Currents in English Literature in the Seventeenth Century* reminds us of the difficulty which the early fathers of the Church found when they tried to reconcile their former cultural pursuits with the new Christian Gospel. They ceased to find pleasure in what had before been their pride. Many of them tried to renounce as completely as they could even the conscious use of the rhetorical skills they had formerly acquired. These things now seemed to belong to a world alien to the Kingdom of God into which Christ had given them entrance. Grierson likens this to the experience which people underwent in the sixteenth century as they

---

[17] Servetus himself was typical of this cast of mind which would rather speculate about whether the Son of God would have been bi-sexual if he had been born of a woman, than think positively about the message of the incarnation itself. We find echoes of Calvin's criticism of the Libertines in the *Institutes*; cf. 1:9:1; 2:1:10; 2:7:13; 3:3:14; 3:20:45; etc. Cf. "The description of the spirit of libertinism" in Paul Hazard, *The European Mind, 1680-1715*, Pelican Books, 1964, p. 155. Since Calvin's opponents in Geneva tended to be of this spirit they were no doubt called the "Libertine" party.

found themselves caught up on the one hand by the Reformation and faced on the other hand the Renaissance:

> In Italy in the 15th century the Renaissance quickly revealed itself as a thoroughgoing secular if not necessarily religious movement; and when the Reformation followed there stood face to face a reasserted, self-conscious secularism, and the reawakened temper of early Christianity, other worldly, intransigent in its attitude towards any acceptance of the world as an end in itself, as something to be enjoyed.[18]

Grierson was referring primarily to the experience of the English Puritans. But Calvin was there before them, and they could learn from his experience of the same kind of conflict a century earlier. We shall see that he tried to encourage what he believed was genuine humanism in Geneva, and to do justice to the obvious goodness that was there in things human, and in life itself. Had not Paul commended "whatever is excellent and admirable"? And was not David's immortal elegy on Saul and Jonathan the most perfect example of humanistic praise for what was merely human?[19] But he believed that it was only within a community where the Word of God was being freely preached and respectfully received that a true humanism could develop and bring its benefits.

The Fall of the Libertines

After Calvin's moral victory in the Berthelier affair in 1553, the political situation in Geneva seemed to grow more dangerous for him. Perrin, Berthelier, Vandel and their associates exercised their power in council affairs to pack committee meetings and to manœuvre their own supporters and relations into important offices. Perrin himself had the office of captain-general of the republic, and he was able to draw after himself in the streets a crowd of young supporters for a demonstration of loyalty to Geneva.

They had all the power and privilege necessary ultimately

[18] *Op. cit.*, p. 26.   [19] Phil., 4:8 (N.E.B.), 1 Sam. 1.

to destroy Calvin, but they pushed things too far and began
to display arrogance. Public opinion therefore began to turn
decisively against them. They lost heavily in the elections
which took place at the beginning of 1555 and their
opponents managed to purge the council and its offices in
their own favour.

What brought matters to a head was a move on the part of
Calvin's supporters to admit sixty more French refugees to
citizenship in Geneva. The town had already given this status
to many French immigrants, and previously even the
Libertines had welcomed such decisions because they helped
to lower the Genevan tax level. But now, too late, they were
wakening up to realise that the presence of the French
protestants in Geneva increased greatly Calvin's influence.
By organising threatening deputations to the council the
Libertines tried to block the plan to receive more immigrants,
and they tried also to have regulations adopted restricting the
privileges of the French already admitted.

On the morning of May 16 they led a mixed anti-French
demonstration to the Hotel de Ville, some of them with
swords, to emphasise the strength of their case. Rebuffed,
their leaders then met in taverns and houses. Wild talk of
resorting to force began to take the shape of a determined
conspiracy, though no definite plans were made. Then, in the
evening things misfired. Some of the party could not wait,
and went out into the street looking for victims. They found
no Frenchmen. Calvin, in a contemporary letter thanked
God that he had made them all sleepy that night so that they
had kept indoors. The mischief makers, however, did meet
and assault a member of the council and finally Perrin
wrenched the baton of office out of the hand of one of the
Syndics who had come to order an arrest. Some blood was
drawn before the tumult was quelled.

The aftermath brought disaster to Perrin and his followers.
He, Vandel and Berthelier, the leaders of the party, had to
flee. They were condemned to execution in their absence, and
were executed in effigy. Other ringleaders were beheaded.
There were stories that Calvin made himself present at their
torture and was active behind the scenes, but there is no

reason to doubt his affirmations in his letters to Bullinger at the time that he kept himself severely out of all the proceedings and visited the prison only because the victims asked for his pastoral help. It is unfortunate that in a letter to Farel, referring to the arrest of the toughest of the gang, he wrote, "we shall see what torture wrings out of them".

We can understand something of their deep resentment over the flood of immigrants. They were quite certain that if the Reformation happened to find favour in France itself, most of them would have gone back there and would have been content to leave Geneva in a mess. But their policies were entirely negative. Doumergue makes the comment that "Geneva from that moment began to make universal history".[20]

[20] *Op. cit.*, vol. II, p. 118. For account of events leading to the fall of the Libertines; cf. H. R. Reyburn, *op. cit.*, ch. XII.

CHAPTER 6

RUMOURS, SLANDERS AND CASES

AS the fame of Calvin's achievement in Geneva spread, rumours about him also spread. These were especially rife around Bern where the exiled libertines found refuge and where the local pastors hard pressed for sermon subjects were finding that they needed only to preach against Calvin to gain approval. The exiles spread exaggerated and distorted stories about what was taking place in Geneva. Calvin therefore found that since they could not destroy him in Geneva they were determined everywhere to make him "an object of detestation".[1] As far away as Poitiers they were saying that Calvin had surrounded himself with pomp and now made everyone kiss his slipper.[2] Other exiles who had somehow fallen foul of Calvin in Geneva told their own side of their story and wherever there was a real dislike for Calvin's teaching and policy such cases gave his enemies outside the city grounds for personal criticism of the man himself.

Though Calvin found the rumours vexatious and humiliating, he finally realised that however clearly he vindicated himself the stories would still circulate, so that his pen would never be out of his hand. Three of the cases which created most rumour and caused him most trouble were those of Sebastian Castellio, Jerome Bolsec, and Michael Servetus.

Castellio

Sebastian Castellio was six years younger than Calvin. When he was a student he stayed for a short time in the Reformer's house at Strasbourg. Calvin, he felt, insulted him. He was

[1] I.C.P., pp. xlv-xlvii, C.L. to Bullinger, June 15, 1555.
[2] C.L. to Bullinger, September 18, 1554; to Church at Poitiers, February 15, 1555.

asked to vacate his room to accommodate the servant of a French madame who came seeking refuge in the house. Having put him out, Calvin then called him back in as cavalier a fashion to do some nursing when the same servant fell ill. The free-board that Castellio was given at Calvin's table at the time was no compensation for the hurt he felt.

In 1541 he was invited, on Farel's recommendation, to go to Geneva as headmaster of the school which, after some trouble, had been reopened at the convent of Rive.

After Calvin arrived, and there was talk of financial stringency, Calvin made it clear that he would prefer to recall Mathurin Cordier whom he had placed in the position during his first period in Geneva. But Castellio's position was eased and he stayed. He and Calvin seemed to clash in personality as much as they did in opinion. When he consulted Calvin about a French translation of the New Testament that he was engaged in producing, he found the senior man impatient and anxious to economise in the time he gave him. When he applied to be given the status of pastor in Geneva Castellio was rejected on the ground that he regarded the Song of Songs as a rather lascivious product of Solomon's youth and therefore uncanonical, that he could not accept the "descent into hell" in the creed, and was unconvinced by Calvin's own interpretation of it.

Calvin on his side found no merit whatever in Castellio's attempts at translating the New Testament, and found him hopelessly arrogant and incorrigible in his own opinions. He grudged wasting his time with him, and he felt it would be impossible to have as a colleague in the ministry a man who was so aggressive over such differences. Yet he raised no question as to the desirability of his continuing to be headmaster of the school in Geneva. He gave Castellio a generous reference for another post explaining that it was due to no personal or moral defects but only on account of two outstanding doctrinal issues that Geneva had refused to make him a pastor.

In 1544, Castellio himself, having demanded public debate and been refused it, forced the issue by giving vent to his feelings in a bitter public attack on the sincerity and good faith of Calvin and his colleagues at a meeting for doctrinal discussion. The matter had to be taken to the magistrates who supported Calvin, and Castellio felt he had to go. Some years later he became a lecturer in Greek at Basel. After he heard of the burning of Servetus he wrote a pamphlet attacking Calvin, expressing views well in advance of his time, and pleading for toleration of all kinds of opinion. Calvin and Beza regarded him as the author of two bitter anonymous attacks on Calvin's doctrine of Predestination.

Castellio had a very hard time in his later life, being forced even to forage the river bank at Basel for wood so that he could burn a fire in his house late into the night in order to finish his work of Bible translation. Some people saw him and spread the news that Castellio was stealing things. Calvin seized on the gossip in Geneva and brought the accusation of theft into one of his published attacks on the man. Castellio let the truth of his plight become openly known in his reply. He died of starvation. Montaigne remarked that the world ought to have been ashamed of its neglect of so distinguished a scholar. Those who do not like Calvin tend to exaggerate Castellio's ability. Those whose instinct is always to support the under-dog find it easy to depict him as a martyr. All in all, there is no doubt that the later part of his controversy did not bring out what was best in the Genevan reformer.[3]

Bolsec

With Jerome Bolsec, Calvin was involved in quite a different affair. He was at one time a Carmelite monk and had been converted to the reformed faith. After flight to Italy he arrived at Geneva among the refugees. He settled down and practised medicine in the environs of Geneva, one of his patients being de Falais, the French nobleman who himself had been attracted to Geneva because of Calvin and with whom Calvin had kept up years of warm and personal friendship through correspondence.

Bolsec himself admired Calvin's teaching on most things

[3] Cf. C.L. to Viret, September 11, 1542; to Viret, March 1544; to Farel, May 30, 1544.

except on the matter of predestination. How was it possible to imagine that God had determined the lot of a man before his birth? Did not this make him like Jupiter, the author of sin and the origin of evil? Unfortunately he let his views be known in a rather dramatic outburst at a congregational discussion after a sermon by one of Calvin's younger colleagues. In delivering his attack, like Castellio, he seemed to raise the question of Calvin's honesty and integrity. The suggestion was that Calvin knowingly twisted Augustine's teaching to suit his purpose. Calvin seems to have arrived in the church unexpectedly as Bolsec was launching out on his attack. The ex-monk found himself completely floored by a reply in which Calvin with his usual unsurpassed skill in argument and his unerring ability to quote the right thing at the right place and time refuted every point he had made. This happened in October 1551.

Soon Bolsec was to find himself banished from the town of Geneva. The town authorities took the trouble, on Calvin's advice, of asking the pastors of the neighbouring Cantons for their opinions about the matters raised by Bolsec, and kept him in prison while they waited for the replies. In one of these queries the pastors of Geneva made their wish clear that the Church should be "purged of this pest in such a manner that it may not, by being driven thence, become injurious to our neighbours". They wanted Bolsec banished from the whole Swiss environment. They were disappointed with the replies. The neighbouring Cantons, on the whole, advised caution against making predestination too decisive an issue. But when all the issues were weighed they found themselves solidly behind their preachers on the matter. People like Bolsec could easily afford to settle down wherever they heard preaching they liked better. They suspected too that Bolsec had been put up to it by those who wanted to foment trouble on other grounds and they did not want any more trouble in Geneva. They preferred Calvin to Bolsec.

There is no doubt that Calvin felt he could not carry on his work in Geneva if people were allowed to go round suggesting in public that his teaching was deliberately founded on lies. He was deeply grieved however with the lack of support that he received both from Bern and Zurich. The affair also terminated his friendship with de Falais. As things worked out, Bolsec, unlike Castellio, proved he was hardly worth the protection of his patrons and that Calvin was well justified in wanting to be rid of him. He created other trouble. The Bernese had to put him out of their territory. Having later applied for a pastorate he again proved his instability by reverting to the Roman Church when things became too difficult. After Calvin's death Bolsec published a life of Calvin full of bitter and ridiculous slanders. It is a pity that those have sometimes been taken seriously by otherwise creditable Roman Catholics in their anxiety to find something to say against Calvin.[4]

Servetus

On October 27, 1553, Michael Servetus was burned at the stake in Geneva as "a warning to all who blaspheme God". He was accused of "terrible blasphemies against the Trinity and against the Son of God". The executioner was inexpert and the onlookers, appalled by the long drawn-out shrieks of the victim, out of pity tried to help the fire to burn more quickly by throwing faggots in to him to hurry up the process of death. The only devices in the whole affair that worked efficiently were the chain which kept the body tightly fixed and a thick cord wound several times round his neck. It took half an hour to kill him in this way. Calvin wasn't there. He had not wanted Servetus' death to be by burning. We are told that Farel was made so speechless by what he saw in the end that he went straight back to Neuchâtel without calling on Calvin. One malicious account of the day relates that he did go after the execution to report to Calvin, and that the conversation turned to the theoretical necessity of burning heretics.

Before he died Servetus was heard to cry out to Jesus for mercy. It was no doubt the genuine cry of an utterly broken

---

[4] A very full account of the Bolsec affair with the documents and minutes is to be found in R.C.P., pp. 137-186. Hughes' introduction to the Register (pp. 20-4) puts the affair in a true perspective. Cf. Doumergue, *op. cit.*, vol. VI, pp. 148ff.

man turning to a merciful God. But there was no comfort in it for those who wanted to know whether the fire had really purified the man's soul. Servetus had been for weeks challenged to put his trust in Christ, the Eternal Son of God. His final cry was to "Jesus thou Son of the Eternal God". Therefore neither the burning, nor Farel's anxious entreaties up to the last moments, clearly decided anything. It was the last and only time that men in the Reformed Church were going to play with fire as a means of purging heretics.

But at the time, everyone of note who was consulted approved of the deed. Servetus was well known and was detested in many places besides Geneva. He had had a remarkable career. Born in Spain, from quite early in his life he had had the idea that he was called to push the Reformation of Church and world further than men like Luther or Calvin had been willing to go. Like Calvin himself he gave up a career in law in order to devote himself to theology. He resigned a secretarial post in the Roman Church to become a freelance theologian mixing with the well-known Reformed teachers in Basle and Strasbourg. Owing to his extreme positions and attitude, however, he could not draw any of them into serious dialogue, and he felt rebuffed.

In his frustration he took to writing, and in his twenty-second year in 1531 he published one of the first significant attacks on the doctrine of the Trinity every written: *De Trinitatis Erroribus*. The Trinity was dubbed a Cerberus, a deception of the Devil. Even Bucer, the sage apostle of love, said from his pulpit that the author was worthy to have his entrails torn out, and the Roman authorities condemned the book. Servetus, under pressure to retract, published a second work in which he disowned his earlier opinions as merely immature. He then decided to hide himself. He changed his name to Villeneuve, travelled about, and took up medicine. Some think he must have gone to Italy for a year or two because a brand of anti-trinitarianism similar to his own cropped up here and there in the Italian provinces at this time.

In 1535 he went to Lyons and was employed as a printer's

reader while he published an edition of Ptolemy's *Geography*. Then he returned to Paris in 1536 where he achieved a reputation as one of the cleverest physicians in France, gave lectures in medicine and wrote a book on syrups. Among his writings there is a passage which suggests a theory about the circulation of the blood. He believed that astrology gave the clue to medical practice, published a book to prove it, and pitied his colleagues in the profession for their ignorance of the stars. He became as obnoxious to the medical establishment in Paris as he had become earlier in the theological world round Basle and Strasbourg. He had to leave.[5]

In 1540 he seems to have tried to settle down quietly at Vienne in Dauphigny where one of his friends had become archbishop. He could have done so comfortably, for he was always able to make money. But he kept hearing the old call radically to reform the Church, and he corresponded with Calvin whose writings and image seem to have inspired him with admiration and hatred. If Calvin in his reforming zeal could write an *Institutio* he would go one step further still and write a *Restitutio*. He sent Calvin several letters which Calvin felt to be full of rubbish, and finally he sent him a manuscript of his great new work which Calvin described in a letter to a mutual friend as "a long volume of insanities". Servetus was hurt when he found he could not draw Calvin even into a controversy which would show that he was taken seriously as a theologian. He reacted and sent Calvin a copy of his own Institutes full of abusive comments in the margin.

It thus happened that Calvin was put quite unwillingly into the position of being able to expose Servetus for both his hidden past and his present opinions. Ultimately a printed copy of the *Restitutio* which had been published secretly in Vienne in 1553 reached him in Geneva. The exposure began when someone from the district of Vienne wrote to a friend, de Trie, in Geneva reproaching him for all the heresy that was being taught in his town. De Trie replied with the gibe that

---

[5] It is said that Servetus made an appointment to meet Calvin in Paris for theological discussion, and that when Calvin kept the appointment Servetus failed to appear.

no one in Vienne should talk too loud about purity of doctrine while they were harbouring in their district someone who was not ashamed to print the very worst kind of blasphemy. Some pages of a printed copy of Servetus' *Restitutio* were enclosed as proof indicating that this kind of thing had been printed in Vienne.

This letter of de Trie is taken as a proof that at this stage Calvin took the initiative in exposing Servetus, and he has also been made responsible for the subsequent transfer of documents from Geneva to Lyons revealing the true identity of the author of the *Restitutio*. It is possible, however, that Servetus himself, in his anxiety to spread his teaching, had sent a batch of copies to Robert Estienne, a Genevan bookseller. There is no reason to suppose that Calvin in the first place prompted de Trie to open the fatal correspondence, because he was determined to hunt Servetus. As in many of the controversies over Calvin's part in affairs it is a matter of how one chooses to read evidence which is clearly open to a variety of different interpretations. Servetus was kept under arrest to await his trial for heresy at Lyons, and he would undoubtedly have been burned at the stake by the Roman authorities there. But he escaped.

It is difficult to understand exactly why he ultimately turned up in Geneva. It is true that he had been for years fascinated by Calvin, but he had also conceived an intense hatred for him. He had such a confidence in his destiny and in his own ability that he was capable of thinking that he could conquer Geneva as he had almost conquered the medical world of Paris, and thus take over from him. It is significant that he arrived just at the time when things were most difficult for Calvin, and he received the backing of the leaders of the Libertine party. At any rate Calvin was bound to interpret his appearance at Geneva as a frank declaration of war and a challenge to everything he stood for in the place. He knew by past experience that those who claimed enlightenment in seeking to further their views by policy could be as ruthless as any of those who opposed them.

Servetus was arrested in Geneva on August 13, 1553, a day after he arrived. Calvin lodged a complaint against him, preliminary hearings took place, and the authorities in Geneva decided to initiate trial proceedings. The prosecution was conducted by the attorney-general, Claude Rigot, one of the Libertine party. Calvin was of course chief witness for the prosecution. His evidence was damning, and sometimes it was given with a passion that could be felt to have personal overtones. Only one or two in the city who were against Calvin on other grounds disapproved of the action against Servetus. Calvin, indeed, pled with the council to use a more merciful form of punishment than burning, but that body did not alter its determination to conform to the customary way of dealing with such heretics.

After the execution Calvin sought, and received such universal approval from all over the world for what had been done in Geneva, even to the burning (of which he himself disapproved) that it was obvious that the world of his day felt that it could not allow such a radical fanatic the least opportunity to conduct a militant crusade for his views. As time passed, however, some people began to be not so sure about it, and it would have been better had Calvin and Beza not tried so hard to keep on justifying it.

In 1903 a committee from the Reformed Churches set up a granite monument to Servetus at the place of his death and inscribed: "Respectful and grateful sons of Calvin, our great Reformer, but condemning an error which belonged to his century and firm believers in freedom of conscience according to the true principles of the Reformation and the Gospel, we have raised this expiatory monument."[6]

---

[6] Calvin's action in the Servetus case here provided a field for a vast amount of research. W. Niesel lists fifty books and articles which appeared on the subject between 1901 and 1959 alone (*Calvin — Bibliographie 1901-1959*, München, 1961). Over a century ago, Bonnet pointed out that this has been "an eternal subject of accusation to the enemies of the Reformer" and Calvin is still pictured as "God's bloodhound". Most of Calvin's friends admit, like Doumergue who drew up the inscription for the expiatory monument that "his mistake was the mistake of the age". Emmanuel Stickelberger (*Calvin*, London, 1959) defends him more valiantly and records that when Servetus was executed Calvin spent the hour "on his knees", collecting his thoughts which were "powerfully upon him". We wish we could know those thoughts here. Dr. Henry Stebbing, an Anglican who translated Paul Henry's *Life and Times of Calvin* in 1849 affirmed that "only if Calvin had prayed to be set free from the bondage that made him a persecutor" could this "one blot which mars his otherwise spotless reputation" ever be condoned.

The Contemporary Situation and Practice

In reviewing such cases we have to remember not only the prevailing mood and customs of the day, but the contemporary situation in Geneva. In the case of Castellio the main issue at first was his suitability as a candidate for the ministry.

Geneva had a college of ministers called the "Company of Pastors of Geneva" which met often and regularly. Any candidate for the ministry was first examined by this body and then, if found suitable, recommended to the town council, who made the appointment. The detailed minutes of this company show that Calvin's was often only one respected voice among many during his years in Geneva, though he was always asked to be in the chair.

Once a minister was appointed he could be removed from office only by the decision of the town council. A pastor with a grudge against his colleagues could therefore ingratiate himself with those on the council who were unsympathetic to the ministry. He could thus win freedom to live in the town in a way unworthy of the ministry. In Geneva the Company of Pastors had serious trouble for many years over fellow pastors who spread gossip and false teaching, and tried to create disunity and scandal.[7] Calvin and his colleagues were therefore bound to proceed towards a recommendation to the ministry only with the utmost caution.

Moreover Calvin regarded it as one of the basic articles of the confession of the Reformed Church that the whole of Scripture was inspired by God. He had no doubt that in the composition of Holy Scriptures, the writers gave full expression to their true humanity, and at certain points we can distinguish his view of Scripture from what is today called "fundamentalism". But he believed that the Holy Spirit would give the believer an "efficacious confirmation" of the Word of God in its unity so that "above human judgment"

---

[7] See the account in Hughes, *Introduction* to R.C.P., of the case of the Pastor De Ecclesia who for years was allowed to create scandal and was a thorn in the flesh of all his colleagues because the city council refused to allow him to be disciplined. Pp. 13-16.

we can affirm with utter certainty that it "has flowed to us from the mouth of God by the ministry of men". He believed that we could, in addition to this, produce many proofs of its credibility.[8] Castellio obviously disagreed. It was not possible within the united Commonwealth which Calvin envisaged for his city, to allow a teacher to spread doubts on such an important matter.[9]

Castellio was not persecuted for his belief nor was he exiled. He was free either to leave Geneva, or stay there. When Calvin and Beza later attacked him because he advocated freedom to express any opinion within a community, they were replying to what was then in their eyes a political attack on the way Geneva was governed. Jerome Bolsec, however, attacked the authorities in Geneva on their doctrine of predestination. If he had chosen to confront them on a matter less central then he would not have found himself expelled. But the Reformation itself had arisen out of the discovery that when God shows mercy, he finds the cause of his mercy in himself alone, and not in the merits or works of those on whom he had pity. When he seems to choose and favour one man prior to another in his desire to save the world, the cause of this can be found to lie only in his grace and good pleasure. The people of Calvin's day were everywhere struggling, above all, for religious assurance. Therefore, the doctrine of predestination required to be stressed rather than questioned. In Calvin's mind it stood for the fact that God's love is such that it goes out to each particular individual in a special and individual way.[10]

Some parts of the doctrinal framework which Calvin and his followers erected in order to support this teaching may seem to us today unfortunate. But they could think of no other framework to safeguard it in their day. Bolsec was bound to

---

[8] Cf. *Inst.*, 1:7:5; 1:8:4.

[9] Lord Haldane in his *Autobiography* (London, 1929), pp. 5-6, tells of how he was taught Bible at school by Dr. Clyde. Though the teacher's duty was simply to teach the Old Testament stories without expressing opinion, "he could not help letting us feel that he himself did not accept what they recorded". The result was: "I soon became detached in my attitude to the earlier Bible teaching." Haldane concludes that it is never wise "to let religious teaching be given by anyone who is not in real sympathy with it". [10] Cf. *Inst.*, 3:22:6, 3:21:1-3.

be regarded as attacking the heart of the Gospel as the Reformers saw it.

Bolsec was, in fact, treated in a comparatively lenient way. Certainly he was exiled, but he was well used to travelling around and he could seek and find a community that was more congenial to himself. In taking this course the authorities in Geneva were following the then progressive example that had been set by the Lutherans in Germany who allowed dissenters freely to emigrate if they wished. Karl Holl, referring to this initiative in Germany, calls it "a departure from a tradition of more than a thousand years, the first fundamental limitation of its own powers by the state, and the first formal recognition of individual right in matters of faith", and he draws a contrast between Protestant custom here and the denial of even this right to the Huguenots by Louis XIV.[11]

Why then was such severity shown to Servetus? Simply because the Reformers were also Catholic in their faith as well as Reformed. They always made a claim to be the true extension in history of the Holy and Universal Church. But belief in the Trinity had been the foundation not only of all the Catholic doctrine but of Christian civilisation itself. To spread denial of such a doctrine was an act of treason and an attempt to spread anarchy.[12] Here was a basic issue on which only madmen would even attempt to speculate, on their own freedom. Here individual consciences, however free to differ from the authorities on other matters, could make only a decision of faith. There was no place in the world of the day either Protestant or Catholic where Servetus would have met with anything but a sentence of death. There had been controversy about the manner of death which should be given to such a heretic[13] and it is certainly strange that against Calvin's wishes the Genevan authorities should have insisted on burning him.

A further explanation of Calvin's concern over Servetus

[11] K. Holl, *The Cultural Significance of the Reformation*, New York, 1959, p.54.

[12] W. Ullmann points out that the first article of the Justinian code was "On the Trinity and the Catholic Faith", *op. cit.*, p. 48.

[13] Cf. J. Lecler, *Toleration and the Reformation*, New York, 1960, vol. I, pp. 80, 85, 88.

can be found in the intensely critical political situation into which the latter had intruded himself and in which he seems to have decided to play an active opposition role. The Church and the State were so closely bound up in Geneva that a serious attack on the confession of faith was a serious attack on the political establishment. As Elton remarks: "As long as membership of a secular organisation involved membership of an ecclesiastical organisation, religious dissent stood equal to political disaffection and even treason."[14] It was a case in which religious toleration was "inconsistent with the maintenance of government".[15]

Though what happened in Geneva, and especially the case of Servetus, has linked Calvin's name especially in many minds with intolerance, he did not differ in this matter from most of his contemporaries. Erasmus certainly spoke in favour of a wide toleration. But he was not involved in the necessary action of changing things and then of holding things together, which forced the Reformers to think about the subject in a way more closely related to the real issues of their day. J. W. Allen has given a useful account of Luther's attitude. At first Luther expressed himself nobly on the subject of dissent: "Heresy can never be contained by force ... Heresy is a spiritual thing, cut with no iron, burned with no fire, drowned with no water. It is God's word only that avails." He asserted that "all should preach freely and stoutly as they are able and against whom they please ... let the spirits fall upon one another and fight it out". But after his later experiences of the consequences of the freedom accorded to Anabaptists and others, "circumstances were too much for him, and after 1531 he went over almost completely to the side of those who, for one reason or another, believed in the maintenance of pure religion by force".[16]

Karl Holl, defending the Reformers on the subject of Toleration, claims that never "at any time whatsoever did the Protestant states brand a Catholic a 'heretic' for his faults, let alone punish him". Catholics, he asserts, were not

---

[14] In *New Cambridge Modern History*, vol. III, p. 5.
[15] J. W. Allen, *A History of Political Thought in the Sixteenth Century*, London, 1961, p. 42.   [16] *Ibid.*, p. 26.

disturbed as long as they kept quiet — even in England they were persecuted only because they were suspected of treason. Heresy was regarded as occurring only where such doctrines as the Trinity or the divinity of Christ were in question. Holl reminds us that Calvin too adopted this lenient attitude towards Catholics.[17]

The Cost and Reward of Involvement

The strength of the political tension which prevailed often within the city can be gathered from the reaction of the authorities to Jacques Gruet, one of Calvin's early opponents. In 1547 a piece of paper was found attached to Calvin's pulpit: "You and yours shall gain little by your measures; if you do not take yourself away, no one will save you from destruction, you shall curse the hour when you forsook your monkhood. Warning should have been given before that the devil and his legions were come here to ruin everything. But though we have been patient for a time, revenge will be had at last. Defend yourself or you will share the fate of Verle of Freibourg. We do not wish to have so many masters here. Mark well what I say." Gruet, one of an old Genevan family, was suspected. His house was searched and writings were found containing abuse of Calvin, of ordinary common standards of morality and of the apostles. But there was also a letter to the king of France which roused suspicion of sedition. Gruet was tortured by the authorities in order to see if he had any accomplices, and then executed, not because of Calvin nor because he was a moral delinquent, but because of his treason.

Calvin could not have remained aloof from such a man, nor could he have detached himself or his name from accepting the support of those who executed Gruet and who wished to keep Geneva an independent and secure haven for many in the city who had already fled from the tyranny in France.

[17] Karl Holl, *op, cit.*, p. 55. J. W. Allen points out (*op. cit.*, p. 34) that Melanchthon regarded Roman Catholicism as a heresy which "erred only by addition". Such heresies could be tolerated in a well-ordered community — not so heresies which "blasphemed by denial".

Such political tension was a continuing factor in the struggle between Calvin and the Libertines. At one time the French king had been reported as saying that "he would give two millions to be master of Geneva", and Ami Perrin was reported to have replied that "two hundred horse would be sufficient to conquer the city". People felt on edge, and any suspicion of treason tended to provoke merciless reaction.

It was because Calvin allowed himself to become caught up in this kind of political activity in Geneva that he found himself so closely involved in actions that seem today ruthless in their cruelty. He had to make a choice between very restrictive alternative courses in which even the style of his activity was to some extent dictated by his contemporary allies. He felt all the more constrained because he knew that God had placed on him the burden of leadership — in such times "The trepidation of a general or a leader", he wrote to Melanchthon, "is more dishonourable than the flight of a whole herd of private soldiers."[18]

He believed that his times called especially for measures of control harsher than normal. He had argued in his *Institutes*:

> There are countries which, unless they deal cruelly with murderers by way of horrible examples, must immediately perish. There are ages that demand increasingly hard penalties ... There are nations inclined to a particular vice, unless it be most sharply repressed.[19]

During his conflict with the Libertines in Geneva there were periods when, as a prelude to the second coming of Christ, he seemed to fear that the great beast of the apocalypse was going to appear in the very streets of this town to bring to a climax the tortures and indignities which he and his fellow French exiles had for many years so meekly borne. "The last act is now played; for after many victories, the enemy meditates a splendid triumph over Christ, His doctrine, His ministry and in a word, over all His members." In the demand of the Libertines for the lifting of the discipline and the freedom of all and sundry to sit at the Lord's Supper,

[18] C.L. to Melanchthon, June 18, 1550.
[19] *Inst.*, 4:20:16 (Westminster Press Translation).

Calvin saw a final sinister threat of anti-Christ: "Their profligacy has now reached such a pitch ... that they obstinately desire to convert the house of the Lord into a brothel."[20]

At no time in his active life was Calvin ever able to forget that many around him were still being martyred for the faith God had placed him in Geneva to defend. "For my own part I wish that the duty of my office and my conscience would permit me to keep silence in the same manner that I have steeled my heart to endure everything. But when I see the heavenly doctrine of Christ, of which he has been pleased to make me a minister, everywhere contentiously outraged, how disgraceful it would be for me to hold my peace as if I were tongue tied! Should I defraud the doctrine of the defence of my words, for which holy martyrs did not hesitate to pour out their blood?"[21]

[20] C.L. to the Pastors and Doctors of the Church of Zurich, November 26, 1553.
[21] C.L. to the Pastors of Bern, May, 1555.

CHAPTER 7

ECONOMICS IN GENEVA

Towards a Healthy Commerce

WHEN Luther looked at the whole area of life being covered in his day by trading companies, it seemed to reveal such a "bottomless pit of avarice and wrong-doing that there is nothing that can be discussed with a good conscience".[1] To him every merchant was inevitably a trickster. The English and the Portuguese and the traders with India and Calcutta were draining Germany of its gold. A wise government would stop up the hole. "How can there be anything good in trade?"[2]

During the sixteenth century world trade had expanded enormously with the discovery of the Americas and the opening up of trade routes. The increase in the supply of gold and the minting of coins had produced widespread inflation. The new commerce seemed to be making the poor more poor. Churchmen and pastors became sensitive to the problems it seemed to cause. In England both Roman Catholic and Protestant preachers in some of their sermons effectively exposed the commercial rackets that were taking place, and castigated the merchants.[3] No doubt sometimes as these listened patiently in the pews they attributed the attacks to the conservative snobbery of the minor gentry whose place in society they were now comfortably usurping.[4]

Calvin himself was well aware that in his day the merchant

---

[1] L.W., vol. 45, p. 270.
[2] *Ibid.*, pp. 246-7; cf. Karl Holl, *The Cultural Significance of the Reformation*, New York, 1959, p. 79.
[3] Cf. J. W. Blench, *Preaching in England*, Oxford, 1964, pp. 133, 244, 270. M. MacLure, *St. Paul's Cross Sermons 1534-1642*, Toronto, 1958, p. 123.
[4] Cf. H. Holborn, *Ulrich von Hutten and the German Reformation*, New York, 1965, p. 45.

was beginning to take the place of the prince. "The merchants of Venice in the present day think that they are on a level with princes, and that they are above all other men except Kings . . . I have been told too, that at Antwerp there are factors who do not hesitate to lay out expenses which the wealthiest of the nobility could not support."[5] He was as bold in condemning the "unacceptable face" of the newly established commercial system as many other preachers of his day. He could himself describe the life of a merchant as "closely resembling the life of a harlot" full of tricks and traps and deceits, and "many new and unheard of contrivances for making gain".[6] But he recognised that in the sixteenth century there could be no movement back to an "ideal" primitive agrarian society.

He decided to cast his vote not against but for the development of the whole risky business of which he knew to be already causing such damage to human character.[7] He saw that the mutual exchanges involved in a healthy commercial intercourse between individuals and different sections of society could play an invaluable part in creating good community life. He was aware of the importance of money for human well-being and even for the Christian good of men. He likened the revenues collected by civil authorities to "almost the very blood of the people".[8] He was quick to point out, when he expounded Isaiah's apocalyptic vision that the first calamity with which God would visit a people in judgment for the wickedness would be that "buying and selling would cease".[9]

Bieler points out that to Calvin material trade is the sign of the spiritual communion of the members of society. The

---

[5] *Comm. on Isa.*, 23:8.
[6] *Comm. on Ezek.*, 23:17.
[7] Cf. R. H. Tawney, *Religion and the Rise of Capitalism*, Penguin Ed., p. 92. Commenting on Calvin's decision on this matter, Tawney observes: "that acceptance of the realities of commercial practice as a starting-point was of momentous importance. It means that Calvinism and its offshoots took their stand on the side of the activities which were to be most characteristic of the future, and insisted that it was not by renouncing them, but by untiring concentration on the task of using for the glory of God the opportunities which they offered, that the Christian life could and must be lived."
[8] *Inst.*, 4:20:13.   [9] *Comm. on Isa.*, 24:2.

greater and richer the commercial interchange, the greater and richer could become the moral and cultural lives of those involved. Social welfare and economic health were bound up together. "No public government can be lasting without the transactions of commerce."[10]

It was his belief in the power of the Gospel to make all things new that gave him his extraordinary optimism in this matter. He took comfort, for example, in Ezekiel's vision of the conversion of the whole, once sordid, commercial life of Tyre to the glory and service of God which proved to him that God could make even the merchant cease his wicked practices and change his disposition. It did not worry him at all, as it did others, that incomes from business enterprise were proving in his day to be bigger than those from landowning. Why not? he argued. Merchants had even to risk their lives in trading their goods, and they earned their profits by sheer diligence and industry.[11]

Usury

For centuries before Calvin's day, the Church and most other authorities had applied the Biblical condemnation of usury quite directly to commercial practices, and had prohibited loans at interest. Exceptions had been allowed. Interest had been deemed payable, for example, when the loan could be shown to have caused loss to the lender or made him miss opportunities of otherwise profiting from the possession of it. But Holy Scripture seemed to draw no such distinctions in its prohibition of "usury". To Luther it did not seem right for men to profit merely from lending money without working or taking any personal risks. However, the practice of taking interest on loans had been growing, and governments were busy trying to regulate the rate at which the interest was to be taken.

Calvin was the first to question the older method of interpreting the Bible on this matter. He insisted that "usury"

[10] *Ibid.*, cf. A. Bieler, *The Social Humanism of Calvin*, Richmond, 1964, p. 51.
[11] *Comm. on Ps.*, 15:5, E. Troeltsch, *The Social Teaching of the Christian Churches*, London, 1931, vol. 11, p. 642.

in the context of the Biblical world was not entirely the same as in that of the sixteenth century. In Biblical times, he argued, business enterprises required little capital and it is obvious from the contexts that the loans there referred to were purely loans given to people in necessity. It was only in relation to such unproductive loans, given for relief and consumption, that usury was forbidden. But the loan most common in the sixteenth century was of another type. It was the loan given for production, so that the borrower could profit from the use of it in his business or commercial enterprise. Even though man might not like this kind of usury there was, Calvin argued, no ground for suggesting that it is forbidden in the Word of God.

He denied the teaching of Aristotle that money is sterile and cannot therefore beget more of its kind. He argued that it was wrong that a rich and monied man who has borrowed in order to buy a piece of land should be allowed to profit from the proceeds of the farm without paying to the lender some part of the revenues as interest till the principal is repaid. The usury forbidden in the Bible "is only as to the poor, and consequently if we have to do with the rich ... usury is freely permitted".[12] Calvin thus gave a clear and bold alternative to the traditional teaching, and people found his arguments much more convincing than the sophistries by which exceptions were allowed against what seemed a straightforward blunt prohibition. In place of the arguments for such complicated, casuistical exceptions he laid down one simple rule: "how far it may be lawful to receive usury upon loans, the law of equity will better prescribe than any lengthened discussions".[13]

While Calvin thus clearly admitted that usury was allowable he constantly expressed his personal dislike for its practice. He insisted that no one should be allowed to adopt usury as a profession. It was to him a strange and shameful thing, while all other men have to toil or expose themselves to danger to earn their living, that "money-mongers" should sit

---

[12] *Comm. on Exod.*, 22:25; *Comm. on Ezek.*, 18:1-9; cf. Letter of Calvin on this subject to a friend (presumably Sachinus) in C.O. 10a: 245-9.

[13] *Comm. on Exod.*, 22:25.

at their ease without doing anything and receive tribute from the labour of all other people.[14] Therefore he believed that no usurer should be tolerated in a well-ordered community, and he found support for this view even in heathen writers.[15]

To prospective investors who wished to receive interest without adopting the ignoble profession, however, he repeated the Biblical warnings against the "unjust and crafty arts of gaining" by which the rich devour the poor[16] and he suggested as a rule for exacting interest, a saying that was well known in other connections "Neither everywhere, nor always, nor all things, nor from all".[17] The interest must be moderate, no one must be lending all the time, within the Church fellowship there must be none of it at all, and no one must ever exact interest from the poor. As to the rate of interest he preached that men should not always expect even the five percent allowed by the law.[18]

The Production and Distribution of Wealth

The spiritual wealth of the Church, according to Calvin, depended on what could be called a "mutual communication" of gifts within the body. Christ bestows on each member a gift from which he means the whole body to benefit. Each member therefore must depend on the other and share with the other in a freely given interchange of services — a sharing from which competition is excluded, and the only concern is love.[19]

Calvin believed that, in much the same way, the health of the political and social body would also depend on the mutual communication of goods and services. He realised that such interchange would depend on the flow of money, the life-blood of the community, to and from each member.

If wealth was to flow it must first be produced. Those who have done careful research on the city records give an impressive acount of how the authorities, during Calvin's time in Geneva, encouraged the establishment of new

[14] *Comm. on Ps.*, 15:5.   [15] *Comm. on Ezek.*, 18:5-9.
[16] *Comm. on Ps.*, 15:5.   [17] *Comm. on Ezek.*, 18:5-9.
[18] *Sermon on Deut.*, 23:8-20, C.O., 28:117 and 121.   [19] Cf. pp. 94f, 117.

business enterprises. Cloth manufacturing and printing were encouraged. Mention is made of a pharmaceutical plant. The silk industry was expanded, young people being taught skills in silk spinning by an expert from Lyons, and mulberry trees were cultivated for the culture of silk worms.

The records show the civil authorities involved in decisions over trade disputes, freezing wages in 1559, forbidding both masters and journeymen in the printing industry to form pressure groups calculated to push the wage level down or up, obtaining guarantees of job security for the workers, and a guaranteed efficient day's work for the masters. Calvin and the ministers are shown often to have intervened when there was trouble — after all, Calvin was the most expert lawyer the town had, and was a skilled negotiator. It has been pointed out that during his time in Strasbourg he must have noticed that the whole cultural and community life of a city could be raised by prosperous industry and trade, and was bound to desire the same high level of prosperity for Geneva.[20]

On the subject of the distribution of wealth Calvin stated. his mind clearly and frequently. He realised that the natural tendency was for wealth to flow to those who had it, who could indeed use their wealth to draw from others what they had. Therefore the civil authorities required not only to stimulate commerce but also, to some extent, to direct the flow of wealth downwards so that it could reach the poor as well as the rich.

Firstly he insisted that as a law of life, where there was lavish wealth there must also be lavish giving by the rich to the poor. In the Middle Ages the relief of the poor had to a large extent been left to personal and charitable giving. The poor had been regarded as the responsibility of the wealthy who should regard it as a privilege as well as an obligation to provide food and shelter to the destitute. Where this had been taken seriously it had meant that sometimes a desirable element of personal communication could enter into the

---

[20] See e.g., A. Bieler, *op. cit.*, pp. 49-50. E. Troeltsch, *The Social Teaching of the Christian Churches*, London, 1931, vol. II, p. 912. W. Fred Graham, *John Calvin, the Constructive Revolutionary*, Richmond, 1971, pp. 136f, 142.

charity. Calvin still regarded the exercise of personal charity from the rich to the poor as an important part of social and economic life of a community as God had designed it, and he called on the rich to fulfil their obligation to charitable giving as if it were an aspect of the law by which they must live.

Certainly he held that every man had a right to own property. This was so basic to his theological outlook that he did not seek to justify the ownership of property to anything like the same extent as did Luther and Zwingli.[21] If a man becomes wealthy this is "not due to his own skill but is the fruit of God's blessing". "Men obtain nothing by their own vigilance and diligence except in so far as God blesses them from above."[22] Since wealth is thus given from above it cannot but be justifiable. But if a man has his *own* property given to him by God, he equally, has his *own* poor whom he must also see as placed strategically around him by God. Such poor people belonged to the rich as did their own families.

One of the texts he most frequently echoes in his writing and teaching is the appeal of Isaiah to the rich man in Israel to "hide not thyself from thine own flesh".[23] In one of his sermons on Deuteronomy he actually reads into the text what he finds as a reference to "thy poor". It is in a passage where the rich man is called to "rejoice before the Lord" not only with his son and daughter and wife "but also with his poor ones". "God mixes up rich and poor so that they may meet together and hold fellowship with each other so that the poor receive and the rich give."[24]

God himself is the receiver of what is given to the poor, and he enters into debt to those who give. Though we must not imagine ourselves able to explain all the ways of God, in making some rich and others poor, we can at least see that the

[21] See G. W. Locher, *Der Eigentumsbegriff als Problem Evangelischer Theologie*, Zurich, 1962, pp. 36ff; cf. Mellone, *Western Christian Thought in Middle Ages*, Edinburgh, 1935, pp. 211-12.

[22] *Comm. on Deut.*, 8:17.

[23] Isa. 58:7, cf. e.g., *Sermon on Deut.*, 15:7-10, C.O., 27:326; *Sermon on Deut.*, 15:11-15, C.O., 27:349.

[24] *Sermon on Deut.*, 15:11-15, C.O., 27:342.

rich are constantly being tested by their attitude to, and use of, wealth, as the poor themselves are being tested in their poverty.[25]

Calvin saw in this interchange of goods from the rich to the poor, an aspect of the ordinance of God by which money and goods were made to flow downward through the community in a healthy and natural way.

But Calvin saw that in the developing commercial age even the utmost personal generosity could not be relied on to ensure the welfare of the poor. No private man could be expected to be able to seek them out or fully understand their need. Therefore it was the office of the deacon to keep in contact with them through visitation, to cooperate with the pastors and thus to become familiar with the actual problems of the home and to administer public welfare. The deacons who both administered and distributed relief to the poor were officials whose task was modelled after the pattern of the deacons of the early church.[26] One of them in Geneva was to be an "adequately paid", full-time and capable administrator.

The ordinances which Calvin drew up in 1541 speak of the "communal hospital" which had to be "well maintained" with amenities available for the sick and the aged who were unable to work, a quite separate wing for widows, orphaned children and other poor persons, and a hospice for wayfarers. Moreover, "it will be necessary also, both for the poor in the hospital and those in the city who have not the means of assisting themselves, that a physician and a surgeon should be specially appointed at the city's expense".[27]

The Spirit of Capitalism

It is to be noted that Calvin did not envisage the disappearance from the community of those who would require to be given charitable financial help either through

---

[25] *Sermon on Deut.*, 15:7-10, C.O., 27:333, *Sermon on Deut.*, 15:11-15, C.O., 27:338.
[26] *Inst.*, 4:3:9, see R.C.P., p. 42.
[27] *Ibid.*, p. 43; cf. *Sermon on Deut.*, 15:11-15, C.O., 27:341.

public or private channels. He did not see how the wealth of the community would be able to reach all and help all, apart from such deliberate communication. Just as business and social life required the distinction between master and servant, so he believed that the transactions of commerce required the distinction between rich and poor. His idea seems to have been that some would require to possess wealth to the extent of being able to ensure its circulation.[28]

He did not believe therefore that the rich should share with the poor to the extent of banishing the distinctions between them. But though he believed in the necessity of some distinctions remaining, he believed that the appearance of extreme differences in wealth and poverty within a community was inexcusably evil. His comment on Paul's ideal that "through giving there should be equality" is illuminating. "Equality", in Paul's mind, he thinks means a "fair proportioning of our resources that we may, so far as funds allow, help those in difficulties that there may not be some in affluence and others in want".[29] The vision given in Christ's parable of Lazarus in heaven lying in the bosom of Abraham implies that riches do not shut against any man the gate of the Kingdom of Heaven but that it is open alike to all who have either made a sober use of riches, or patiently endured the want of them.[30]

Calvin believed that Christ's command to us to "sell your possessions and give alms" might under certain circumstances demand the giving away of capital as well as current income. It enjoined that "we must not be satisfied with bestowing on the poor what we can easily spare, but that we must not refuse to part with our estates, if their revenue does not supply the wants of the poor. His meaning is 'Let your liberality go so far as to lessen your patrimony and dispose of your lands.' "[31] While a man, therefore, has a right to be rich,

[28] *See Comm. on Isa.*, 24:2.
[29] *Comm. on 2 Cor.*, 8:14.
[30] *Comm. on Luke*, 16:25.
[31] *Comm. on Luke*, 12:33. John Wesley, here as elsewhere slightly more legalistic than Calvin, taught that Christ's command, "Lay not up for yourselves treasures on earth", forbade the rich to increase their capital. "As it comes, daily or yearly, so let it go." Cf. *Works of Rev. John Wesley*, London, 1811, vol. X, p. 143.

he has no right to remain very rich while a deep gulf is maintained between him and the poor around him. He must regard himself as a steward of what he possesses. The answer the Lord gives to the greedy who argue too much about their rights to keep their own is, "It is indeed thine, but on this condition, that thou share it with the hungry and thirsty, not that thou eat it thyself alone."[32]

Calvin's spirit, in all his teaching about the possession and flow of wealth, seems to be quite different from the "Spirit of Capitalism" with which his name has become too closely associated. Indeed on the matter of the ownership and stewardship of wealth his preaching moves towards the doctrine radically expressed by Lever and others in the St. Paul's Cross sermons in England. Lever declared that though there was "no anabaptistical communism in the early church" yet "Christian men in that they are Christian men have all things comen even to this day." "The rich", he declared, "keep to themselves what they need and give to the poor as much as they need". A Christian man's goods are "comen with every man's need and private to no man's lust".[33] This teaching tends to have more in common with mediaeval thought than that which lay behind the vigorous growth of Capitalism.

It must be noted at this point that Calvin could never have approved of the idea of a competitive society. Rivalry and struggle of one member with another is impossible within a true Christian body. No member is living in full health while competing with another. It is interesting to find how closely on this matter Calvin's thought comes to that of Kropotkin the anarchist. In contrast to Hobbes, and to all thinkers who look back to the natural state of man in society as being one of continuous struggle, Kropotkin believed that "the law of

[32] *Comm. on Isa.*, 58:7. Calvin here appears to be accepting the division of property into "mine" and "thine" as a necessary evil due to our need for peace in a world of selfishness. Possibly he would have agreed with the mediaeval doctrine that in Paradise there need be no "mine" or "thine" (cf. Mellone, *op. cit.*, pp. 211-12). Pascal thought that the instinct for plunder was the origin of private property.

[33] Quoted in MacLure, *op. cit.*, pp. 124ff. It should be noted that Calvin rejected any enforced community of goods. Commenting on Acts 2:44, he says: "This place needs some exposition because of fanatic spirits."

nature was the law of cooperation, of mutual aid rather than struggle. Within each species mutual support is the rule. . . ."[34]

Moreover, Calvin was always warning about the deadly effects of covetousness — an unquenchable and irresistible fire in the soul destructive of all individual and social good.[35] He called those who extorted cheap labour from the poor, blood-suckers, murderers of a worse type than any street thug.[36] He was never weary of castigating those who used their financial power to draw money from others to themselves.[37] He expresses his dismay that when prices were so high wealthy merchants could keep their granaries closed in order to raise the price even higher and thus to "cut the throat of poor people".[38] Nothing in the commercial world, he believed, could be lawful which was hurtful to other people, and "all bargains in which the one party unrighteously strives to make gain by the loss of the other party" are condemned.[39] The idea that any form of rivalry in commercial enterprise could help society or that self-seeking could further the common interest could never have entered his mind. He believed in restraining rather than in setting free the competitive spirit.

The spirit of Calvin has therefore nothing in common with the "Spirit of Capitalism". Troeltsch's suggestion that in the ethic of Calvin "there is a door into which capitalism was able to steal"[40] shows a lack of understanding. Certainly he *did* approve of the development of commerce, and he *did* clear up men's muddled thoughts on the subject of usury. But to say that he "provided a religious justification for the competitive

---

[34] James Joll, *The Anarchists*, London, 1964, p. 155. I remember reading somewhere that F. D. Maurice, too, reacted from the idea of a competitive society on the ground that there is no trace of competition within the Holy Trinity — on the model of which human society is created by God.

[35] *Comm. on Amos*, 8:5; *Comm. on 1 Cor.*, 11:3.

[36] *Comm. on Jer.*, 22:13.

[37] Cf., e.g., *Comm. on Jer.*, 5:28.

[38] Cf. A. Bieler, *op. cit.*, pp. 52-3. On this point W. Fred Graham quotes *Sermon on Deut.*, 20:16-20, C.O., 27:639.

[39] *Comm. on Ps.*, 15:5. Calvin here appeals to his readers not to imagine "that anything can be lawful . . . which is hurtful to others".

[40] Cf., e.g., Troeltsch, *op. cit.*, pp. 644-5, 915.

individualism of commercial enterprise"[41] is as far from the truth as the claim that Christopher Columbus was responsible for the American Civil War. Certainly he was to blame for being so naïve as to believe that philanthropy could to a large extent help to palliate social injustice. He had obviously at this point a more naïve trust in the potential goodness of human nature under the power of the Gospel than many have today.[42] Yet it has to be noted that where the cost of social welfare has begun to grow prohibitive, some who knew the value of the voluntary spirit and of what used to be called "charity" are beginning to wish again that we had more of it. Calvin obviously did not wish poor relief to become a prescribed tax, and was anxious to preserve the voluntary spirit.[43]

[41] P. A. Micklem, *The Secular and the Sacred*, London, 1948, p. 174. For a relevant rejection of any suggested relationship between Puritanism and Capitalism, cf. Harold Laski, *The Rise of European Liberalism*, London, 1958, pp. 92ff.

[42] Cf. R. Niebuhr, *An Interpretation of Christian Ethics*, London, 1937, p. 19.

[43] Cf. *Sermon on Deut.*, 15:7-10, C.O., 27:333-4.

CHAPTER 8

EDUCATION AND THE HUMANITIES
IN GENEVA

The Founding of the University

AFTER he had succeeded in ensuring a secure place for
the Word of God within the city Calvin directed his
attention to founding a university. From the beginning of his
work as a Reformer, like Luther and Melanchthon, he had
been concerned about the schooling and catechising of
children. People had to be taught the elements of the faith,
and they had to be able to read and understand the Word of
God.

It is not surprising that when the citizens of Geneva
accepted the Reformed faith, they also at the same time
agreed to make a new start with the education of the young.
During his earlier period in the city, in 1537, Calvin wrote his
first Catechism — his *Instruction in the Faith.*

In Strasbourg during the years 1538-1541 he was in a city
where schooling had a first priority and where some of the
greatest educational experts of the time were at work. He
therefore returned to Geneva in 1541 with more far-reaching
plans which he indicated in the ordinances he then submitted to the Council. Not only were the present schools to
be improved, but a "College" was to be established with a
view to "preparing our children" both for "the ministry and
civil government".[1]

The catechising of the young remained always his first
priority. "Believe me, my Lord," he wrote to Somerset, "the
Church of God will never preserve itself without a
Catechism." "True Christianity" should be taught in "a
certain written form". Such catechetical instruction would

[1] 1541 Ordinances, R.C.P., p. 41.

promote unity, supply the deficiencies even of some "pastors and curates" and help people not to be led astray by "presumptuous persons". But it had to be a "good catechism", brief and in "language level to their tender age".[2]

He therefore wrote a catechism for Geneva in 1545.[3] But he had to wait a long time for his "College". At first he and his fellow pastors contented themselves with minor improvements to the existing system of primary education and with caring as far as they were personally able, for the brighter pupils who had come through it. It was not till 1557 when most of his controversies with opponents were over, that he began to push for action. A committee was appointed in January 1558 and a site selected. Nothing was to be second-rate. Though Geneva was a comparatively poor city with a large proportion of refugees from France struggling financially to re-establish themselves the whole venture must have seemed over-ambitious to many.

The cost of building was met from money which came when Geneva, having submitted its case against Ami Perrin and his allies to a neutral court in Basel, finally won its suit and was able to auction off their estates. But much finance was required, and a public appeal was made. Lawyers were encouraged to arrange for legacies to be given. Calvin himself took part in the house-to-house collection from rich and poor. The project could not have succeeded without an enormous united public effort. The goodwill which the large majority of the people in the town had towards Calvin is evident in the way they supported him. The new foreign residents and the old Genevese families cooperated generously.

He did not realise his aim to have a full university with every faculty but he insisted that the standard of teaching was to be the highest available anywhere. In his correspondence there is a letter to a prominent teacher at Paris tentatively seeking to woo him from his chair to be his colleague. Fortunately Calvin's problems in finding a faculty were solved for him when troubles occurred in Lausanne between the authorities and the faculty of the Academy. Viret and

---

[2] C.L. to Protector Somerset, October 22, 1548.
[3] Cf. C.Tr., vol. II, pp. 33ff.

several well known professors left and came to Geneva. These included Theodore Beza who became the first Rector of the new Academy.

There were two sections in the whole institution. A child went first to the college or *Schola Privata*, with seven grades, gradually leading up to ability in reading Greek and Latin and in the study of dialectics. Among the authors read were Virgil, Cicero, Ovid, Caesar, Isocrates, Livy, Xenophon, Polybius, Homer, Demosthenes. After this came the academy or the *Schola Publica*, where different elective courses could be taken in a variety of offered subjects — Theology, Hebrew, Greek, Poetry, Dialectic and Rhetoric, Physics and Mathematics.

At the opening of the Academy there were six hundred students. The enrolment rose in the first year to nine hundred. They came from all over Europe and the list of famous teachers and pupils is impressive. Calvin himelf wrote the regulations for it. Teachers had to subscribe to a confession of faith which did not, however, include predestination. Kampschulte, Calvin's Roman Catholic biographer of last century, points out that a few decades later, when Acquaviva, the General of the Jesuit order, drew up his educational curriculum he borrowed extensively from the Geneva academic regulations and was greatly indebted to Calvin for his whole outlook on scholastic affairs.

W. Fred Graham brings to our notice the evidence which some of the regulations written by Calvin himself, give us about his own personal attitude to the humanities. The professors are warned that "they are not to make invectives against the authors whom they expound, but they are to apply themselves to explicate the sense faithfully". The principal "must be of a *debonnaire*" spirit, having neither a rude nor a bitter disposition, so that his whole life may give the scholars a good example, and must carry the vexations of his charge quite peaceably (*doucement*). McNeill thinks it was Calvin's modest ability to recognise his own limitations in the above respect that prevented him from taking the post himself, as he well might have done.[4]

---

[4] W. Fred Graham, *op. cit.*, p. 150. John T. McNeill, *op. cit.*, p. 194.

In appointing Beza as head, he chose an internationally known humanist and man of letters who wrote and loved poetry and had published a play. Beza gave the address at the inaugural ceremony on June 5, 1559. He gave a history of education in the past, referred to how Moses learned wisdom from the Egyptians, and congratulated the council on giving Geneva a share in the glorious work of diffusing knowledge that was free from superstition.[5]

Two Worlds in Geneva

The reader will have noticed that in his statement of the aim of the College, in the 1541 ordinances, Calvin mentioned preparation for "the ministry", before "civil government". His primary concern in founding the academy was obvious. In Geneva humanistic studies were to be directed to the service of the Word of God. The understanding and the preaching of the Word required the kind of skill which ordinarily the pastor could acquire through such education. The people themselves must be given preaching which, instead of coming always down to their level, would constantly raise the standard of thought and discourse in every sphere of the life of the city. They, too, had to be trained to read the Word for themselves, and judge the preaching against the authority in Scripture.

Certainly no man should become a minister of the Word of God unless he knew something of the humanity to which the Word was addressed.[6] He had therefore to be trained in the humanities as well as in Christianity. Calvin believed that a man could be helped to become "human" by such education. He himself, in his *Institutes* quotes a wide range of classical authors, now criticising them, now following them, using what he can of their wisdom to illustrate his exposition of the Biblical text. He is ready to acknowledge it gratefully when he finds a spark or two of insight into divine matters in Plato, and

[5] Cf. Reyburn, *op. cit.*, p. 285.

[6] For centuries in Scotland, e.g., the minister of the Word had to take a first degree in "humanities" before he was allowed to enter the study of "divinity". With such a basic beginning it was not considered as necessary as we find it today to try to train candidates for the ministry through more direct psychological or social study.

he certainly was helped by Aristotle in his understanding of human psychology.[7]

Beside his concern to produce an educated ministry for the Church Calvin realised that education in the humanities had its own power to enrich the whole life of Geneva as a city and thus promote "civil government". "How richly deserving of honour", he wrote, "are the liberal arts and sciences which polish man so as to give him the dignity of true humanity."[8] "The things which the philosophers teach", he insisted, "are true, not only pleasant to learn, but useful, and well put together by them."[9] He was certain that "the Lord has been pleased to help us through physics, dialectics, mathematics and other similar sciences, by the work and ministry of the ungodly".[10]

"Those who have pursued philosophy", he wrote to Bucer, "have been incited thereto by God himself."[11] In his comment on Paul's quotation from Epimenides in Titus 1:12 he refers to an essay of Basil in which he instructs the young people of his day "as to what help they should receive from heathen authors", and he adds: "Since all truth is of God, if any ungodly man has said anything true, we should not reject it, for it also has come from God. Besides, since all things are from God what could be wrong with employing to his glory everything that can be rightly used in that way?"[12]

Calvin planned therefore that Geneva should be a city open to two quite distinct sources of inspiration and life, both coming from God, and both being good — a city, indeed, open to two worlds — to the great world of the Bible, of Christian and eternal values, and to the world of what has been best in human culture from time immemorial — to both "heavenly" and "earthly" things.[13]

He refused to follow those who in his own day read only a note of contempt in Tertullian's famous question, "What has

---

[7] Cf. *Inst.*, 1:3:3; 1:5:3; 1:15:6, etc.   [8] *Comm. on 1 Cor.*, 1:20.
[9] *Inst.*, 1:15:6.   [10] *Inst.*, 2:2:16.
[11] C.L. to Bucer, February 1549.
[12] *Comm. on Titus*, 1:12. Later in his life Basil became deeply suspicious of the education and morals of his day, and excluded the pagan classics from his monastery schools. Calvin seems to have forgotten this.
[13] Cf. *Inst.*, 2:2:12-13.

Athens to do with Jerusalem?"[14] and decided to find their culture only in the Bible. For Calvin, no kind of teaching that made men unconcerned about anything that affected man's life deeply even in his purely human concerns could possibly be Christian. If he was opposed to the falsehood of the Roman Church, he was equally opposed to the over extreme radicalism that was so exclusively concerned about the Kingdom of God as to be careless of man's earthly well-being. He desired that the life of Geneva should remain always open to the same stream of vitalising and human culture which had flowed through Athens and Rome, and which produced what was best in the world he knew apart from Christ himself. When he wrote to Protector Somerset in England that "our type of Christianity" in no way thwarts true humanity, he was dissociating himself from those who minimised the value of those things which he believed could flourish naturally in human life lived under stable social conditions.

One of the reasons he gave for writing *The Institutes* was to counteract the unjust charge that the Reformed doctrine encouraged men to rebel against human authority, and to despise the prevailing establishment. He believed that Satan was using the confusion and turmoil caused by a necessary and genuine opposition to Rome to raise his own kind of chaos and disorder in which everything good and human would be destroyed. Therefore the Reformed Church had now to fight against these Satanic enthusiasts who despised humanity itself, as well as to continue against Rome.

The Origin and Sphere of the "Liberal Arts and Sciences"

It helps us to understand both Calvin's motives and his policy on these matters if we understand his views, drawn from the Bible, on the origin and purpose of human culture and its relation to the spirit of God.

As a result of the fall, man was deprived by God of all his "spiritual gifts". He lost his ability to understand what Calvin calls "heavenly things" — those things which belong to the pure knowledge of God and his Kingdom, to true justice, and

---

[14] *De Praescr.*, 7; *Apol.*, 46.

the blessedness of the future life. When it comes to the knowledge of such things all the philosophers, said Calvin, are "blinder than moles".

The consequences of the fall, however, did not deprive man of his "natural gifts". Man's ability to deal with "earthly things" (i.e. government, household management, mechanical skills and the liberal arts) was only partially impaired.[15] Therefore the natural man still retains a significant measure of ability to conduct political affairs, and a certain measure of moral discernment. Some seed of political order has been implanted in all men and no man is without the light of the reason required for the arrangements of this life. One has only to read the history of man's achievements in government, the arts and sciences and one is forced to marvel. "Can we deny that the truth must have beamed upon the ancient jurists who arranged civil order and discipline with so much equity? Shall we say that the philosophers were blind in their exquisite research and skilful description of nature?"[16]

Calvin has no hesitation in attributing the fact that mankind at the fall was not deprived of all that was good, to the same grace of God that meets us in Christ. It is by this grace of God that the image of God has not been totally annihilated or destroyed. He therefore speaks of a "general grace of God"[17] manifest in the good things that are left in us and by which we differ from the brute beasts. He includes amongst the signs of this general grace of God not only man's ability to conduct himself in decent social relations but the "universal apprehension of reason and intelligence implanted" in men. It is only by the grace of God that we are not all imbeciles.[18]

Sometimes this aspect of Calvin's doctrine of Grace is called his doctrine of "Common Grace". It must not be

---

[15] *Inst.*, 2:2:12-13. In making this distinction between things heavenly and things earthly, Calvin is following a tradition common in the Church. Paul, after all, referred to "carnal" things and "spiritual" things, and Walter Ullman has pointed out that Gregory the Great believed that man's occupation with carnal matters was denoted in Scripture itself by the collective term *humanitas* (*The Individual and Society in the Middle Ages*, Baltimore, 1966, p. 8 n.). In distinguishing between "supernatural" and "natural" gifts he is following Augustine.

[16] *Inst.*, 2:2:13, 15.   [17] *Inst.*, 2:2:17.   [18] *Inst.*, 2:2:14.

thought, however, that for Calvin there are two types of grace
— redeeming grace and common grace. This general grace of
God is simply the turning of the same grace as we know in
Christ towards man in his fallenness. It is in itself the refusal
of redeeming love to let man go.

Moreover Calvin regards the operation of the general
grace of God as being the work of the Son of God. Christ
himself according to Calvin sheds light on the world in two
quite distinct ways. Firstly being the eternal creative Word of
God, He keeps all things in life and being, adorns man with
understanding, and retains for man what measure of light has
not been destroyed by his fall. Secondly he renews and
restores fallen nature.[19]

Calvin emphasizes that the good natural gifts which we
admire so much and use so gratefully belong primarily to
man in his essential secularity, and indeed in his fallen
perversity. He points out that the Old Testament assigns the
gifts that produce human culture in most full measure to the
family of Cain by whose sons, though deprived of the Spirit of
regeneration, some of the arts were invented. The study of
history since then, he affirms, will teach us how widely the
rays of divine light have shone on unbelieving nations for the
benefit of the present life. The liberal arts and sciences
therefore "have descended to us from the heathen. We are
indeed compelled to acknowledge that we have received
astronomy and the other parts of philosophy, medicine and
the order of civil government from them."[20]

The Development and Control of the Secular

Calvin recognised that there was a natural inclination within
men and women to artistic and cultural pursuits and their
development. "There were, among the sons of Adam,
industrious and skilful men who exercised their diligence in
the invention and cultivation of the arts."[21] This inclination
they owe directly to God the Creator and Redeemer. "The
swift and versatile movements of the soul", he writes further,
"in glancing from heaven to earth, connecting the future with

[19] *Comm. on John,* 1:15.   [20] *Comm. on Gen.,* 4:20.   [21] *Comm. on Gen.,* 4:20.

the past, retaining the remembrance of former years, nay, forming creations of its own — its skill moreover in making astonishing discoveries, and inventing many wonderful arts, are sure indications of the agency of God in man."[22]

Some kind of artistic talent, he believed, was widespread in human life and could be found in quite ordinary people. "All of us", he writes, "have some degree of aptitude for the arts." Some, it is true, are not as able as others to learn them. Yet there is hardly anyone "who does not display a talent for some particular art".[23]

We can see how well he improved his own talent in his superb ability to write beautiful prose, and though he did not write much verse he confessed late in his life that he had a natural propensity to poetry.[24] But, he admitted, for outstanding progress in the arts we must wait for the appearance of genius. Most people in their artistic pursuits go no further than "to improve on something learned from a predecessor". There are however some who can "devise something new" in various arts.[25] In other words, popular culture must be stimulated and guided by a cultural elite, able in different generations to break through in creative ways and open new avenues in which others can follow them in the expansion of new cultural forms.

While he relates human culture to the grace of God in Christ in such a decisive way Calvin at the same time emphasises the entirely limited sphere to which its influence has been restricted and the subordinate place assigned to it in God's scheme of things.

Calvin in his day had seen in many places how even the Word of God and the new life of the Spirit had become perverted by the libertines and the enthusiasts keen to propagate destructive heresy, justify outbreaks of bloody revolution, and lawless lust. He realised that artists and leaders of culture could become no less open to the same destructive and lawless spirit and that under its influence they could soon become degenerate. Therefore in his day, for the

---

[22] *Inst.*, 1:5:5. [23] *Inst.*, 2:2:14.
[24] To Conrad Herbert, May 19, 1557; cf. M'Neill, *op. cit.*, p. 232.
[25] *Inst.*, 2:2:14.

sake of the basic decencies of life and stability of society, those whose calling lay within this secular sphere had to be reminded of the law of God in order to find their own best self-expression. The Word of God has something to say even to the "natural man" precisely about this activity as a natural man. "Let each of us, therefore, in contemplating his own nature remember that there is one God who governs all natures and who would thus have us look unto him, and make him the object of our faith, worship and adoration. Nothing indeed is more preposterous than to enjoy these noble endowments which attest the divine presence within us, and to neglect him who, of his own good pleasure bestows them upon us."[26]

Calvin therefore believed that the "human" needs the Christian alongside of it. It can find direction and help in its own pattern of life only by looking constantly at the pattern of life manifested within the Church. The light of the Gospel must be allowed constantly to shine from the Church into the surrounding community in order to help the whole of humanity to find the best directions and limitations for its self-development in personal, family, social and cultural life, and to come to a true understanding of itself. There are limits beyond which if men seek to go in their self-expression and self-development they begin to destroy their own humanity.

The liberal arts and sciences must therefore, for their own health, accept the place in life accorded to them by God. In practice, for Calvin this means that their use will be largely confined to the secular sphere in which their true worth will be adequately revealed. Obviously he believed that the Church can use human culture to help it to understand the Word of God, and it can harness the expressive gifts to enable it to give God a worthy response to his grace — especially in its church buildings, and in aspects of its liturgy and worship. Therefore to this extent art, music and architecture can assist though in a limited way the orientation of our life both towards God and the life to come.[27] Yet he would not have us overestimate the power of such arts in themselves to lift up our

[26] *Inst.*, 1:5:6.
[27] Cf. A. Kuyper, *Calvinism*, Edinburgh, 1898, pp. 208-9.

souls to the Lord in such a way as to bring us into contact with the saving power of the Gospel.

He was convinced that it was both dangerous and wrong for God's majesty to be debased through unseemly representations.[28] He approved of the arrangement of the ten commandments to include the second commandment distinct from the first, forbidding the worship of man-made images. We have to curb the licentiousness which would represent God to our senses or represent him under any visible shape.[29] He admitted that human nature needs to be appealed to in worship through visible rites as well as through the spoken word. But he believed that God had amply provided for our need in this respect by the institution of Baptism and the Lord's Supper. The Word, and these two sacraments constitute the image in which God Himself has chosen both to represent and present Himself to His people. It is not for man to seek to improve on what God has ordained. Since these are the mirror in which we see the face of God we must not try to transform that face in case it becomes unlike God. Since these are the appointed signs of God's presence in our midst, we must not devise other signs, for these are bound to prove completely empty of the reality of His presence. We must not make worship a game, when it is meant to be an encounter. If the preacher is faithfully setting forth the true image of God in Christ through the preaching of the Word and the administration of the Sacraments, no man should need more by which to enable him to grasp Christ and therefore give Him true worship.

It is to be noted that Calvin directs his criticism of visual art in the Church mainly against its use to stimulate devotion or response in the acts of worship where the gracious presence of God alone can give true reality and life. He does not to the same extent criticise the building of spacious and beautiful churches and he acknowledges that within the Church visual arts could be useful in giving instruction, for the artist can reproduce historical events which are "useful for instruction and admonition".[30]

---

[28] *Inst.*, 1:11:12.
[29] *Inst.*, 2:8:17.   [30] *Inst.*, 1:11:12.

To Calvin, then, the "instruction" of the people in the events of Bible and Church history, and their meaning, was quite distinct from the activity of worship itself and could be furthered by the use of the visual arts. It may be, therefore, that he had no objection to the Romanesque carvings of historical scenes and the statues which ornamented the mediaeval churches as long as these were not used for worship. He expressed strong disapproval when he heard of the destruction of images. His statements in this matter seem to be slightly broader than those of Zwingli who had allowed the representation of historical events to have a place around the churches, and admitted that art might have a Christian use, but had voided art entirely "not only of any liturgical or ecclesiastical content or purpose but also of any spiritual dimension".[31]

The Reformers earlier than Calvin had discussed the part that might be played by music and musical instruments in Church and secular life. Luther had had no hesitation in affirming that the "Holy Spirit honours music as a tool of His work" using the effect of David's harp on Saul as an example. In spite of men like Carlstadt who had spoke of the "lascivious notes of the organ", and had wanted to relegate them along with trumpets and flutes, to the theatre, the Lutheran Churches had retained the use of instrumental music in worship. Zwingli had disagreed. He had acknowledged that music could have a powerful and deep but purely psychological effect of a temporary nature on men, and this alone was the explanation of the effect of David's playing on Saul.[32] He had agreed that music had a unique place in human life above all the other arts. The capacity to respond to it was profoundly and universally rooted in human nature. He argued that its main function was to moderate and soothe savage passions, and he believed that it was abused when it was used to stimulate the passions. But he believed that music should be confined for man's use and pleasure as a purely secular gift of God. Within the Church, his decision was, "I disturb no one with my music." The New Testament, he

[31] C. Garside, *Zwingli and the Arts*, New Haven, Conn., 1966, p. 172.
[32] 1 Sam. 16:23.

believed, did not inculcate vocal singing in Church, but rather told men to sing in their hearts, and we must not add our own ceremonies to those instituted by Christ. Therefore Zwingli's influence excluded all singing from worship in Zurich for two generations. But Zwingli composed music, and it played a large part in his home life.[33]

With regard to music Calvin took a middle line between Luther and Zwingli. He believed that music should be allowed to play a part in the "offices of religion" from which he excluded the visual arts. Music, he believed, had a nature adapted to make it profitable in this connection.[34] Therefore, as we have seen, he encouraged congregational singing. Moreover, in his explanation of the effect on Saul of David's music on the harp, he referred to an inward inspiration of the Lord in the heart of Saul, accompanying the music. But Calvin believed that under the New Covenant many of the more elaborate ceremonies of the Old Testament had been abolished or simplified and he believed that under this new dispensation the use of instrumental music had been excluded from Church worship. The use of instruments in worship was suited for those "yet tender, like children" being trained under the law, but "the voice of man ... assuredly excels all inanimate instruments of music". Moreover, he suggested that purely instrumental music was too much like the "unknown tongue" in which according to St. Paul we are forbidden to praise God.[35]

Therefore Calvin relegated instrumental music to the secular realm where it "may minister to our pleasure, rather than our necessity", yet "it is not to be thought of as altogether superfluous" and it must not in any way be condemned.[36]

[33] *Op. cit.*, pp. 59f, 67.

[34] *Comm. on Gen.*, 4:22.

[35] 1 Cor. 14:13; cf. *Comm. on Ps.*, 33:2, *Comm. on Ps.*, 81:2, *Comm. on Exod.*, 15:20.

[36] *Comm. on Gen.*, 4:20. In small cities such as Zurich when the Church ceased to employ the artists and craftsmen they found new patrons in the wealthy burghers. This meant a development in portrait painting, in the interior decoration of houses. It also meant that artistic craftsmanship was lavished on secular rather than on religious articles. This movement took place wherever the Reformation went.

CHAPTER 9

TOWARDS A CHRISTIAN SOCIETY

Sixteenth Century Trends

IT enables us to evaluate Calvin's aim and his actual achievement in Geneva if we view these in the light of certain developments which were taking place both in the thought and in the social structure of the age in which he lived.

For centuries within Christendom both Church and civil government had been closely involved together in all the important affairs of social life. Each had felt that God, the giver of all power, had bound them up in this way. At one time the State, and at another time the Church, had dominated the partnership, but each had tended to cling to the other within a unified Christian society. Life in this world was too hard and dangerous for the Church not to require the support of the civil arm. Faith in the life-to-come was too strong for earthly rulers to imagine that they could do without the Church.

In Calvin's day things had changed. People had begun to alter the focus of their attention. The claims of earthly business were proving more pressing than those made in the name of a distant world-to-come, and earthly comforts were proving more satisfying. As Maynard Smith puts it: "The hearth had conquered the cloister."[1]

Calvin often deplores the fact that the leaders of the Church had allowed themselves to be caught up in such a change. They, too, had altered their priorities. They had become more concerned to wield temporal power for temporal ends than spiritual power for spiritual ends. They had therefore denied their true calling, exposed themselves to

[1] H. Maynard Smith, *Pre-Reformation England*, London, 1963, pp. 516ff.

just contempt and lost their true status and moral authority. An important development in the thought of the Church about man himself took place in the thirteenth century when Thomas Aquinas brought about a union of Aristotle and Christianity. Aquinas conceived of our life as being lived in two distinct realms, the natural and the supernatural, and following Aristotle he evaluated man's natural gifts and his natural ethical and religious potential very highly.

Nature was an element that contained its own force, its own principles of operation, and those who simply followed nature could live with immensely rich resources and achieve important and well-definable ends. A "natural" man living merely within this realm of nature, with its natural resources, its own virtues, and limited ends, was thought of as having an independent worth and identity of his own, even though his life did not aim at being also specifically Christian.[2]

As the distinction between the natural and the Christian (or supernatural) sphere was clarified it brought far-reaching consequences also in the political and ethical thought of the Church. It became possible to conceive of the state with its civil government, adapted for this realm of nature, as itself the reasonable product of human nature. Man was seen as naturally a political animal. Theologians could now clearly develop their ideas about natural law as well as about natural theology. The state with its civil and natural laws seemed now to have a sphere which was peculiarly its own. It could feel called on to develop man's own natural and essential humanity quite apart from a need to make him Christian.

The result was that, guided by its own wisdom and trusting

[2] W. Ullmann, *op. cit.*, pp. 175, 184. For Thomas of course there was always a living and close connection between God and nature, and thus between grace and nature; but the idea of a natural law, reasonable in itself, gave a certain independence to the State in its secularity. Thomas also so underlined the distinction between man as a natural being and man as a Christian as to make them two potentialities capable of quite distinctive self-realisation, the natural aspect of man being worthy of its own free self-expression and sufficient to achieve its own natural end. Cf. also Ullmann, *op. cit.*, pp. 128ff, 134ff and A. Lang, "Reformation and Natural Law" in *Calvin and the Reformation*, New York, 1909, p. 90. Francis Schaeffer blames Aquinas for beginning the movement which has set the secular realm free and unrelated to that which is Christian thus allowing nature to become not only "autonomous" but to control and "eat up" grace. Cf. *Escape from Reason*, London, 1968, pp. 10ff.

in its own earthly resources, the State tended to feel it could find its own way through life without the guidance of the Church. There was an increasing tendency for any unity of Church and State to break up, and for the State to go it alone — a process which Butterfield has called the "great secularisation".[3] The Reformation itself had not so far helped to heal the breach, for it had taught those who ruled secular affairs about the priesthood of all believers, and therefore about the responsibility and privilege of the layman, following his secular calling in direct obedience to God, to find his way himself.[4]

Moreover, the unity of Church and State had been largely forged within the wide dimension of the Holy Roman Empire. As the unity of the Holy Roman Empire broke up, regional and national states themselves became centres of their own sovereign power. It was often to the rulers of these national states that the Reformers had to appeal to effect the needed changes within the Church.[5] This very process itself weakened the status of both the universal and the national churches.

Individual men and women who were living through these great social changes were also being deeply affected by them. The Reformation had succeeded in delivering many of them from the religious fears and superstitions which the corrupted Church had foisted on their minds. But there were many other troubles and questions facing the minds of ordinary people in the sixteenth century making them feel powerless and anxious. Changes in the social structure were breaking up the old associations that had given the individual a helpful measure of group support, and competition was beginning to take the place of cooperation. People in trade and commerce were beginning to feel the pressure of "market-forces". The individual, especially the unsuccessful one within this process, was in danger of finding those ties broken "which used to give him security and a sense of belonging". The world around

---

[3] H. Butterfield, *Christianity in European History*, London, 1952, p. 37.

[4] Cf. *Karl Holl, op. cit.*, pp. 45-6.

[5] E.g. in Germany; cf. O. Chadwick, *The Reformation*, Penguin Books, 1964, pp. 27f, 68.

was becoming bigger and more threatening than he had ever
before imagined. He was "losing his fixed place in a closed
world at the centre of which was man".[6]

A Commonwealth under the Word of God

Calvin's concern in Geneva was to bring Church and State
closely together again in mutual interdependence, in such a
way that the Church had its spiritual independence restored
to it, and civil government was allowed to retain its full power
over every decision proper to its own sphere. T. M. Parker has
pointed out that the distinction and yet the close union of
Church and State which Calvin achieved with the precision
possible in the self-governing city state was an important
factor in the spread of Calvinism, and "expressed its
characteristics on a larger stage almost as well as upon the
narrow platform of Genevan politics".[7]

Moreover, Calvin also showed concern that the individual
of his day should not only find salvation by faith in Jesus
Christ, but should also discern that he mattered in his
community. Calvin tried to ensure in Geneva that each
individual should find that he himself was reached, and cared
for by others, and should discover that his own contribution
to the social group was of value to them. What Calvin lived
to achieve in Geneva deserves to be called a commonwealth
in which both Church and State serve each other in serving
the Word of God, and the individual is nurtured and trained
to true freedom and responsibility in the community.

Some Church historians have described the regime Calvin
set up in Geneva as a theocracy; some have called it a
clerocracy. Troeltsch, reviewing Calvin's work in Geneva,
pointed out, rightly, that Calvin's concern was "the
organised rule of Christian thought over society" but he
added "society cannot be influenced in this way unless the
Church is supreme over society", thus controlling the State

[6] Cf. Erich Fromm, *The Fear of Freedom*, London, 1942, pp. 52-3.
[7] T. M. Parker, *Christianity and the State in the Light of History*, London, 1955,
p. 160.

and social life in general. In practice, he affirmed, Calvin made the State subordinate to the Church.[8]

The latter statements do not reflect accurately either Calvin's thought or his achievement. He was not concerned to make either the Church or the clergy supreme. All he was concerned about was that what the Church offered should be supreme. Troeltsch himself is more correct when he speaks of Calvin seeking to develop the necessary organs by means of which the community can be moulded by the Divine Spirit and the Divine Word in every aspect of life.[9]

To achieve this miracle within the life of the Church and community the Word of God had to be allowed its full freedom to influence both spheres. In their action in the Berthelier case, Calvin saw a threat by the civil authorities to the welfare of the whole church-city. The Word, indeed, would have become a choked and useless seed in thorny ground, if the fellowship of the Lord's Supper had been marked by the scandals which the council was ready to tolerate. Calvin's concern, therefore, was for the freedom of the Word of God to produce the fruits of the Spirit.

For the sake of its own health, therefore, the city authorities needed not only the Word but a Church which was ready to preach it without contamination. Calvin could not have imagined a purely secular government which did not in some way give special acknowledgement and encouragement to such a Church. For him even heathen governments necessarily acknowledged some form of religion. The Church itself however must not live apart, but must act as the most vital organ of the whole community. Otherwise it could not justly claim the help of the civil power to establish and support it. The Christian, too, must realise that he himself cannot break away from all the outward associations of the civil society in which he is meant to give his witness clearly.

For the Church to be free to preach the Word unhindered did not necessarily involve its being given a position of supremacy or even of high privilege within the community. Calvin knew that in fulfilling its task the Church might have to accept, as Christ did, the lowly, even abject, "form of a

[8] *Op. cit.*, pp. 627-8.   [9] *Ibid.*, p. 591.

servant". Precisely in such a form would the radiating truth of its Word be more clearly seen. No matter how low its fortunes might sometimes seem to sink in the course of history, it would always be brought again into new life and freedom by the power of the resurrection of Christ. Calvin found the course of Church history foreshadowed in what happened to young Joseph: "although the Lord took pity on Egypt, yet he did it not for the sake of the King, or of the country, but that Joseph might, at length, be brought out of prison; and further, that, in the time of famine, good might be supplied to the Church; for although the produce was stored with no design beyond that of providing for the Kingdom of Egypt; yet God chiefly cared for the Church, which he esteemed more highly than ten worlds".[10]

Civil Government, "Humanity", and the Church

As regards civil government, Calvin gave due weight to the idea that it has to do with law and order. Its task was to see that there is "no idolatry . . . no blasphemy . . . that the public quiet be not disturbed, that every man's property be kept secure".[11] Moreover, sometimes, "it has the power to take up arms in order to execute public vengeance".[12] Therefore he fully acknowledges the importance of the use of sheer force in the hands of the ruler. But in the *Institutes* this aspect of the State's function is introduced in such a way as to suggest that it is secondary.[13] Basically, for Calvin, the political government of man is there for man's education, cultural advancement and social welfare in its widest and most positive implications.

Therefore in thinking about the structure of human society we should think, as Raymond Williams suggests,[14] in terms of a "human order" rather than of simply a "political and economic order".

Twice in the *Institutes* Calvin briefly summarises his conception of the function of civil government in terms that

---

[10] *Comm. on Gen.,* 41:9.   [11] *Inst.,* 4:20:3.
[12] *Inst.,* 4:20:11.   [13] *Inst.,* 4:20:3 and 9.
[14] *Culture and Society 1780-1950,* Pelican, p. 131.

are positive rather than negative. "In short, it provides that a public form of religion may exist among Christians, and humanity among men."[15] "It exists to adapt our conduct to human society, to form our manners to civil justice, to conciliate us to each other, to cherish common peace and tranquillity."[16] In reading his definitions we manage to get away from the traditional ideas expressed too often even by Luther that civil government is for the bad and the weak and that its main business lies in exercising force over men. Calvin would have approved of John MacMurray's contention that "the intention of politics is not the use of force, but the elimination of force and the achievement of freedom through justice", that force if it has to be used by the State shall be used only as a last resort when all else has failed.[17]

The "order" which should chiefly concern the politician is therefore a social order in which the health and the cooperation of each individual is of primary importance — indeed, an order, the shape of which is itself to some extent determined by the thinking and aspirations of individuals which make up the society.[18]

But how are we to know what true "humanity" is — and how are we to foster it? Earthly rulers may have good political instincts, a natural conception of justice and human rights, and in addition may be able to conduct exhaustive and efficient psychological and sociological research into the state of affairs before them, yet it still remains true that "government by itself cannot govern";[19] moreover, no amount of research into human behaviour and conditions, as John MacMurray points out, "can form a basis for the essential understanding of human nature. The doctrine of the fall stands within the Christian faith as a continual witness to such brutally negative but most important facts."[20]

---

[15] *Inst.*, 4:20:3.   [16] *Inst.*, 4:20:2.   [17] *Op. cit.*, p. 33.

[18] Cf. J. Bronowski and Bruce Mazlish, *The Western Intellectual Tradition*, Penguin, 1963, p. 549: "The way in which human beings think and feel must somehow shape the structure of human societies."

[19] Jacques Maritain, *The Rights of Man*, London, 1945, p. 50.

[20] John Macmurray, *Clue to History*, London, 1938, pp. 36f. This observation is important in view of the fact that today in governmental decisions, the results of research tend to replace "natural law".

Calvin therefore believed that we can know what true humanity is, and how this life is meant to be lived only if we know Christ and the Word of God. Neither the meaning and destiny of human life, nor the true nature of its orders can be properly understood apart from divine revelation. The Church was there to offer to the civil rulers the extra insight and wisdom they must have, through its contemporary interpretation of the Word of God.

Calvin believed that what happens when humanity is redeemed in Christ gives us a true picture of what was meant to happen originally in society in its natural form. For grace always tends to reveal and restore the original form of nature. Therefore he found the ideal human order described for him in Paul's account of the Church in the New Testament — an organism, or a body, in which each member derives its life and health and nourishment from the whole body, and has a quite unique and irreplaceable function.[21] In Geneva he wanted even civil society to reflect as far as it could the pattern of mutual dependence, cooperation, close intercommunion between the whole body and its members which he expected to find first especially in the Church. Earthly citizenship was to be patterned on heavenly citizenship. The whole social body in the city itself, therefore, was meant to be an organism with a great variety of members, each member finding significance in his part in, and service to, the whole body, and the health and wealth of the whole depending on the faithful functioning of each.

His first concern in Geneva was therefore to create at the heart of the city a community of the faithful in Christ whose ways of mutual forbearance, love and forgiveness would provide a pattern for the rest of civil society. By nurturing its own members within its fellowship to a life of true Christian sanctification, the Church would at the same time produce a pattern for good earthly citizenship not attainable through any kind of purely secular education. Moreover the free and yet controlled self-expression offered to the individual within the life of the Church would produce for society the individual who could face the challenge of leadership and

21 Cf. 1 Cor. 12:14-26, Rom. 12:4-6.

responsibility in the wider affairs of society. Only thus could the Church become the instrument for the reordering of the whole of human life.

The Church had to give its witness to the State in these important matters not only by preaching the Word, and by passing resolutions at its assemblies, but also by showing what it all meant in the life it lived. It had to manifest in its own life of flesh and blood the new humanity and divine order that was now being reintroduced into this creation by Jesus Christ through the renewing work of the Spirit. Its task was not simply to teach, for example, that the meaning of sex can never be found in permissiveness, that marriage is sacred, monogamy healthy, and that divorce is wrong. Its task was, rather, to show the true meaning of marriage by producing living examples of married life based on love and faithfulness, and patterned after the relationship of Christ and the Church. Only by paying heed to such a Church could the State begin to understand properly the human nature it was dealing with, the true nature of marriage, of parenthood, of the purpose of life itself, or of the nature of evil.

Before we pass on from Calvin's plea to governments to cultivate "humanity" as a first concern in all this activity, it can be illuminating to take note of his attitude to war in his time. The magistrate has the right to wage war and incurs guilt if he does not defend his people. He must prepare soberly for war in time of peace, post garrisons, enter defensive agreements with neighbouring princes, and even engage in the manufacture of armaments. In inflicting punishment he acts not of himself, but executes "the very judgments of God".[22]

It is doubtful however if Calvin would have ever allowed himself to go the length of Luther's utterance on this subject: "It is not man, but God who hangs, tortures, beheads, kills and fights. All these are God's works."[23] His own sermons, on the contrary, are full of expression of horror at what happens in war. He stated clearly from his pulpit that no war can be justified when it leads to widespread and extreme confusion, and when men made in the image of God are wantonly

[22] *Inst.*, 4:20: 10 and 12.   [23] LW, 46, p. 96.

destroyed. He lamented that modern war, as they knew it in the sixteenth century, was little better than brigandage, marked by such inhumanity that all order was overthrown and men became no better than furious beasts.[24] "We know with how many miseries war is replete, for when once men begin to take up arms, the gate is open for robberies, rapines, burnings, slaughters, debaucheries and all violence; and in war all humanity and equity is buried." Therefore "all other means must be tried before having recourse to arms".[25]

War must always be only a desperate last resort. We will take note that Calvin deliberately refused to encourage the start of war on religious grounds,[26] and there is no suggestion in the *Institutes* that a religious war could be justified. He was obviously deeply concerned by the thought that the civil magistrate might allow a policy of war, or the conduct of a war, to be dictated by passion or by rash motives rather than by the reasonable practical necessity of a desperate situation. During a war, he insisted, God allowed the use of force only when it was carefully restrained and all excessive cruelty was avoided. "Unless such moderation accompanies the performance of their duty, it is in vain for kings to boast that they are commissioned by God to execute vengeance."[27] Calvin obviously believed that in his day, with the armaments then available, it was possible so to control the events and the fighting that some measure of humanity was preserved. What would have been his preaching in face of the devastating effects of modern armaments?

The Clear Boundary Lines

Calvin, as we have seen, drew strict boundary lines between the two spheres of human concern, which he called the heavenly and the earthly, and which we sometimes refer to as

---

[24] *Sermon on Deut.*, 20:16-20, C.O., 27:636, *Sermon on Deut.*, 2:1-7, C.O., 26:14.
[25] *Comm. on Ezek.*, 6:11, *Inst.*, 4:20:12.   [26] Cf. pp. 162ff.
[27] *Comm. on Ps.*, 18:48. Cf. *Sermon on Deut.*, 20:10-18, C:O., 27:617ff. In *Sermon on 2 Sam.*, 2:17ff, Calvin dwells on Abner's inability to spare Asahel once the fighting broke out. These sermons were probably preached against the background of the first war of religion in France, and Calvin draws the moral (cf. pp. 44-6). *Supplementa Calviniana*, 1961, *Sermons on 2 Samuel*.

the sacred and the secular. In his thinking these lines never
become blurred. He had no thought of ever fusing one realm
into another.

It is sometimes claimed, however, that Calvin aimed to
produce in Geneva what can be called a "Christian culture".
Such a phrase is confusing. He certainly did believe that a
transformation could take place in the heart and life of the
individual so that he can now become a "Christian" man or
woman, and through the Word and the Spirit develop a new
outlook which can indeed merit being called a "Christian"
world-view. He believed, moreover, that the whole realm of
human and secular affairs in Geneva, in spite of its frailty and
its persistent tendency to alienation from God, could become
penetrated and invaded powerfully by the Word of God, and
thus, by the influence of the grace and Kingdom of God. The
proximity of the realm of grace could thus powerfully affect
the realm of nature, and the life of the "world" could in
Geneva become dominated and moulded by the same
regenerating divine influences as were at work within the
Church. Calvin therefore expected to see great changes
taking place in how Geneva as a secular city worked and
lived.

However great the change effected within the sphere of the
city, it can nevertheless be argued that to Calvin it always
remained a "secular" city. Calvin did not believe we could
blend the Christian with the human. Just as there were for
him no close relationships between the truths put within the
grasp of man's natural reason, and the truth of the Gospel, so
there are no vital points of contact between the gifts bestowed
by God on the "natural man" and those "delivered to guilty
man for their sanctification".[28]

We find, therefore, that Calvin differs greatly from
Aquinas in his view of how these two realms are related to
each other. Aquinas attempted to bring about a unified
synthesis by establishing points of contact and transition from
one realm to the other. What was highest and noblest in the
sphere of the human touched what was supposedly the lower
levels of the spiritual realm. The upper reaches of the realm of

[28] C.L. to Bucer, February 1549.

nature, indeed, seem to lead us smoothly into the realm of grace, and grace brings nature to perfection. The whole sphere of the natural is thus a substructure to the kingdom of grace. With Calvin, however, we do not find this tendency to weld the two realms together in a unity. What was "natural", he believed, was too much subject to frailty and vanity, and tended to be too much perverted by our persistent human sinfulness ever to be trusted to lead us in its highest reaches towards the Kingdom of God. Therefore Calvin simply allowed the two spheres, that of our human culture, and that of our central Christian concern, to lie side by side in their parallel co-existence, and in the tension which was bound to exist especially when in the human sphere there is always a confusion of merely human aims and purposes. He did not attempt any facile or unrealistic reconciliation in theory between what went on in each sphere.

That the realm of the secular and natural is on a lower level than that of the Christian does not mean that it is further from God. In Calvin's view those whose life and work lay within the realm of the secular were no way more distant or less responsible to the one living God than those whose life and ministry lay within the Church. The God we know through our redemption in Christ as the giver of salvation and heaven, is also the giver of creation and the earth, and the same self-giving grace and power as brought about redemption also brought about creation itself. Calvin, who recognised the glory and goodness of God shining so clearly in redemption, did not fail to recognise the same glory and goodness also reflected in the natural realm which waits to be redeemed.

Calvin never seems to concede the possibility that the secular world of Genevan affairs in which he called men and women to live the Christian life could ever become so transformed that it was no longer simply the "world" about which the New Testament has so many words of warning. Certainly he tried to make the Church and its members in Geneva truly and fully Christian. He wanted to see this holy and healthy Church developing within a community life as rich, varied, and flourishing in its secular pursuits as is possible while this world lasts. He sought to achieve a truly "human" culture and a "human" society within the Christian commonwealth.

Though Calvin always tried to hold Church and State as closely together as possible, his thought about the Church itself tended to establish it in separation from civil society. In his approach to most of the problems of Geneva he accepted the view which had prevailed since the Roman Empire professed Christianity, that the Church and State were one and the same people. Yet his mind was also beginning to move in another direction as well. Gaining ground in Europe at this time were the views of the Anabaptists and the Independents of history which ultimately led to the emergence of the voluntary Church separate from the State. In their view, the Church was a voluntary association composed of those who from their own personal conviction professed the faith and whose life was in accordance with their profession. There were many aspects of the Anabaptist view of the Church with which Calvin could have had no sympathy. They had abandoned completely the idea that Church and State were two aspects of the one community. They believed only in Adult Baptism. They were suspicious of civil power, and often refused to co-operate with it. But they believed in strict ecclesiastical discipline, in the right of the Church to impose its own required standard of membership, in the need for personal confession of a body of teaching by those who belonged to the faithful. Calvin agreed with them on these latter points. He can freely speak of the Church universal being divided and dispersed in separate places and concedes that such "individual Churches" "each rightly has the name and the authority of the Church".[29]

It is sometimes asserted that the voluntary Church in actual fact appeared first in England in the independent Churches of Cromwell's time, but the Huguenot Calvinistic Churches in France have the same appearance of being freely gathered voluntary groups quite distinct within the civil community. There is truth in Ronald Bainton's assertion that with Calvin "the concepts of the Church embracing the

[29] *Inst.*, 4:1:9; cf. *Comm. on 1 Pet.*, 5:3.

entire community and of the Church as a sect comprising only the saved were ... combined".[30]

Today we tend to diminish in our thinking the role of the "State" within society. We tend to resist the thought that it can be identified with society. We think rather in terms of a "government" set up by society, and within society, to assist in its welfare, protect its freedom and preserve its best values. The Church is regarded as simply one voluntary organisation taking its place alongside many others, possibly more powerful than itself — trades unions, industrial confederations, cultural bodies, sporting associations, etc. We call the agglomerate "pluralistic society". The State, too, has forced the Church to assume this voluntary form by vigorously asserting its own secularity, and by affirming its belief that it can think out and solve the problems of government quite apart from any reference to its former teacher and ally.

Calvin's thought about the Church and society is thus adaptable to the conditions in which it must accept a non-established position and form, and can no longer reckon its membership to be even the majority of the community. The Church in many places has to think out afresh its task, understanding itself as the servant people of God within a largely alien world to whom it again has to give the uncompromising witness and leadership which can only come when it clearly understands both its limitations and the glory of its position in the world.

The Individual within the Community

Calvin often reveals a sensitivity to the position and needs of the individual within society — especially of the under-privileged and the poor. From the pulpit he often went out of his way to stir the conscience of his hearers about their duty to the apparent waifs and strays around them. When he preached on the Old Testament prohibition to deprive a poor debtor of an upper millstone as a pledge for his debt, he spoke with overtones which can be heard today as a claim that no society must ever deprive any man of the opportunity to work

[30] *The Reformation of the Sixteenth Century*, London, 1963, p. 121; cf. Troeltsch, *op. cit.*, vol. II, pp. 627-8.

for his living. "God speaks here of millstones, but it is an illustration of a universal principle.... You cut the throat of a poor man when you deprive him of the tools by which he gains his living.... If a man is deprived of his work he is degraded."[31]

Of course he continually reminded the individual that as a soul loved by God he was of far greater value than even the status of an important place in the social organism could give him. He tried therefore to help people, even as they found their due place within the community, also to see themselves as dignified by the personal love of God, and as working under a personal call from God himself. "We must perform our duties as to God", he repeats again and again. We must "serve God himself", have God "fixed before our eyes". Even the woman in the kitchen with her hands in the pastry must remember "that she serves God".[32] Each had to be made to feel that he or she had a destiny far greater than can be found merely within the structure of Church and society. "We must take pleasure in his service. It must be all joy and delight. This bondage must be more sweet and precious to us than all liberties, and than all the realms and kingdoms of the world." "Let us assure ourselves that our state is not a scrap lower before God than if we were kings and princes, and all men trembled before us."[33]

Such teaching was certainly not new. It had filtered down from New Testament times. In the Middle Ages, however, the importance of an individual simply as an individual had become obscured. Persons were often thought of as deriving their significance simply from the vocation they filled in society. Here Calvin makes his contribution to the recovery in his day of an important aspect of the Biblical view of man — that each individual is to be regarded as of infinite worth, simply as an individual.

Therefore society had to be organized and disciplined in order to find each individual and to help each to attain this sense of his worth. We have already noted that in the Church

[31] *Sermon on Deut.*, 24:1-6, C.O., 28:161-2.
[32] Cf. *Sermon on Eph.*, 6:5-9, *Sermon on 1 Tim.*, 2:13-15, C.O., 53:228-9.
[33] *Sermon on Eph.*, 6:5-9, E.T., pp. 639, 641.

discipline and pastoral work carried out by the elders of Geneva no one was to be missed. This was why the parish was divided into districts and elders were given supervision of manageable areas.

We see again here how Calvin's thought about Church structure could provide him with the model of an ideal social structure. Geneva as a city had to be organised so that no one was missed, or might become "lost". Calvin's plan was to ensure that the whole community was closely knit, each one being personally given as close a tie as possible with someone in the neighbourhood who had immediate contact with the source of real authority and power. Perhaps Calvin in his own day sensed the fact that as urban communities grow in size the ordinary individual begins to be left to the mercy of an impersonal bureaucracy that can often fail even to be able to weigh up his particular desert and needs.

The city authorities themselves had to be encouraged to think of their work in government as involving a social care for the welfare of each individual corresponding to the pastoral care exerted by the ministry of the Word. The local magistrate, according to Calvin, must live up to the name given to him from time immemorial — the "father of his country ... the shepherd of his people". His people, moreover, are meant to see the image of God reflected in his pastoral and sovereign rule.[34]

The individual must respond to the approach and concern of the community and gladly fulfil his vocation within it. Whatever his work he is to try to see it as a sacred calling, and through doing it he will be helped to find and fulfil the will of God. In such obedience his life is given stability and purpose. "Every man's mode of life is ... a kind of station assigned him by the Lord, that he may not always be driven about at random."[35] In the Middle Ages of course the same kind of thing had been said. But it was then believed that a higher and more perfect calling could be pursued through giving up the secular vocation and choosing a monastic life apart from the world. Luther had taught, and Calvin followed him, that true Christian perfection was to be found, and the

[34] *Inst.*, 4:20:4.   [35] *Inst.*, 3:10:6.

sanctification of the individual was to be fulfilled, not apart from, but within the fulfilment of the earthly task, whether it be that of a married man, a wife, a tradesman or an artist.

Though Calvin can speak of an earthly occupation as "a burden laid on us by God",[36] he does in his working and preaching, try to stir up the mind with a vision of the glory of even a humble task in a community that is itself worthy to be called "holy" and "Christian".[37]

It is sometimes asserted that Calvin left no freedom for anyone to change the vocation which Providence seemed to have assigned to him. There are slight hints of this in his discussion of the matter in the *Institutes*. Yet in one sermon he warns everybody, especially the parents of children, that there are occupations which "serve only for outward show and pomp, and for I do not know what delights and allurements, but which do nothing but debauch men". Many, he asserts, if they examine what purpose their occupation serves "will find it to be nothing but infection and stench . . . a wasting and perverting of what God has given to men". "It is not enough," he appeals, "when a man can say, oh, I labour, I have my craft or I have such a trade. That is not enough. But we must see whether it is good and profitable for the common good."[38]

All this certainly sounds like an appeal to choose an occupation carefully and even to move out of one kind into another. It is a reminder, too, of how important it is that each individual should be able to feel that the community in which he has to live his life is worthy of devoted service. Of course Calvin stresses the fact that all other reformation is in vain unless each has learned to love his neighbour — or the person he works or lives with.

When Calvin, discussing the Christian life, says "The gifts

---

[36] *Inst.*, 3:10:6.

[37] Troeltsch affirms that for Luther the vocational system was simply accepted as a divine arrangement for the individual within society, and was not consciously designed for the purpose of producing the holy community — as it was in Calvinism. Cf., *op. cit.*, p. 610; Raymond Williams (in *Culture and Society 1780-1950*, p. 210) quotes D. H. Lawrence: "men are free when they belong to a living, organic, believing community, active in fulfilling some unfulfilled perhaps unrealized purpose", from *Studies in Classic American Culture*, p. 12.

[38] *Sermon on Eph.*, 4:26-8, E.T., p. 457.   [39] *Inst.*, 3:7:5.

we possess have been bestowed by God and entrusted to us on condition that they be distributed for the good of our neighbour",[39] a study of the context and his language will show that he is talking at the same time both about the spiritual gifts we have from Christ through the Spirit for the benefit of the Church, and also about the possessions, wealth and natural abilities we have as privileged citizens for the benefit of the social community. He is talking about our "neighbour" in the Church pew and in the city street in the one breath. "No manner of life", he says elsewhere, "is more praiseworthy to God than that which yields some advantage to human society."[40]

Though Calvin stressed the need for the cultivation of a sense of brotherhood and solidarity, he did not say that all men are equal. Though he affirmed that all men are made in the image of God,[41] and that each must be treated by his -neighbour with dignity and honour, "God's intention", he declared, "is not that all men should be jumbled together ... but that some should rule ... and that they who are under them should obey."[42] Christ did not come "to make a confused equality, so that it should not be known who is great and who is small".[43]

All our equalities and inequalities belonged therefore only to what was superficial in life. Even slavery, Calvin believed, belonged to this merely external order of affairs. There must be mutual regard and love between master and slave, and if the slave is obligated to the master, the master is also obligated to the slave. The master must say, "I am master, not in tyranny, but on this condition that I am also brother: I am master, but there is also a common master in heaven for me, and those who are under me. We are here as if we were all one family."[44] We must not forget "the nature common to all men by which God joins us all together". The master-servant relationship must always be regarded as ephemeral; "Bondmen ought to be regarded as paid servants

[40] *Comm. on Matt.*, 25:24.
[41] Cf. *Inst.*, 3:7:6.
[42] *Sermon on Eph.*, 6:5-9, E.T., p. 637.
[43] *Ibid.*, p. 640.
[44] *Sermon on Deut.*, 15:16-23, C.O., 27:357; cf. *Comm. on 1 Cor.*, 11:3, *Comm. on Eph.*, 6:9.

who are engaged only for the day" for "in God's school where there is brotherhood between both great and small ... they share one hope of eternal life".[45] An off-the-job class structure should not be allowed to develop even though a hierarchy may be necessary within the job.

Calvin himself was able easily to forget human rank because when he thought of other men and women his own mind became powerfully gripped by the certainty that for each soul only one thing counts: its relationship to Christ. This is why he writes with such ease, and indeed, often in such a familiar way, to the nobility and rulers everywhere in Europe. Occasionally in a superficial and formal way he shows signs of deference. But chiefly he writes as a brother and a comrade. The other person of whatever rank is to him another soul struggling desperately before God, and Calvin hopes, in Christ.

[45] *Sermon on Eph.*, 4:31-5:2, E.T., p. 480; *Sermon on Eph.*, 6:5-9, E.T., p. 646.

PART II

CHURCHMAN AND PASTOR

CHAPTER 10

REFORMER AND CHURCH ARCHITECT

The Servant of the Word

NO matter how involved he had to allow himself to become in civic affairs Calvin's first loyalty was always the Church. His call from God was to the ministry not simply of the Geneva congregation, but of the Church universal. He made its welfare and wider problems his first concern, entered fully into its controversies, gave his enthusiastic support whenever he heard of a helpful plan for its reconstruction, and corresponded with nearly all its leaders.[1]

He believed that the part which he and others in his day had to play as reformers of the Church was quite unique, and due entirely to the emergency of the times they lived in. In the short autobiography introducing the Psalms, he likened the intervention he had to make in Church affairs to that of King David "taken from the sheepfold and elevated to the rank of supreme authority".[2] In his Epistle to Sadoleto, he likened himself to a common soldier of the line who, seeing the others on his side routed, scattered and abandoning the ranks, raises the leader's standard and recalls them to their posts.[3]

Later on, in his letter to the King of Poland on December 5, 1554, he again insists on the uniqueness of this personal calling which, he felt, forced himself along with some others to take responsibilities and make decisions not given to men in the normal course of human events:

This office which the Lord laid upon us when he made use of our services in collecting Churches is altogether

---

[1] Cf. J. H. Kromminga, "Calvin and Ecumenicity", p. 156 (in *J. Calvin, Contemporary Prophet*, Grand Rapids, 1959).   [2] I.C.P., p. xl.
[3] C.Tr., vol. I, p. 59 — Calvin saw the Reformation as the restoration of the true Catholic Church; cf. McNeill, *op. cit.*, p. 216.

anomalous. Those, then, who in an unwonted manner, and so contrary to the expectations of men, appeared as defenders of true religion, ought not to have their vocation judged by the common rule. They were divinely called for this special purpose.[4]

No regular pastor could ever arrogate to himself the part that he himself or Luther or their reforming colleagues had undertaken within the Church! We have no record of his ordination to the priesthood, or to the ministry, or to this particular task he felt he had to fulfil within the Church. He never refers to such an occasion. It is possible that he felt that his task was too irregular for it ever to be justified by a ceremony involving regular Church authority.

Calvin certainly regarded such ordination as essential within a well-ordered Church, and realised its value as an outward sign of historic continuity.[5] He believed, however, that the Word of God is the foundation of the Church.[6] The Apostolic and Catholic Church has to be recognised where the Word of God is rightly preached, and the sacraments are rightly administered.[7] Word and Sacraments are signs of Christ's presence and the marks of a Church. Where these signs are, we must recognise a Church, even though there may be many imperfections and sins within its fellowship. The Old and New Testaments show us a God who patiently holds on to his delinquent people and congregations, and Church history confirms that the Church has always lived by the forgiveness of its own sins. Though we ourselves should not patronise even the minutest error in our Church, we must not, therefore, separate from it on the grounds of its impurities.[8]

By the preaching of the Word, Christ not only calls, and holds his Church together, he also exercises his rule over the hearts and minds of his people. Whereas David ruled over his earthly kingdom by a golden sceptre, Christ's heavenly kingdom is presided over by the sceptre of the preached

[4] C.L. to the King of Poland, December 5, 1554.
[5] Cf. *Inst.*, 4:3:16; 4:19:31; C.Tr. III, pp. 264, 266; C.L. to King of Poland, 1554.
[6] *Inst.*, 4:2:4; 4:8:10ff.
[7] *Inst.*, 4:1:9.   [8] *Inst.*, 4:1:11-29.

Gospel.[9] When Christ gave Peter and the apostles the promise that they would be given the keys of the kingdom of heaven, and would be able to "bind or loose" people on earth, he was referring to the effect their preaching of the Word of God was to have on its hearers.[10] The authority thus attached by Christ to preaching must be accepted without question by all who will have anything to do with Christ and the Church.[11]

A true Church in Calvin's eyes, will therefore be a Church that seeks and allows the Word to have such rule within its worship, counsels, and activity. If the Church continually hears, and obeys the Word of God, allows its sins to be continually cleansed and its human tendency of growing corrupt and deformed, to be continually corrected by such hearing and obedience, it will be kept in health and faithfulness. If the Church in any generation, however, allows its own human wisdom and perverse desires to dominate its life, and refuses to allow the converting and constraining power of the Word to alter its ways and thoughts, it will begin to lose all claim to truth, and will become like the salt which has lost its savour.

It had become clear to Calvin that the Church of Rome had so broken with truth and with Christ that it had lost continuity with the ancient Catholic Church. In doctrine and worship it had gradually grown away from its origin till its form had no recognisable relation to a true Church. At the time of the Reformation it had been challenged again to become a Church reformed under the Word of God. But it had decisively refused. It had preferred hardening itself more and more in its false dogmatic and institutionalised forms, and was becoming more and more irreformable.[12]

An Architect of the Church — External Order

Calvin thought of himself in relation to the Church as an architect of reconstruction. In the letter dedicating his

[9] *Comm. on Isa.*, 49:2; *on Hosea*, 1:11.
[10] *Comm. on John*, 20:23; *on Matt.*, 16:19; *Inst.*, 4:11:1.   [11] *Comm. on Eph.*, 4:11.
[12] Cf. T. F. Torrance, *Conflict and Agreement in the Church*, London, 1959, vol. I, pp. 96-7.

Commentary on Isaiah to King Edward VI he described the state of the Church. It had become like the ruined temple of God, utterly deformed, having lost all the glory of the early centuries of its life. But God had begun to raise it up so that men might begin again to see the beauty and glory of the former outline, and Calvin describes himself as one of many inconsiderable persons selected by God "as architects to promote the work of pure doctrine".[13] In his important letter to the King of Poland, he refers again to his call to "build up the Church now lying deformed among the ruins of Popery".[14]

Calvin was more concerned about the externals and the general shape of the Church's life than many of his contemporaries. "Should some one object", he wrote to the Duchess of Ferrara, "that externals of religion are quite indifferent, that what is required is only that the heart should be upright, to that our Lord answers, that He will be glorified in our body, which He has purchased with His blood, that he requires the confession of the mouth, that all our prayers should be consecrated to his honour without being in any way contaminated or defiled by anything despleasing to Him."[15]

He felt that carelessness about external matters denied the wholeness of Christ's redemption, and his lordship over the whole of life. For the Church to seek good and worthy external forms of expressing its faith, its inner life and love, and its devotion to God could greatly enhance and stabilise its witness to true doctrine. Practices within the Church which were not in accordance with its faith could destroy its witness to the truth either by their falsity or by their very emptiness.

Some, in Calvin's day believed that the externals could be left to sort themselves out gradually, as long as the Word was being heard and received. Luther himself had sometimes given the advice that we must "leave it to the Word". Calvin, however, was not content with such a policy. The "reformation" of the Church meant a deliberate restoration of good order. A Church must therefore *ensure* that it has a "true and lawful constitution".[16] "Let us understand that

---

[13] *Comm. on Isa.*, vol. 1, pp. xxii-xxiii.   [14] C.L. to King of Poland, 1554.
[15] C.L., October, 1541.   [16] *Inst.*, 4:2:12.

some kind of government is necessary in every human society to ensure the common peace and to maintain concord. . . . This ought especially to be observed in Churches which are best sustained by a constitution in all respects well-ordered, and without which concord can become no churches at all. Wherefore if we would provide for the safety of the Church, we must carefully attend to Paul's command that 'all things be done decently and in order'." Calvin believed firmly that there was such "diversity . . . in the customs of men, such variety in their minds, such conflicts in their judgments and dispositions" that the Church would disintegrate if it did not lay down some set-forms.[17]

In deciding the external forms of Church order which are in keeping with the Word of God, Calvin recognised that Holy Scripture does not always lay down definite rules. Many of the English Puritans later felt that all the rites introduced since the days of the New Testament could be abolished and that there should be placed in God's Church "those things only which the Lord himself in his word commandeth".[18] Though Calvin occasionally makes statements which can be misunderstood to teach this view,[19] in other places he insists that even in matters which he regarded as of vital importance for the life of the Church, its practice must be decided otherwise than by "distilling constitutions from Biblical texts". While God has prescribed clearly and carefully in Scripture everything relating to man's salvation "yet in external discipline and ceremonies he has not been pleased to prescribe every particular that we ought to observe. He foresaw that this depended on the nature of the times, and that one form would not suit all ages.[20] "We know", he writes, "that every Church has liberty to frame for itself a

[17] *Inst.*, 4:10:27.
[18] Cf. *Puritan Manifestos*, W. H. Frere and C. E. Douglas, London, 1907, p. 8. J. L. Ainslie, *op. cit.*, p. 23, quotes John Udall: "God doth describe perfectly unto us out of His word that form of government which is lawful, and the officers that are to execute the same; from which it is not lawful for any Christian Church to swerve."
[19] Cf. C.Tr., vol. II, p. 126. During his absence from Geneva, for example, he wrote to the Seigneury: "I beseech you well to consider all the means of rightly ordering your Church, so that she may be ruled according to the scriptural method of our Lord." C.L., February 19, 1541.
[20] *Inst.*, 4:10:30.

form of government that is suitable and profitable for it, because the Lord has not prescribed anything definite."[21]

He believed that there were fundamental articles of the faith which should be recognised by everyone, "such as, God is one, Christ is God and the Son of God. Our salvation rests on God's mercy and the like."[22] He would not tolerate deviations from such basic doctrines or ambiguities in their expression. Yet he recognised that in his day Church matters were in an unsettled and precarious state. Therefore excessive rigidity in matters of order was foolish; many things had to be tolerated which could not easily be allowed in more settled times.[23] No Church, he believed, was pure enough to be meticulous on non-fundamental issues. "There is scarcely any Church which does not retain some remnants of former ignorance. It is sufficient for us if the doctrine on which the Church of God is founded be recognized and retain its place."[24]

His strict and fairly clear definition of the area in which there could be no compromise, left him a much wider field than had many of his contemporaries, in which there could be a wide variety of choice and opinion, and when controversy arose on such matters he is nearly always found on the side of leniency,[25] trying to moderate those who were over zealous either for conformity or non-conformity. Many things, he felt, were so "indifferent" as to be not worth fighting about. Vestments came under this category. When Hooper in England, on being appointed Bishop, was imprisoned because he refused to wear the required vestments ("Aaronical habits", he called them), and take the oath prescribed for his installation, Calvin wrote Bullinger saying, "I had rather he had not carried his opposition so far with respect to the cap and linen vestment, even although I do not approve of these."[26]

---

[21] *Comm. on 1 Cor.*, 11:2.   [22] Cf. *Inst.*, 4:1:12.

[23] C.L. to the Church of Frankfurt, December 22, 1555; to Somerset, October 22, 1548.   [24] Cf., the plea for concord in C.L. to Zebedee, May 19, 1539.

[25] C.L. to Somerset, October 22, 1548: "We must observe moderation ... overdoing is, neither discreet nor useful ... forms of worship need to be accommodated to the condition and tastes of the people."

[26] C.L., March 24, 1551.

Similarly we have seen that Calvin desired to see the Church celebrating the Christian festivals but he submitted to other arrangements because he did not wish to fight about it. Moreover, in the midst of very high feeling amongst others about the exact locality in the Church at which Baptism should be celebrated — whether at the door, or in face of the congregation, he refused to commit himself in the quarrel because he felt it was not important enough.[27]

Since Calvin's name has been usually associated with an extremely bare and simple type of worship, it is worthwhile looking at what he wrote on such a matter. He believed that as well as deciding its discipline, its doctrine, and its form of government, it was also important that the Church should exercise control over its forms of worship.[28]

He was sensitive about the details which affected the interpretation which people could give to central acts of worship. He hated especially the unauthorised ceremonies and prayers, and the false interpretation, by which the heart of Christian worship had been corrupted in the mass, which he believed firmly to be idolatry and to cut us off from Christ. Every action and word, no matter how trivial in themselves, must be controlled when they obtrude into the centre of the Church's service of God. Nothing in this area should be tolerated which does real violence to doctrine. The Church's public worship must always provide the framework within which the truth of its teaching can be clearly illustrated.

It is at this point that his preference for simplicity becomes obvious. Under the Old Covenant the ceremonies instituted for the Church's worship had to be elaborate and multiplied because everything was as yet obscure. But under the clarity of the New Covenant it had pleased Christ to give himself under forms that were much more simple, in order that men might not be distracted by the ceremonies themselves from realising His own presence in the midst.

True it is, Sire, that there are things indifferent which one may allowably tolerate. But then we must always

[27] C.L. to Seigneurs of Bern, March, 1555. Cf. C.L. to the English at Frankfurt, January 13, 1555; to Knox, June 12, 1555. He refers to things he did not like as "tolerable fooleries".　　　　[28] Cf. *Inst.*, 4:8:1; 4:10:1; 4:11:1.

carefully insist that simplicity and order be observed in the use of ceremonies so that the clear light of the gospel be not obscured by them, as if we were still under the shadows of the law; and then that there may be nothing allowed that is not in agreement and conformity to the order established by the Son of God, and that the whole may serve and be suited to the edification of the Church.[29]

Therefore he felt that "when a pure and simple order of worship is in our power", to burden the ritual with "lighted tapers and crucifixes and other trumpery of the same description" was not only frivolous but "pernicious" and was bound to give rise to superstition.[30]

Calvin's main criticism of most of the trivialities which men indulged in at public worship was that being unrelated to true doctrine, and established for purely emotional or aesthetic considerations, they obscured the truth which the service of worship, centred on the preaching of the Word and the simple celebration of the Sacraments, was meant to exhibit clearly. All ritual was bound to be interpreted by those who indulged for long in it. A ritual that had not its roots in true doctrine was bound to be interpreted in terms of false doctrine, for the natural human mind is full of a pagan theology contrary to the Gospel, and when Christians busy themselves inventing ritual from the rash movements of their own minds they usually outdo the pagans in the absurdities they produce. Therefore superstitions and false doctrines were bound to proliferate and to become confirmed in the minds of those who were trained to observe the "false" ceremonies. This is why the second and third commandments were directed against the false elaboration of ceremonial religion. "God does not allow his name to be trifled with — mixing up silly frivolities with the holy and sacred ordinances."[31]

The whole chapter in the *Institutes* which Calvin devotes to a discussion of the history of the corruption of worship in the

[29] C.L. to King of England, January, 1551.
[30] C.L. to John Knox, 1555.
[31] C.L. to King of England, January, 1551.

Roman Church, the extent of its abuse, and of the current trends of his own day both among the enthusiasts and the traditionalists, is well worth studying today both by those who want to introduce new forms of liturgy and by those who want to resist all change.[32] It is in this chapter that he refers with approval to the post-apostolic customs in celebrating the Lord's Supper which "are not to be disapproved",[33] and to the good traditions of the apostles which were "not committed to writing".[34] Calvin was willing to learn important things about Church liturgy and Church government simply from good apostolic tradition within the Church.

Ministry within the Church

Each member within the body of Christ was to serve and care for each other member and for the whole body. Calvin regarded all ministry and service within the Church as participation in the one ministry of Christ, who is himself the active and powerful inspiration of all Christian service. But he also believed that some within the Church were specially called and gifted by Christ to exercise an official, public, and thus perhaps a more full ministry.[35]

For such a public ministry Christ makes certain men the substitutes for himself, choosing them as his ambassadors, "to represent his own person".[36] They are appointed to certain regular forms of service within the congregation, or larger Church, and given the necessary talents or gifts in order to fulfil these.

After an examination of the three lists given by St. Paul of the kinds of ministry practised by the Christians to each other in the early Church,[37] Calvin found four permanent and ordinary offices which should always be filled and efficiently carried out in any Church. The first two offices, those of pastor and teacher (or doctor) are most closely related to the ministry of the Word. The latter is responsible mainly for

[32] *Inst.*, 4, ch. 10.   [33] *Inst.*, 4:10:9.   [34] *Inst.*, 4:10:31.
[35] *Inst.*, 4:12:1.   [36] *Inst.*, 4:1:3.
[37] In Eph., 4:11; Rom., 12:7-8; 1 Cor., 12:28.

directing the interpretation of Scripture within the Church and of keeping doctrine pure.[38] The main function of the pastor is to preach, and to have the charge of discipline and the sacraments, being, indeed, a successor of the apostles in the ancient Church.[39] He may be called "bishop", "presbyter", "minister" as well as pastor.

To pastors and doctors there are added "governors" or "elders chosen from the people" whose responsibility is the "censure of morals and the exercise of discipline along with the bishops".[40] Finally there are the deacons of whom he found two kinds described in the New Testament, namely those who administered alms, and those who cared for the poor and the sick.[41]

Though his ministry is closely associated with other ministries in the Church, the pastor or bishop, with his special charge of the Word and Sacrament has a unique responsibility for representing Christ and ministering in his Name.[42] He has a unique relationship to the whole flock. He is more than a leader or mouthpiece within a corporate ministry. His task is at times to stand on the side of·the Word of God quite apart from all other members of the flock and at times over against them. His ministry does not rise out of the universal common priesthood. God Himself in Christ gives it specially to the Church for a purpose comparable to that of no other member, indeed comparable only to that of Christ's own unique ministry or that of the Apostles, who, as P. T. Forsyth once put it: "descended on the Church, and did not rise from it".[43] Moreover when he teaches others, and they receive the common doctrine from a single mouth, the pastor can be seen as one whom God uses to bind the members together in his service and in the exercise of mutual charity. As the Church is thus gathered round him, the pastor is a sign of the unity of the Church in its relation to the one Christ. Therefore his ministry is the "chief sinew by which the believers are held together in one body".[44]

---

[38] *Inst.*, 4:3:4.   [39] *Inst.*, 4:3:6.   [40] *Inst.*, 4:3:8.
[41] *Inst.*, 4:3:9.   [42] *Inst.*, 4:8:2; 4:12:14.
[43] *Church and Sacraments*, London, 1917, pp. 133, 140. Cf. also A. A. Van Ruler, "Das Leben und das Werk Calvins", in *Calvin Studien*, 1959, ed. J. Moltmann.
[44] *Inst.*, 4:3:1-2.

It is likely that Calvin, in the language often used in ecumenical discussions today, would claim that the ministry of the pastor or bishop belongs to the *esse* rather than to the *bene esse* of the Church. "It should be carefully noted that Churches cannot safely remain without the ministry of pastors, so that, wherever there is a considerable body of people a pastor should be appointed over them."[45]

The Scriptural basis which Calvin gives for the office of elder is so flimsy that many Calvin scholars have felt that he was simply trying to find sanction for an institution that had been devised to meet the urgent needs of the Church of his day, and that was proving itself vital for a healthy reformed Church life. He had seen the eldership working to good effect first in Basel and later in Strasbourg. As Basil Hall writes, Bucer himself, who was largely responsible for clarifying the nature of the office, believed that "in different nations, and under different governments, there will be different ways of arranging the ministry of the Church, which is not a matter for Christians to quarrel over".[46] Calvin, too, often insisted that the needs of different times and the differences in locality, and in other local institutions, would give rise to minor differences in discipline and ceremonies in the Church.

Calvin believed that the office of deacon must not be regarded as a menial task, but as one inspiring reverence, and to be filled by carefully chosen men. It had been degraded and trivialised in the practice of the Roman Church, which had regarded it as merely a step to the priesthood, nothing more being demanded of its holder than that he should assist at the altar, chant the gospel, and "goodness knows what other trifles".[47] That this apparently humble office is placed alongside the obviously more directly "spiritual" offices reminds us that the work of the Church in its more social and "wordly" dimension, must not be in any way neglected in favour of the more obviously Godward or liturgical aspects of its ministry.

Calvin assumes that though none of the Apostles had

[45] *Comm. on Titus*, 1:5.
[46] In *Service in Christ*, London, 1961, ed. J. I. M'Cord and T. H. L. Parker, p. 99.
[47] *Inst.*, 4:15:5.

prominence over the others, one of them would have to act as moderator when they met together. Calvin did not regard it as a serious aberration when as a "human arrangement" in the early Church, the local presbyters in a town selected one of their number to whom they gave the special title of "bishop", and who permanently acted as moderator of their meetings. At this stage in the history of the Church "these ancient bishops had no wish to frame a form of Church government different from that which God has prescribed in his Word". This "bishop" was "not so much higher in honour and dignity as to have lordship over his colleagues". He was simply a kind of permanent moderator — a *primus inter pares*.[48] In his letter to the King of Poland, Calvin suggested that in reforming the Church there, the present bishops would continue functioning, holding the first place in the synods for the sake of order, and would cherish a holy unity between his colleagues and brethren.[49]

Calvin himself did not rigidly insist that there could be no deviation from the order he himself found in the New Testament, or that such an arrangement must be adhered to if a proper Church was to be constituted. His teaching is often examined today to find out to what extent he would have approved of the setting up of some form of monarchical episcopacy within the reformed Church. There are many statements which show him concerned to maintain an essential parity among all pastors.[50] He asserts that there is no such thing as monarchy among ministers, or the government of one over the rest. Christ alone has superiority amongst the ministers of the Church "in such a way that they are colleagues and companions of one another".[51] In New Testament times no difference had developed between the rank of bishop and that of presbyter, though it is to be noted that the case of Titus proves that one had authority and judgment over others.[52] There is not a trace of evidence suggesting that in Calvin's view Cranmer was not fulfilling a high Church office to which God had appointed him.

[48] *Inst.*, 4:42 and *Inst.*, 4:4:4.
[49] C.L. to King of Poland, December 5, 1554.
[50] *Inst.*, 4:8:10.   [51] *Comm. on Eph.*, 4:11.   [52] *Comm. on Titus*, 1:5.

Amongst his own fellow-bishops in Geneva Calvin himself moderated, as a kind of permanent president, at their common meetings. There is on record the report of a conversation in which Beza affirmed that "Mr Calvin who had rejected episcopacy was in fact bishop of Geneva, and that a little before his death he had proposed to Mr Beza to make him his successor, but that the latter had refused the offer."[53] Beza not only refused the offer, but after actually being forced to hold the office of permanent moderator for sixteen years after Calvin's death, he became responsible for instituting a rotation of moderators. A letter from Beza to John Knox in 1572 reveals an intense hatred of anything in Church government savouring of episcopacy, and it is to him, rather than to Calvin, that we can trace the abhorrence of even the idea of a bishop which has been found among presbyterians.[54]

Even though he approved of monarchical bishops being allowed to remain where the system worked well, however, Calvin himself was deeply suspicious of making the rule of one man too decisive in any sphere of Church affairs. "In the Church", he wrote to Melanchthon, "we must always be on our guard lest we pay too great a deference to men. For it is all over with her, when a single individual, be he whoever you please, has more authority than all the rest, especially when this very person does not scruple to try how far he may go."[55] Cyprian, he believed, taught correctly about how episcopal authority should be used.

> This power ... did not belong to an individual who could exercise it as he pleased, but belonged to a consistory of elders, which was in the Church what a council is in a city. Cyprian, when mentioning those by whom it was exercised in his time, usually associates the whole clergy with the bishop (Cyprian Lib III Ep. 14, 19). In another place he shows that though the clergy presided, the people, at the same time were not excluded

---

[53] Cf. Henry, *op. cit.*, vol. I, p. 401.
[54] Cf. Beza's letter to Knox, April 12, 1572, in Knox, *Works*, (ed. Laing), vol. 6, pp. 613f.
[55] C.L., June 28, 1545.

from cognizance; for he thus writes: from the commencement of my bishopric, I determined to do nothing
without the advice of the clergy, nothing without the
consent of the people.[56]

In his commentary on Ephesians 4:11, Calvin noted that
Paul himself aimed at overturning the fictitious primacy of
any individual in the Church other than Christ. He thus
confirmed the view that there is only one *episcope* (i.e.
oversight or episcopate) and one primacy within the Church,
that of Christ alone. Therefore whenever oversight is
exercised it is always simply a participation in this one
episcopate of Christ which can never be held by a single
individual or exercised by a single individual apart from all
the others who must be his "colleagues or comrades" in its
exercise. Here, Calvin noted that, "Cyprian followed Paul,
and defined briefly and clearly what is the lawful monarchy
of the Church. There is, he says, one episcopate, a part in
which is held by individuals collectively (*in solidum*). This
episcopate he claims for Christ alone. He assigns a part in its
administration to individuals, and that collectively, lest one
should exalt himself above others."[57]

What concerned Calvin most of all in his thought on the
ministry was that power should never be regarded as being
transferred from Christ himself to the persons of those who
ministered in his name.[58] Certainly he always constantly
urges the local pastors to magnify their episcopal office and to
live up to all the titles — minister, pastor, bishop, father — by
which their office "not without reason", is described.[59] Yet
the pastor or bishop must beware of arrogance.

No matter how highly Calvin speaks of the power and
dignity of the office of preaching, he stresses the fact that "as
far as men are concerned, it is not so much power as ministry.
Properly speaking, Christ did not give his power to men but
to his Word of which he made men the ministers."[60] When
the Spirit is joined to the Word all power of action "... resides
in the Spirit Himself", and God can withdraw the Spirit

[56] *Inst.*, 4:11:6.
[57] *Comm. on Eph.*, 4:11.
[58] *Inst.*, 3:1:1.
[59] *Comm. on 1 Tim.*, 3:1; 4:6.
[60] *Inst.*, 4:11:1.

when He wishes.[61] "All the power of the pastor", says Calvin, "consists in ruling the people according to the Word of God so that Jesus Christ may ever remain supreme Pastor and sole Lord of his Church, and alone be listened to."[62] There is no suggestion of Christ's transferring to the pastor his own right or honour. He uses men instrumentally "only doing his own work through their lips, just as an artificer uses a tool for any purpose". He acts always so that he Himself retains the sole Lordship and immediate authority. He wills "that He alone should preside and be conspicuous" in the Church.[63]

"Government of the Church by the ministry of the Word", then, does not mean government by the ministers of the Word. "As Head", says J. K. S. Reid, "Christ exercises a lordship over the Church which does not set Him at such a distance that some kind of subordinate lordship can arise; on the contrary, as Head He is never without the members that constitute His body: "Rule in the Church belongs to the Head Himself. Where therefore Christ is given His place, there the Church which is His body may be said to obtain the Kingdom; for Christ wishes nothing in separation from His members."[64]

Each within the Church, moreover, has to submit to the other. Even those who rule must submit to those who are ruled. Just as in certain matters in human life a husband must be subject to his wife or a father to his children, so "when authority is granted to the elders, they are not given the right or the liberty of throwing over the rein, but they are also themselves to keep due order that there may be mutual subjection".[65] The ministry therefore must fulfil its function after the pattern of Christ's own ministry. When Paul describes his attitude amongst the Thessalonians as that of a mother nursing her infant,[66] Calvin interprets this as giving us the pattern for the exercise of authority in the Church according to Christ, refraining from all show of dignity, pomp

[61] *Comm. on Mal.*, 4:6; *on Ezek.*, 2:2 and 7:26; *Inst.*, 4:1:6.
[62] *Geneva Confession*, 1537. C.Tr., II, p. 134.
[63] *Inst.*, 4:3:1.
[64] In *Service in Christ*, ed. M'Cord & Parker, p. 102, quoting *Comm. on Zech.*, 2:9.
[65] *Comm. on 1 Pet.*, 5:3-6.
[66] *Comm. on 1 Thess.*, 2:7.

and boasting and arrogance, "for a mother in nursing her infant shows nothing of power and dignity".

This meant, of course, for Calvin, that the ministers of Christ should not on any account live in too much wealth or with any pomp whatsoever. The fact that a minister was a bishop would not have worried him more than the fact that he was too obviously wealthy. He was especially afraid not of "episcopacy" but of prelacy and pride whether these developed under a system that might be either episcopalian or presbyterian.

CHAPTER 11

CHURCH LEADERSHIP

Ecumenical Concern

THE unity of the whole Church in Christ was a central
doctrine of Calvin's faith. He liked to quote Cyprian:

There is one Church, which, by the increase of its
fruitfulness, spreads into a multitude, just as there are
many rays of the sun, but only one light, many branches
in a tree, but one trunk, upheld by its tenacious root: and
when many streams flow from one fountain, though
from the superabundance there seems a division into
parts, yet at the source unity is preserved. Separate a ray
from the body of the sun, the unity of the light is not
divided. Break a branch from a tree, that which is
broken cannot germinate. Cut off a stream from the
fountain, and it dries up. So also the church illuminated
by the light of one God, sends its beams over the whole
earth, yet it is one light which is everywhere diffused.[1]

When we believe in Christ, Calvin said, we embrace the unity
of the Church. It is there before us in Christ, and when we are
united with him we ourselves are one in heart and soul with
an innumerable multitude of believers, within his one body.
The Church is thus called "Catholic" or "Universal", Calvin
explained, and there cannot be two or three churches,
"without tearing Christ asunder ... and this is impossible".[2]

The Reformed Church was therefore pledged to express
before the world the unity it believed itself already to have.
Calvin saw around him what he described as "the fearful
devastation of the Christian World ... the few churches

---

[1] From Cyprian, *On the Unity of the Catholic Church*, Bk. v; quoted in *On the Necessity
of Reforming the Church*, C.Tr., vol. I, p. 217 and *Inst.*, 4:2:6.   [2] *Inst.*, 4:1:2-3.

which truly worship God . . . scattered and hedged round on all sides by the profane synagogues of Antichrist".[3] Their lack of fellowship and unity was "to be ranked among the chief evils of our time",[4] since "God chiefly aims at gathering us into one body".[5] He therefore responded enthusiastically to Archbishop Cranmer's suggestion in 1552 that learned and godly men from all over the Reformed world should come together to promote theological understanding and common forms of expressing the faith. "The members of the Church being severed", he wrote to Cranmer in reply, "the body lies bleeding", and affirmed that he "would not grudge to cross even ten seas"[6] to be present at such a conference. He dreaded the effects of schism. He concluded his letter to Cardinal Sadoleto with the prayer that Christ would "gather us out of our present dispersion, into the fellowship of his body, that so, through his one Word and Spirit, we might join together with one heart and one soul".[7]

Calvin certainly believed that as people came close to Christ together in heart and living communion they would begin to find their doctrinal differences becoming less.[8] Those who are united to him in pure faith, are beyond the risk of schism, for "all heresies and schisms arise from this, that men neglect to look to the ground of truth, or to seek the head, the doctrine of the heavenly master".[9] Yet he insisted that there could be no true unity unless it was sought on the ground of truth. When even Renée, the Duchess of Ferrara, seemed to incline to compromise in the name of what she believed was Christian "love", he reminded her that St. John, from whom she seemed to have retained nothing but the word "love", forbade his disciples even to salute those who turned aside from the pure doctrine.[10] He suspected all attempts to win a

[3] *Dedication to Geneva Catechism*, C.Tr., vol. II, p. 35.
[4] C.L. to Cranmer, April 1552 (cf. appended footnote by Bonnet); C.L. to Melanchthon, February 16, 1543.   [5] *Comm. on Isa.*, 33:20; 66:7.
[6] C.L. to Cranmer, April 1552; cf. Letter to Churches of Lower Saxony, January 5, 1556.   [7] C.Tr., vol. I, p. 68.   [8] *Comm. on Matt.*, 24:8.
[9] *On the Necessity of Reforming the Church*, C.Tr., vol. I, p. 217.
[10] C.L., January 24, 1564. Cf. Luther: "No gentlemen, none of this peace and love for me! If I were to strangle someone's father and mother, wife and child, try to choke him too, and then say, 'Keep the peace dear friend, we wish to love one another.' Oh how he would love me." L.W., 37:24f.

mere show of unity through compromise with formulae which merely covered over fundamental disagreement.[11] Apart from the Lord's Word there "is no union of believers, but a faction of the ungodly".[12]

Those who differed must meet for dialogue. To try to avoid conferences as some in his day did, was, he believed, to try to avoid the light.[13] "The less interchange of opinions the greater will be the danger of pernicious dogmatisms."[14] There must be no despair even when the difficulties facing unity seemed impossible to overcome. "If only we could talk together for half a day", he wrote to Bullinger once, "we would agree without difficulty."[15] With fuller discussion new expressions could be found to illuminate the differences and bring the sides together. The Spirit could come and reveal truth in such a way that it had convincing and unifying power. "At the commencement of our deliberations", he wrote, on one occasion, to Bucer, "agreement seemed really hopeless. Light suddenly broke forth."[16] The agreement which Calvin obtained eventually amongst the Swiss churches on the doctrine of the Lord's Supper — the *Zurich Consensus in regard to the Sacraments* of 1549 was the result of several years of patient discussion.

His personal attitude towards colleagues in such ecumenical discussion is always interesting. He was always frank towards them. He frequently reproaches Melanchthon for his lack of forthright zeal and his tendency to compromise.[17] He thought Bucer also tended to give way too easily on essential matters and he said so to him. "My love and reverence for him [i.e. Bucer] are such that I freely admonish him as often as I think fit."[18] But on several occasions when he heard that

---

[11] C.L. to Farel, May 12, 1541.   [12] *Inst.*, 4:2:5.
[13] C.L. to Bullinger, April 22, 1556 and July 1, 1556.
[14] C.L. to Wolfgang Musculus, November 28, 1549.
[15] C.L. to Bullinger, November 1544.
[16] C.L. to Bucer, June 1549.
[17] E.g., C.L., June 28, 1545, June 18, 1550, August 27, 1554. On August 23, 1555 he warns his friend that people are wondering if he is ever going to fulfil his promises, and that "if this warning, like a cock crowing rather late and out of season, do not awaken you, all will cry out with justice, that you are a lazy fellow!"
[18] C.L., June 26, 1548. Bullinger tended to distrust Bucer: "Let us not be suspicious where there is no call for it", wrote Calvin.

people were suspicious or unfriendly to either of these two he wrote in their defence.[19]

Calvin's attitude to Luther was one of great reverence. He knew the man's faults in his old age. He could accuse him of arrogance and of disregard for the public peace, but when he heard that Luther had attacked Bullinger he wrote to the latter pleading with him to be considerate in his reaction:

> I do earnestly desire that you would consider how eminent a man Luther is, and the excellent endowments wherewith he is gifted, with what strength of mind and resolute constancy, with how great skill ... he has hitherto devoted his whole energy to overthrow the reign of Antichrist, and at the same time to diffuse far and near the doctrine of salvation. Often have I been wont to declare, that even though he were to call me a devil, I should still not the less hold him in such honour that I must acknowledge him to be an illustrious servant of God ... Flatterers have done him much mischief since he is naturally too prone to be over-indulgent to himself. It is our part, however, so to reprove whatsoever bad qualities may beset him as that we may make some allowance for him at the same time ... Consider ... that you have to do with a most distinguished servant of Christ, to whom we are all of us largely indebted.[20]

Calvin's hopes of any conversion of mind on the part of Rome suffered a severe blow when the Council of Trent authoritatively adopted irreformable positions in opposition to the Reformers. His later attempts to find agreement with the Lutherans over the Lord's Supper were gradually frustrated too. But even after the death of Melanchthon in 1560 when it seemed as if controversy was replacing dialogue, he proposed that a council should meet, free as well as universal, to "appease all the troubles of Christendom".[21] He was willing to agree that the Pope could chair it — provided the latter agreed to submit to the decisions of the assembly!

[19] Cf. C.L. to Farel, May 12, 1541; to the Seigneurs of Geneva, October 6, 1552.
[20] C.L., November 25, 1554; C.L. to Farel, November 20, 1539.
[21] Cf. Memoir of December 1560, C.O. 46:286.

The whole Church must become involved in the ecumenical discussion. Church leaders, however, must not seek to impose agreements that might cause hurtful division and controversy within the local Church, where different, less advanced, though permissible, views might prevail. Authoritarian carelessness in Church government should never be allowed to scatter sheep whom Christ had gathered together in his flock. There is always need on the part of those in Church government to "accommodate to the condition and tastes of the people".[22]

Calvin does not seem to have desired to see a Reformed "World Church" with "one overgrown government" in church affairs. An ideal which he coveted from the early Church was the frequent conferring together of Bishops in local areas over problems as they arose, to maintain fellowship and to seek the guidance of the Spirit.[23] He believed that the normal custom by which the early Church sought to meet their difficulties was by convening provincial synods. Only very occasionally and temporarily were General Councils called. Therefore he pled with the Emperor to seek the Reformation of the Church through a provincial synod in Germany rather than through the Council of Trent.[24] It seems possible that, had he been here today, he might prefer the Church in its re-groupings to move towards federal associations of local or provincial autonomous churches, rather than towards huge bureaucratic structures — with "world councils" again becoming occasional and temporary.[25]

Diplomatic Outreach

Calvin's practical care for the welfare of sufferers involved him in diplomatic missions. For example, when the Waldensians were cruelly persecuted in 1545 he lost no time in visiting the Swiss cantons and organising relief, protest,

[22] C.L. to Somerset, October 22, 1548.
[23] C.L. to the King of Poland, December 5, 1554; C.Tr., vol. II, p. 35; vol. III, p. 30.　　　　[24] C.Tr., vol. I, p. 223.
[25] In Calvin's view the form of the Church would have to reveal its essentially pastoral nature.

and shelter for the refugees.[26] During a later period of further persecution and hardship, he sent Beza and Farel on a mission to the Protestant Cantons and German Princes, to seek ways of bringing them under protection.[27]

Since power in Church affairs in his day had fallen into the hands of the laity he tried especially to enter correspondence by letter with rulers, powerful noblemen and statesmen, everywhere. He believed that the earthly rulers of his day were, within the secular sphere allotted to them, no less bound by Christ than he himself was, to further the work of renewal in society and to assist in the reformation of the Church itself. The Word of God clearly promised that earthly kings would protect the renewed Israel in the days of its future glory, and would bring their tribute to it![28] Therefore he expected the crowned heads of Europe to hear and respond to his call to such a work.

The publication of each new book which he wrote gave him an opportunity to make an approach to people who might prove influential allies. Occasionally he was disappointed. After dedicating his commentary on Galatians to the Duke of Orleans, he complained to a friend that "the illustrious Duke ... never deigned to show by a single word that my courtesy was agreeable to him".[29] But he was never daunted. When Edward VI came to the throne in England he sent an envoy to the court with one letter to Protector Somerset and another to the young king, dedicating to him the newly published commentary on Isaiah.

In his letter to the monarch, he reminded Edward that even in the early days of the Church, the "haughty loftiness of the Roman Empire" yielded submission to Christ, and pled with him to become God's instrument for the work of "carrying forward the restoration of the Church", promising that if he did so it would mean prosperity not only for himself but for his whole Kingdom.[30]

The envoy who was entrusted with these letters was

[26] C.L. to Farel, May 4, 1545; to Viret, May 25, 1545.
[27] C.L. to Bullinger, May 30, 1557.
[28] Cf. Isa. 60.
[29] C.L. to Charles du Moulin, July 27, 1554.
[30] *Comm. on Isa.* (ET), vol. I, pp. xxii, xxv.

prevented from crossing the Channel for seven days by head winds, and even then narrowly escaped ship-wreck. Eventually, however, he returned with good news. The Duke had received Calvin's letter kindly, and had himself set out for court in order to deliver personally the letter to the king. "The Royal Council" was pleased when it was read and the King was "filled ... with extraordinary delight". The Archbishop of Canterbury had sent a personal message to Calvin to tell him that he "could do nothing more useful than to write to the King more frequently". Calvin, in a letter to Farel giving this account of the venture, congratulated himself. He made a short list of the reforms he would now like to see carried out in England. "I will not cease to goad the whole of them", he resolved. Obviously he admired the "Christendom" that had been the result of the cooperation between Church and Empire in the early days and hoped it would make its reappearance in England.[31]

The death of Edward and the accession of Mary made him hold his hand for several years. But when Mary died, a new edition of the Isaiah commentary was ready. This he sent with a fresh letter of dedication to Elizabeth asking her now to protect the book, the banishment of which had caused such a deep sorrow to so many of her subjects, and praying that her reign in England would "restore the doctrine of true godliness ... to its former privileges". He drew the attention of the new Queen to the fact that he had written his letter on the very day he knew to be fixed for her coronation. Moreover as if expecting not only her interest, but also her sympathy, he added a postscript informing her that when he wrote it, he had only partially recovered from "an attack of quartan ague".[32]

But alas, by the time the letter reached England John Knox had written his *First Blast of the Trumpet against the Monstrous Regiment of Women*. In this book, Knox, reacting to such female rulers as Mary of Guise and Mary Tudor, had written sweepingly against all rule by women. The book had

---

[31] C.L. to Somerset, October 22, 1548; to Cecil, January 29, 1559. On the whole we find Calvin expressing himself with the greatest confidence about the future of the Church when he is writing to England.   [32] *Comm. on Isa.* (ET), vol. 1, pp. xviff.

been published in Geneva along with another like it by
Christopher Goodman. Calvin himself would never have
approved of either of these works and it was without his
knowledge that they had both been published in his parish
(another proof that we cannot blame Calvin for all the stupid
things that were done in Geneva). Calvin's courier therefore
came back from England with word that this time his homage
had not been acceptable. It was in vain that he later protested
his innocence and affirmed that if he had known about
Knox's book he would have had it banned.[33] From then on,
though Calvin managed to gain the friendship of Archbishop
Grindal who asked and took his advice, his influence in
England was to depend almost entirely on the translation and
circulation of his writings.

Yet the fact that his influence grew in spite of the failure of
his diplomacy[34] is a reminder to us that the "still small voice"
and the power of the quiet and humble seven thousand who
have not "bowed the knee to Baal"[35] can be far more
powerful than the earthquakes and the fire we hope for when
we have favour with the powers that be. England was a
fruitful field and Calvin could still provide the seed!

In marked contrast to what happened in England, was
Calvin's experience in Poland. Here his diplomacy in high
places was brilliantly successful. King Sigismund Augustus
gladly accepted Calvin's dedication of his commentary on
Hebrews, read the *Institutes* and allowed them to be
expounded to him twice a week by an Italian pastor. He was
pleased to receive Calvin's letters. His regime was tolerant.
The Bohemian Brethren had found refuge there in exile and
their witness strengthened the evangelical cause. The Poles
seemed to be inclined to prefer the Reformed doctrines to the
Lutheran.

Calvin had correspondence not only with the King but
with one of his close confidants Nicholas Radziwill who had
adopted the reformed faith. Calvin was especially active with

[33] Cf. *The Works of John Knox*, ed. Laing, vol. 4, p. 357f. Letter to William Cecil,
Zurich Letters, second series, p. 35.
[34] Cf. C. D. Cremeans, *The Reception of Calvinistic Thought in England*, Urbana,
1949, pp. 73ff.
[35] Cf. 1 Kings 18.

his pen when he knew that important consultations were taking place. On December 29, 1555 there were several letters from him. An invitation finally came to him from Polish nobles to visit them but he had to decline it with regret.[36] In the end, however, it all proved fruitless. The Poles then seemed not only to tolerate heresy but also to love it. The works of Servetus became popular, and even anti-trinitarianism flourished. Successful diplomacy does not sow the Word of God in the hearts of a people, and thorns and thistles can choke weak growth. "Before his death Calvin began to suspect the whole nation", and one of his last works which he dictated to Beza from his sick-bed was an "*Admonition to the Polish Brethren*" — a last warning to a stubborn nation!

We find in his correspondence also a letter written in 1558 to the Scottish Earl of Arran who was in prison in France.[37] It mentioned John Knox, who was then in Geneva, and the hope of a Reformation in Scotland. Possibly Knox had suggested that Calvin write to Arran. Calvin lived to hear of Knox's success in Scotland and was consulted by him on his problems. Yet Knox was Knox, long before he met Calvin, and he did not always take the wise and moderating advice which he sought and received from his Genevan friend. There is no doubt, however, that the theology Knox formulated and preached, owed much to his time of study and ministry in Geneva, and he shared Calvin's vision of the Christian Commonwealth.

Mission to France

Calvin, as we might expect, had a powerful and direct influence in his own native France. He helped many who were adopting the Reformed faith to find refuge in Geneva and elsewhere. And he kept in touch with those who had adopted the Reformed faith but were afraid to avow it openly, still attending mass, and conforming outwardly in all

---

[36] C.L., March 17, 1557. For above see C.L. to King of Poland, December 5, 1554 and December 24, 1555; to Nicholas Radziwill, February 13, 1555.
[37] C.L., August 1, 1558.

the Romish rites. He did not approve of such concealment of the truth, and besides corresponding personally with those whom he knew to be in this difficult situation, he wrote two tracts on the subject addressed to those who, he felt, were denying the faith. He called them "Nicodemites" because they justified their behaviour by the example of Nicodemus who concealed his faith by going to Jesus by night.

In the first *Traité de fuir les Superstitions*, he advises his compatriots to leave their country. If prevented, they should give a clear witness by refusing to take part in superstitious worship. They might have to face death. They would win the contest and obtain a crown of true glory. The second treatise *Excuse de Jehan Calvin à Messieurs les Nicodémites*, written no doubt because his first appeal seemed to be unheeded, was provocatively reproachful. His most trenchant criticism fell on those who knew the truth, but who still luxuriated in the wealth and ease of office within the Roman church, being content with only minor reforms. He also castigated the upper-class laity who would allow their faith to influence them only so far as to remain popular in flippant court circles where, as Dyer puts it, a "tincture of evangelism" was becoming a fashion of the day. Nicodemus, he pointed out, buried only the *body* of Christ after anointing it. These men buried both his body and soul, his divinity and humanity and that without honour.[38]

After the beginning of the year 1555, when Calvin's own troubles in the city were beginning to ease, we find that the *Register of the Company of Pastors in Geneva* refers to ministers being sent abroad on missions beyond the confines of Geneva — France and Piedmont. These notes sometimes indicate their difficulties, imprisonment and martyrdom.

The story behind these notes and minutes is one of great heroism. From 1547 onwards the notorious *Chambre Ardente* was set up in France so that the civil authorities themselves could deal directly with heretics. This court was responsible

[38] Cf. Thomas H. Dyer, *The Life of John Calvin*, London, 1850, pp. 187ff. Some of the Reformed faith in France, perplexed by the severity of Calvin's views on this matter, asked him if he would go to Germany and consult Luther. Calvin would not go, but wrote via Melanchthon who did not feel that Luther, in the mood he was, would take any notice of the letter.

for hunting out, arresting and making very many Protestant martyrs after the most cruel treatment in prison. In 1551 the Edict of Chateaubriand codified the existing laws in defence of the Roman Catholic faith and gave a fresh impetus to the persecution. The fury of the attack, however, made the Protestants all the bolder in their defiance of the statutes. Five young students set an example. They had been trained in Lausanne, and decided to return to France to preach. They were arrested, sentenced to be burned alive, and they were held in prison in Lyons. After a prolonged delay in which protests came with appeals for clemency from many centres, the sentence was executed in May 1553.

In the following years the Reformation spread till, it was reckoned, a sixth of the country had come under a predominant Protestant influence. At first the Protestant adherents gathered in informal groups around the Word of God. By 1555 however, some were beginning to organise themselves after the Genevan pattern with a pastor, elders and deacons. Such a congregation was set up in Paris with a pastor sent from Geneva. By 1559 it was reckoned that seventy two had been thus organized, and many other groups were meeting. In that year there took place a General Synod of the Reformed Church in Paris. A confession of faith, and a book of discipline were drawn up, reflecting the influence of Calvin's thought.

Though the spirit of the men and women in the French Reformed Church was unconquerable, their power as a body to grow with such strength under persecution in France owed something both to the Church structure devised by Calvin and to his pastoral care. He personally kept in touch with the persecuted groups in France who at this time were beginning to form themselves into organised congregations and were now looking to Geneva to help them to find regular pastors. Indeed, his little presbytery in Geneva became like the headquarters of a board of missions. The available minutes contain the names of 88 men sent out between 1555 and 1562. But there is evidence that only a small proportion of those commissioned are actually named in the Register.[39]

[39] Cf. Hughes, R.C.P., p. 27f.

Sometimes pseudonyms are used to refer to persons and congregations because of the need for secrecy.

When Calvin heard of an isolated Christian or even of an isolated group trying to gather by themselves, he was there, on the doorstep, as it were, with a messenger and a letter, seeking to make them feel they were part of a far larger group in touch with the universal church which was praying for them, had a word for them, and was seeking to support them in every possible practical way. Each small local group that appeared, he regarded as the nucleus of a congregation which must be made to grow and define itself to receive as pastor one of the numbers he had trained for the purpose of such leadership under the Word of God. When he sent his man to them, he asked them to see the pastor as one to be listened to for the sake of Christ, and respected as representing Christ in their midst, the good Shepherd.

Within each congregation he sought to develop a cellular structure in which under wise and trained leadership each individual would give the other support, enlightenment and encouragement and in which those who tended to falter would be held to the faith and the standard by the expectations, example, and encouragement of the others and if need be by the discipline exercised by them. Congregations too had to be organized in groups sharing a common concern for each other and a common discipline.

Students of the period of the Reformation and its aftermath agree that what gave Calvinism, as it spread, its ability to survive and even to grow under the most determined and ruthless opposition which it encountered was something Geneva had given it — an essentially cellular organization under which large numbers of men could retain a substantial unity of belief, while yet being trained to worship and fight in the small group.[40] Indeed Calvinism, says J. E. Neale, had often to take the shape of rebellion, and the chief essential for prolonged and successful rebellion is organisation. Neither Lutheranism nor humanism possessed the practical genius necessary for such organisation. "Much of English history, Scottish history, Dutch history in the second half of the

[40] A. G. Dickens, *The Reformation in England*, London, 1965, p. 200.

sixteenth century might be written round the organisation of Calvinism."[41]

We find in Calvin's later correspondence more frequent diplomatic and pastoral letters addressed to members of the French upper nobility who enjoyed immunity from the persecution which was meted out to others. Many of them in the exercise of their rights and privileges adopted the Reformed faith. Calvin seized this opportunity to correspond with people like Antoine de Bourbon the King of Navarre, Louis the Prince of Condé, Francis d'Andelot and Admiral Gaspar de Coligny, and with their wives. He maintained his correspondence with Renée the daughter of Louis XII who had returned from Italy to the French court.

Calvin's teaching and letters were found helpful and acceptable. He was asked to send a pastor from Geneva to preach and work in court circles. As Paul Henry puts it, they listened to him in the same way as the princes of Germany had listened to Luther.[42] In 1561 the Venetian Ambassador to the court of France wrote about it to the Doge. "Your Serenity will hardly believe the influence and the great power which the principal minister of Geneva, a Frenchman and a native of Picardy, possesses in this Kingdom. He is a man of extraordinary activity, who by his mode of life, his doctrines and his writings, rises superior to all the rest."[43]

Calvin's mission to the Reformed Churches in France also involved him in an abortive attempt at mission to the heathen. Admiral Coligny had become interested in the founding of a colony in South America in which French Protestant emigrants might settle, worship, and develop their culture, free from persecution — and evangelise the South American Indians. Two pastors, Pierre Richer and Guillaume Charterier, were sent from Geneva in August 1556

[41] J. E. Neale, *The Age of Catherine de Medici*, London, 1943, pp. 13ff. Neale points out that the power of the Roman Church through the centuries had lain in its organisation and discipline as well as in its dogma, and he quotes an "eminent French historian" as affirming that "Calvin's unique achievement, the sign of his originality, was to construct a new Catholicism outside the old, and opposed to it". Cf. p.17.

[42] Henry, *op. cit.*, vol. II, p. 374.

[43] Quoted by T. M. Lindsay, *History of the Reformation*, vol. II, Edinburgh, 1907, p. 153.

to act as chaplains to a group from the Reformed Church and to the work of evangelism. But the Governor of the colony betrayed his trust, killed some of them and forced the others back home. "Abortive though this excursion proved to be," writes Philip Hughes, "it testifies strikingly to the far-reaching vision which Calvin and the Church in Geneva had of their missionary task."[44]

Counsel to the Church under Persecution

Within the immediate context of the Reformed Church, we find Calvin accorded the same status and reverence as he himself and many others, gave to Luther. In Geneva itself, from the time of his arrival, the "company" of his fellow pastors never thought of electing any other than he as their chairman and leader. A minute written after his death records:

> As for the late M. Calvin ... God had implanted so many graces in him, and had invested him with such authority towards the people, thereby enabling each one of us the better to discharge the duties of his ministry, that, had we been bound to make a choice every year, we could not have considered any other member of the company — which was not to belittle the abundance of the great gifts which were to be found there.[45]

Spontaneously they spoke of him as having been "like a Father in the midst of the company and also to each of its members separately", so that "the company had never been destitute of wise counsel". "Dear brother," wrote Beza to him during his sojourn in France, "as you are unable to aid us by your presence, guide us like children by your counsel! ... I would that our Lord would glorify the praise of his wondrous wisdom by your mouth."[46] Beza, indeed, once affirmed that "on whatever subject Calvin was consulted, his judgment was so clear and correct that he often seemed almost to prophesy;

[44] Cf. Hughes, *op. cit.*, p. 28.
[45] R. C. P., p. 363.
[46] C.L., August 30, 1561; cf. to Peter Martyr, May 22, 1558.

nor do I recollect of any person having been led into error in consequence of following his advice."[47]

The Reformed communities in France recognised that they could trust him, and they continually consulted him on a great variety of questions: Might a widow leave her children if she had to withdraw from a catholic country? Could a true believer attend mass under any circumstances? Was it allowable for a minister of the Gospel to make money by usury? Was it allowable to react with violence against violent persecution? "His opinions had the force of law for the synods," writes Paul Henry, "partly because his voice was as that of a father of the Church, and he might be considered its conscience."[48]

Calvin's advice to the members of the Reformed Church in France on matters that then meant life or death is worthwhile considering in some detail. We have already noted the uncompromising severity with which early in his career he criticised those who were afraid to confess their faith, and take the consequences. "Withdraw before you are plunged into so deep a mire that you are not able to extricate yourself", he had written then to M. de Falais when the latter's conscience was troubled and he wondered if he should leave France.[49]

He continued to the end on the same uncompromising note. To a lady who had been seized while emigrating to Geneva and was under threat, he wrote, "If we find ourselves in such necessity that no other means can be found to deliver us from the tyranny of the enemies of the truth, but those subterfuges which might turn us from the right path, there can be no doubt that God has called upon us to seal our faith with our blood."[50] M. de Crussol asked Calvin if he might attend on his prince when he went to a Roman mass, and the example of Naaman the Syrian[51] was suggested as a precedent. "It is not lawful to do so," replied Calvin, "because such conduct would be a scandal to the godly, and

---

[47] C.Tr., vol. I, p. xcviii.
[48] Henry, *op. cit.*, vol. I, p. 469.
[49] C.L., October 14, 1543; cf. to Monsieur de Budé, June 19, 1547, to a French Seigneur, October 18, 1548, to Madame de la Roche-Posay, June 10, 1549.
[50] C.L., September 13, 1553.
[51] Cf. 2 Kings 5.

an occasion of abuse to the wicked. The example of Naaman is not applicable in this case, for he was the only worshipper of God in Syria and could therefore give no offence to anyone. He had himself also an altar to the true God."[52]

During the period when the law forbade gatherings for Reformed worship and the persecution was especially fierce, Calvin had no hesitation in counselling believers to break the law — but carefully! "Assemble here and there in little parties", he wrote to the congregation at Poitou, "till all the members of the Church are united in the Kingdom of heaven ... Fear of persecution must not deter us from seeking the living pasture, and following our good shepherd." He assures them that if they do this God will care for them. If they neglect to do so they will certainly fall away. He counsels then to take "a middle way between rashness and timidity": "Keep yourselves quietly in retirement but not so as to close the door to those who wish to enter the Kingdom of God with you. Strive to win as many souls for the Lord as possible." He promises them that the influence of such genuine secret community worship will diffuse itself in the manner in which they go about life, at home and elsewhere, and have a transforming effect.[53] In this letter Calvin is obviously giving his approval to quiet and deliberate civil disobedience.

Though Calvin thus went the length of advising Christians to break the law in order to obey God, he did not believe that they should plan or initiate violence, or seek actively to overthrow tyrannous dictatorship. He seems to counsel nothing but patient suffering on the part of individual subjects when rulers and authorities persecute them for their faith. When he heard that some in the Church at Anjou, facing persecution, were determined to resort to violence rather than allow themselves to be hunted down by ruffians, he wrote entreating them to "abandon such designs which will never obtain the blessing of God so as to come to a happy issue, for He does not approve of them". Calvin did not underestimate the extremity of suffering. They might face death, but in such an extremity Christians cannot have any

[52] C.L. to Monsieur de Crussol, July 31, 1563.
[53] C.L. to the Brethren of Poitou, September 1554.

excuse for "refusing to suffer for Him who died and rose again that we might dedicate our lives as a sacrifice to Him". To submit to such suffering, he asserted, is not only involved in our call to be conformed to Christ,[54] it is also the only safe policy, for "our only secure refuge against the heat, the stormy wind and every other danger, is under the shadow of his wings. As soon, however, as we begin to resist by force we put away his hand and his help from us." Though God "will always cause the ashes of his servants to fructify ... excesses and violence will bring with them nothing but barrenness. We must therefore, never abandon the conviction that the hairs of our head are all numbered, and that if God does permit us to go through extremities of suffering he will ensure that not a tear is in vain."[55]

He was consulted beforehand about a plot to destroy the power of the Duke of Guise and his family, and he advised strongly against it. The conspiracy went on, was discovered, and ruthless reprisals were taken on those involved.

The first war of religion in France broke out in 1562. On March 1 a party of troops under the Duke of Guise had brutally massacred a Protestant congregation which had gathered for worship at Vassey. The Reformed leaders felt that a point had been reached which justified them in taking up arms. A battle took place at Dreux in which though the Protestants were defeated, the other side did not gain much. Eventually the Duke of Guise was murdered by a fanatic. Negotiations took place under Catherine de Medici the Queen regent, and Condé the Protestant leader compromised his cause by accepting terms which finally resulted in the Edict of Amboise in March 1563. It allowed personal liberty to Protestants but did not concede the right to meet together for common worship.

With regard to this first war of religion, Calvin was by no means doctrinaire in his advice. He tried to face the changing situation wisely. Before the war, he had given it as his opinion that "if a single drop of blood were spilled, floods of blood

[54] C.L. to Church at Anjou, April 19, 1556.
[55] C.L. to Church in Paris, September 16, 1557, to the Church at Aix, May 1, 1561.

would soon deluge Europe. Thus it were better that we should all perish a hundred times than expose the name of Christendom and the Gospel to such opprobrium."[56]

After the Amboise conspiracy failed, and the persecution increased in ferocity he was again consulted about the advisability of open rebellion, since clandestine plotting had proved so disastrous. He indicated that within the situation then prevailing in France, if several of the princes of the blood royal sought to maintain their rights for the common good, and if the Parliament joined with them, it would then be lawful for all good subjects to lend them assistance. In this case, of course, Calvin is reverting to what he had written in the *Institutes* about the rights of duly constituted authorities within a State to check the unbridled tyranny of a superior ruler within the realm.[57] Calvin, however, admitted that conditions could arise when the outbreak of war could not be avoided and certain rules could no longer hold. Then facts had to be faced and fresh decisions taken.

He was once asked whether it was lawful to help one of the persecuted believers to escape from prison by means of keys surreptitiously obtained by trickery or otherwise. He replied "I should never advise or approve of such a proceeding, but I should heartily rejoice at the deliverance of anyone, and should make it the subject of my prayers if it could be effected without offence to the good."[58] In the same way, once war has broken out and the peace has been violated by others, then the Christian has a right to take stock of the situation and make a fresh judgment as to what action to take in legitimate self-defence in the state of open war. This seems to be the reason why once the religious war in France had broken out, Calvin, having to choose one side or another, sought to "support the side of equity" even encouraging the raising of money for mercenaries, and discussing what strategy was most advisable.[59] Moreover, he approved of Beza's presence as a chaplain, and leader in the battlefield.[60]

[56] C.L. to Coligny, April 16, 1561.
[57] *Inst.*, 4:20:30-1.   [58] C.O. 10a: 257.
[59] C.L. to Bullinger, August 15, 1562; to the Churches of Languedoc, September 1562.
[60] C.L. to Coligny, April 16, 1561.

When the war ended Calvin regarded the terms of the treaty of Amboise as "execrable" but he immediately gave the advice that arms should be laid down since the peace had been made by a "legitimate" council.[61] He wrote to Madame de Roye: "I would always counsel that we should all perish rather than enter again on the confusion we have witnessed."[62]

[61] C.L. to Soubise, April 5, 1563.
[62] C.L. to Madame de Roye, April 1563.

CHAPTER 12

THE PASTOR — THE CURE OF SOULS

The Individual before God

WE have already noted the care which Calvin believed due to each individual as a member of the social group. Such concern for the individual within society arose from his belief in the worth and responsibility of each soul in its secret relationship with God.

Luther has stressed the freedom of the "inner man" from any constraint by others in the call to live the Christian life. He had taught that when each of us is faced with the most important decisions we have to make in life, we stand alone before the Word of God to make our own response of faith to God, or to decide otherwise. Calvin followed him closely. Each of us, he taught, must learn to appreciate our separateness or apartness, as well as our solidarity, within the social body. We have to understand ourselves as living each "in two worlds over which different kings and different laws preside",[1] the outer world the civil kingdom, and the inner world, the spiritual kingdom. Each of us in the outer realm is involved often it may seem inextricably, in having to deal with other men and women, in the organisation and welfare of earthly society, in matters that demand human obedience and involve social and national Church and family loyalties. We live there under the pressure of laws laid down by legitimate external authorities. But always at the same time we live inwardly under another constraint. We live in debate with God alone. In the "inner forum of conscience" we ourselves have to make the greatest decisions of life alone, in complete privacy and lonely personal responsibility before God.[2]

[1] *Inst.*, 3:19:15. [2] *Inst.*, 4:10:5; 4:20:1.

Calvin often underlines this aspect of our life as individuals especially when he is dealing with matters of Christian freedom. For each of us in our inner apartness, our solidarity with others is broken through. In the final decisions we have to make in spiritual matters we need no longer depend on the priest or the group or even on the Church, and we must try to learn to exercise this freedom. Each of us is responsible for his or her self-determination before God. Calvin recommended that confession of sins should be made to God alone. Only in exceptional cases should an individual seek for another to hear.[3]

He taught that this apartness which is so important a characteristic of the human soul must be acknowledged and respected in practice by the community. The veil of mystery which surrounds the life of each human being before God, and which especially covers the life of the Christian in Christ cannot be penetrated by others. Under no pretext should others seek to violate this hidden sanctuary of the person by the exercise of deliberate social pressure. No human being, or court, Calvin asserted, not even a Church court, has the power to make a sound moral or spiritual judgment about what goes on in this realm below the surface of human life.[4] Had he lived today it seems certain that he would have denied also that society's psychoanalytic experts have any true power either to probe, or approve or condemn in this realm. Moreover no kind of invasive force, psychological or otherwise, must be used to make the individual conform in its patterns of thinking or in its final judgments to any external norm.

Today, in the face of all the persuasive and pervasive forces which play upon our human minds through the mass media and the psychological and other techniques that can be used sometimes with good and sometimes with evil intentions to make people conform to common standards, it seems that Calvin here makes an important contribution to thought

[3] *Inst.*, 3:4:8-9; I.C.P., p. xxxviii.
[4] *Comm. on 1 Cor.*, 5:11: "Inward impiety, and anything that is secret, does not fall within the judgment of the Church." Cf. *Inst.*, 4:12:6. Of course the Church has justification and authority to make its judgments about people from their public attitude and behaviour — by their works and fruit.

M

about real human freedom. "The more the separateness and differentness of other people is recognised", wrote Iris Murdoch, "the harder it becomes to treat a person as a thing."[5] A good society must serve the individual in its midst by allowing him or her complete privacy and thus complete freedom at this point. "The group attains its goal", says Maritain, "only by serving man, and realizing that man has secrets which escape the group, and a vocation which the group does not encompass."[6]

Pastoral Concern

When he was engaged in defending Reformation interests at the Assembly at Worms in 1540, he heard that the French congregation he had left at Strasbourg was doing well in his absence. He wrote the locum, Nicolas Parent, discussing Church affairs and saying how proud he was that the Church had kept together; he added, though "a well ordered Church is the pastor's crown and glory, even so he can neither exult and rejoice in anything regarding it, except as far as the salvation of souls is concerned".

Calvin felt that one of the chief needs of his day was to help men and women through the Word to attain assurance in their life before God. The Roman Church had for centuries failed to bring men and women into the knowledge of God's mercy. The obscure and trivial ceremonies which it had invented as embellishments of its confessional and penitential system led nowhere. The Gospel is meant to ensure that the soul attains peace: i.e. to a joyful, continual, radiant assurance. "To have faith is not to fluctuate, to vary, to be carried up and down, to hesitate — finally, to despair: rather, it is to possess continued certainty and complete security of mind, to have a place to rest in, plant your foot."[7] "No man is a believer . . . except him who leaning on the security of his salvation confidently triumphs over the devil and death."[8]

---

[5] *The Sovereignty of Good*, London, 1970, p. 66.
[6] Jacques Maritain, *The Rights of Man*, London, 1945, p. 13.
[7] *Inst.*, 3:13:3.
[8] *Inst.*, 3:2:16; cf. A. N. S. Lane, *Calvin's Doctrine of Assurance*, in *Vox Evangelica*. No. XI.

He believed therefore that one of his first tasks, following his predecessors in the Reformation movement, still lay in this area. No matter how much he was involved in social concerns and in Church affairs, he never neglected his call and pledge to this other work. He would have agreed with Vinet "that the gospel is addressed and the preacher is sent, not to peoples and masses, but to all the individuals of whom the people and masses are composed".[9]

We find him therefore often directing his ministry towards the individual with a special concern to give pastoral and personal care and guidance where there was perplexity of heart, doubt, or spiritual darkness. As Thurneysen has pointed out: the Reformation itself was a pastoral care movement growing directly out of care for the salvation of the soul.

His theological writing was often pastoral in its aim. The pages of the *Institutes* are studded with sentences and even paragraphs written to help the struggling soul. He says in the preface to the book that initially he "toiled" at the task of writing it, "chiefly for the sake of my countrymen, the French, multitudes of whom I perceived to be hungering and thirsting after Christ".

His writing was sometimes entirely pastoral in its direction and motive. Explaining why he wrote his treatise *Concerning Scandals* he says: "a serious book appears because many people create a demand for it", and he later adds: "My concern is for the weak, for when their faith is shaky, then it is our place to support it with a sustaining hand."[10] He wrote this particular book for the sake of those who, committed to the service of Christ, had begun to run the Christian race. He wrote in order to describe clearly for their sake the kind of obstacles that they would meet and the diversions to which they would be tempted, as they tried to make progress. Some of these obstacles were, he explained, part and parcel of the Gospel itself, some were such as occur inevitably wherever the Gospel takes root in a community, and some were due to the persecution and slander of enemies.[11]

[9] Cf. A. Vinet, *Pastoral Theology*, Edinburgh, 1852, p. 229.
[10] *Concerning Scandals*, Edinburgh, 1978, pp. 4 & 12.   [11] *Ibid.*, pp. 13-14.

Even his controversial writings in which he castigates his theological opponents are pastoral in their aims. For the true pastor, he often affirmed, has two different voices — one for calling the sheep, the other for frightening away the destroying wolves. "Then only do pastors edify the Church, when, besides leading docile souls to Christ, placidly, as with the hand, they are also armed to repel the machinations of those who strive to impede the work of God."[12]

When we read his letters to his correspondents amongst the upper nobility in France we find the pastoral motive is nearly always dominant. For instance his first letter to Admiral Coligny is written to "furnish you with a proof of the interest I have in your salvation". He had been informed that Coligny in prison in St. Quentin had nearly died in an illness, had been reading religious books, and was concerned to find hope and comfort. Calvin's letter was about God and his glory, and the promise of Christ. Moreover, on the very same day Calvin wrote an equally encouraging and helpful letter of spiritual counsel to Madame de Coligny whom he knew to be deeply pious.[13]

This pastoral emphasis is all the more remarkable since such letters were often written on Church or national business with some diplomatic aim, to further the Reformation cause in Europe. But often the diplomatic gives way entirely to even an evangelistic motive and we find that his first concern is with his correspondent as a person. Is he or she keeping close to God, listening to his word continually, and likely to continue to resist the temptations of Satan in order to keep running well in the Christian race — in other words, how is it with your soul? Even when he sends an envoy to the King of Navarre with the express purpose of obtaining shelter in his province for Spanish Lutheran refugees some of whom had arrived in Geneva, he cannot keep himself from these other issues too. "Sire ... prepare yourself with the greatest magnanimity in order to bear yourself with constancy when

---

[12] C.Tr., vol. I, p. 29. Cf. A.-Marie Schmidt, *Jean Calvin et la Tradition Calvienne*, Paris 1957.
[13] C.L. to Admiral de Coligny, September 4, 1558; to Madame de Coligny, September 4, 1558.

necessity shall require it. For however you keep yourself in the background, God will put you forward to maintain his cause. So arm yourself beforehand, I entreat you, Sire, exercising yourself in the word of God and suffering yourself to be taught thereby, so that wealth, honours, high rank, royal dignity, shall not prevent you from bearing the yoke of Jesus Christ, and so aspiring to the Kingdom of heaven."[14]

His correspondence with Seigneur D'Andelot, Coligny's younger brother, is typical of his pastoral ministry amongst the great in France. D'Andelot was imprisoned by Henry II for allowing the Reformation to be preached freely in his great estates in Britanny. Immediately he heard of his constancy and sacrifice Calvin wrote him on May 10, 1558 a long letter of personal advice to help him to endure, and encouragement in the faith. This was followed on July 12 by another letter more urgent. Calvin had heard that great pressure was being put on D'Andelot to relent and submit to the King's wishes. Calvin pleads earnestly with him for constancy. God is going to prove him. He can now become fully conformed to the image of Jesus Christ "not only in death but also in burial". His suffering will be mitigated. Let him not turn aside from the simplicity of Jesus Christ but offer the complete sacrifice. In the same month Calvin heard that D'Andelot had given in and immediately he dispatched a third letter. The shame of the public scandal is mentioned, but only in passing. Calvin must have been torn in heart over the possible consequences of his recantation for the many believers in Brittany. But nothing of this is alluded to. The whole letter is one of compassion to a fellow Christian who is beginning to suffer remorse, but seeking to turn it into true repentance. Calvin emphasises the seriousness of the sin and endeavours to show him that the way back is open. He gives him advice on how to become a stronger Christian when he finds this way.

Preaching and Pastoral Care

Calvin believed that God means preaching to be a pastoral event, and seeks through its ministry to bring souls to the full

[14] C.L. to the King of Navarre, December 10, 1558.

and liberating assurance of faith. True preaching is meant to open the door of the kingdom of God to the hearer. Through preaching the fullness of the grace of God promised in the New Testament is meant not simply to be offered to people, but *presented* to them with such reality and power that Christ not only knocks on the door, but also enters to take possession of the heart.[15] Therefore pastoral care should be given to the individual even from the pulpit. "Whenever God speaks to all his people in a body", wrote Calvin, "he addresses himself to each individual."[16] If his sermon is to be a true reflection of the Word which God is seeking to speak to those in the pews, than the preacher should also seek to direct it now and then, even often, to the heart of some individual to whom God is seeking to communicate his grace.

Obviously, then, if the preacher shares such pastoral concern as Calvin had, as well as his view of preaching, this will greatly affect the style of sermon given from the pulpit. The true pastor in the pulpit will never be content with a mere oratorical preparation directed only to the group, or the "type", or the parish, or to mankind in general. He will tend, rather, to fall into a conversational and pastoral manner of addressing the individual, in the midst of the community. He will try to direct his words, as anonymously as he can, yet as personally as he can, so that he enters conversation even from the pulpit with at least some isolated and perplexed heart whom he will know to be there before him. He will preach in this way in the hope, and sometimes with the strange realisation, that Jesus the Good Shepherd who also knows his sheep by name and is to be known by them, is present among his congregation that day, as he was then in the Gospels, seeking out this very individual with a specially intimate word.[17]

Moreover if he has a true pastoral concern for those to whom he is preaching he will seek not to fail to visit them in their homes. Calvin believed that Paul gave a pattern for the

[15] See, e.g., E. Mulhaupt: *Die Predigt Calvins*, Berlin, 1951, p. 29; T. H. L. Parker, *The Oracles of God*, London, 1947, p. 64; R. S. Wallace, *Calvin's Doctrine of the Word and Sacrament*, Edinburgh, 1953, ch. VII.

[16] *Comm. on Ps.*, 125:2.

[17] Cf. John, 10:1ff.

ministry of the Word when he spoke of how he did not cease to admonish both "publicly" and "from house to house". "Whatever others may think," Calvin wrote, "we do not regard our office as bound within so narrow limits that when the sermon is delivered we may rest as if our task was done. They whose blood will be required of us if lost through our slothfulness, are to be cared for much more closely and vigilantly.[18]

Calvin was concerned that the pulpit work of even the most well disposed preacher could often fail to bring the soul to Christ. "It often happens that he who hears general promises that are intended for the whole congregation of the faithful remains nevertheless in some doubt,[19] and still is troubled in mind as though he had not yet received forgiveness." Therefore, he affirmed, preaching itself requires often to be supplemented by a pastoral interview. "It is not enough that a pastor in the pulpit should teach all the people together, if he does not add particular instruction as necessity requires and occasion offers."[20]

Like Bucer, he lamented that many preachers in his day were either too short-sighted in their view of the ministry or too lazy to visit the homes of those who listened to them from the pews.[21] Therefore they failed too often in the task of reaching the individual. They looked on the Church building as an auditorium, on the congregation as an audience. They took the easy way of avoiding the sharp evangelistic edge of the Gospel, and the close application of their teaching to the individual soul. Calvin condemned this approach. "Nothing is easier", he commented shrewdly, "than to lapse into such generalities", and "it is very difficult" to apply such doctrines to everyday life.[22]

Speaking of God's providential love he lamented that far too many people in his day simply contemplated God's

---

[18] *Comm. on Acts*, 20:20, C.O. 33:319. [19] *Inst.*, 3:4:14.

[20] *Comm. on 1 Thess.*, 2:11. Calvin here insists that the pastor must be a "father" to each individual. See also *Order for the visitation of the sick.* C.Tr., vol. II, p. 127.

[21] Bucer wrote Calvin in 1547: "I must greatly praise you for visiting the brethren, for you know with what pain I have observed that the duty of piety and love, on the part of the clergy — to visit, warn, and comfort the people, — is greatly neglected."

[22] *Comm. on Ps.*, 10:14.

promises in this matter "at a distance, and so far removed" from everyday life, "that they will not presume to appropriate them to themselves".[23] Too often, he complained, preaching was given with a lack of the "true and heartfelt conviction" which makes us reverence God so that people were left merely with a "cold and unimpressive knowledge of God in the head".[24]

The result of such generalised oratory was that the preacher too often became to the people "like one who sings love songs with a beautiful voice, and plays well upon instrument".[25] Moreover, tragically, the people sometimes encouraged it. In a letter to Bullinger Calvin laments that the ministers of his day, including himself, were being prized and sought after more on account of their oratory than on account of being pastors of souls.[26]

Calvin encouraged the burdened individual, too, who cannot find consolation through his own private approach to God to seek his pastor for private confession. "Let every believer remember that, if in private he is so troubled and afflicted with a sense of sins that without the aid of others he is unable to find freedom from them, it is his duty not to neglect the remedy which God provides for him, namely, to find relief in a private confession to his own pastor — and for his solace he should privately implore the help of him whose duty it is, both in public and in private, to comfort the people of God by the Gospel teaching."[27]

He felt that it was appropriate that this interview between the pastor and individual Church member should take place regularly before each celebration of the Lord's Supper. In Strasbourg he found himself with a congregation small enough to realise such an arrangement when he was given the care of the French congregation. At this time his mind was much concerned with questions of Church organisation and he was learning a great deal from the experience and insights of Martin Bucer, who recommended such personal and

[23] *Comm. on Ps.*, 125:2.
[24] *Comm. on Ps.*, 10:4.
[25] Ezek., 33:32.
[26] C.O., 10b:154.
[27] *Inst.*, 3:4:12.

private confession. Calvin described his pastoral arrangements then, and his purposes, in a letter he wrote to William Farel: "When the day of the sacrament of the Supper draws nigh, I give notice from the pulpit that those who are desirous to communicate must first of all let me know. At the same time I add for what purpose, that it is in order that those who are as yet uninstructed and unexperienced in religion may be better trained; besides that, those who need special admonition may hear it; and lastly, that if there be any persons who may be suffering under trouble of mind, they may receive consolation."[28]

In Geneva Calvin was not able to achieve this ideal, and the visiting of parishes themselves had to be organised in a way that seems quite formal, each minister being accompanied by an elder, new residents especially being visited, and inquiries relating to discipline being made generally.[29] Great care, however, was taken with visitation of the sick. "No one is to remain three full days confined to bed without seeing that the minister is notified, and . . . when any wish the minister to come, they shall take care to call him at a convenient hour, so as not to distract him from that office in which he and his colleagues serve the Church in common."[30]

It should be noted that such pastoral visitation especially of the sick brought the poverty as well as the physical suffering of the people before the pastor and the Church, and helped to enable the pastoral ministry to become a caring for the whole personal needs of the member. Everywhere the Reformation went, observes Gordon Rupp, "poor relief and the concern for philanthropy was to be an important stress ... running through its story like a gold thread among all too much veniality".[31]

[28] C.L. to Farel, May, 1540. At this point two great concerns, in Calvin's mind, tended to link up together — his concern both for pastoral care and discipline. Concern for pastoral care requires a different approach to Church problems than does concern for discipline, and each concern pulls the pastor in a different direction. It is possible that Calvin too often tended to make pastoral care a means of discipline rather than vice-versa.

[29] Cf. letter to Olevianus, November 9, 1560, C.O., 18:236.

[30] R.C.P., p. 46 (*Ordinances, 1541*).

[31] G. Rupp, *op. cit.*, p. 102.

The Pastoral Conversation

Calvin's first concern in seeking to bring the sinner to assurance in such counselling was to try to get him to look away from his inner state. There had to come a moment when the mind is turned away completely from all psychological problems or past failure. The sinner has to be helped by the counsellor to lift his mind out of the "prison of his introversion". "Our teaching is", writes Calvin obviously going to the heart of his "method", "that the soul should not look upon its own compunction or tears, but should fix both eyes upon the mercy of God alone."[32] "Both eyes" involves at least a willingness to look away in order to let God break through the damnable chain of our self-centredness, which makes us love psychological introspection. Calvin is always pleading with people, as Luther did, to get out of themselves into God. "If you feel in yourselves too much infirmity, have recourse to Him who has every virtue in his hand",[33] he wrote, even to those who were being threatened with martyrdom.

But the soul cannot look away from itself unless it hears the voice of God calling it to look. Only then does it know what it must look towards. Therefore the Word of God must have a determinative place in pastoral counselling, and the counsellee must be encouraged always to listen for a word from God directed personally to himself. "It would not be sufficient for God to determine with himself what he would do for our safety, if he did not speak to us expressly by name. It is only when God makes us understand by his own voice, that he will be gracious to us, that we can entertain the hope of salvation."[34] The pastor therefore, in his conversation will use scripture no less than the preacher in the pulpit. He will do this with the prayer and hope that some word of God will enable the looking away and the lifting up of the eyes to take place.

Calvin, however, warns us against trying to base the

[32] *Inst.*, 3:4:3.
[33] C.L. to the Brethren at Chambery, October 8, 1555.
[34] *Comm. on Ps.*, 12:5.

Christian life on the mere superficial and random use of Scripture texts. He certainly believed in quoting the promises of Holy Scripture in order to help people to grasp them by faith.[35] But he warns against the emptiness which will finally reveal itself within people who have simply "snatched in a passing way a few words of holy Scripture". Holy Scripture is there to introduce us to Jesus Christ himself in his humanity. Therefore the aim of our using the Bible is that we can "become more and more like the Lord Jesus, by beholding him in the mirror of the Gospel". "The better we know Christ", he adds, "the more nobly will his grace and power operate in our souls."[36]

It will be obvious from what has been said that the pastor in his conversation about the Word of God will try to avoid thrusting himself into the field of vision before the counsellee. Of course something within and from the pastor can inspire confidence in the hearer to listen. Yet the pastor's work finally must be simply a pointing away from himself to what he hopes the soul beside him will see. The voice that must be heard is not that of the pastor but that of the true Shepherd of the sheep. The pastor must at times realise that he is merely an instrument and not even a channel.

Moreover, even in the attainment of true hearing, vision, and thus, of assurance, the soul will be led to understand that it is the assurance of faith that has been given. Of course there will be new inner feelings, but the assurance will arise out of what has been heard and seen, and not out of what has been felt. Feelings of anxiety and fear can soon replace any inner feelings of joy and certainty, but the assurance of faith is not affected. Calvin reminds us that we are always "condemned, dead, and lost in ourselves", so that "we should seek righteousness, deliverance, life, and salvation in him",[37] that we have "a victorious assurance to rise above all our fears" at the same time as we "groan under the burden of our iniquities".[38] "If we consider our life to be placed in Christ,

[35] Cf., *Inst.*, 3:2:7. "We need the promise of grace which can testify that our father is merciful."
[36] To a Seigneur of Piedmont, February 25, 1554.
[37] *Inst.*, 2:16:1.
[38] *Inst.*, 3:11:11.

we must acknowledge that we are dead in ourselves; if we seek our strength in him, we must understand that in ourselves we are weak. ... If we have our rest in him we must feel within ourselves only disquietude and torment."[39]

The problem of sin must be frankly faced and dealt with. "None but the afflicted and those wounded by the awareness of sins can sincerely implore God's mercy", wrote Calvin.[40] When he was trying to bring people who had fallen, into a new conviction of assurance, he began his letter with some form of reproach, some measure of exposure of the sin, trying to ensure that there would be deep and genuine sorrow before God. "It is no slight or small offence to have preferred men to God", he wrote to D'Andelot. "Your fall has been very grievous and you ought to remember it with bitterness of heart." It is the pastor's duty, he explained, always to be severe so that the sorrow can lead to repentance. "If you desire to be spared by God, it is good and salutory for you not to be spared by those to whom he has given charge to bring you to repentance."[41]

Calvin always insisted that assurance could not be genuine unless it was accompanied by repentance. "Forgiveness of sins can never be obtained without repentance." He was careful often to add that "repentance is not the cause of forgiveness of sins".[42] Yet certain passages of Scripture forced him to go the length of saying that "we may obtain God's forgiveness by repentance".[43] He was anxious to avoid any kind of cheap grace. At this point we can note his belief that repentance is "induced by the fear of God" and that "before the mind of the sinner inclines to repentance, he must be aroused by the thought of divine judgment".[44] Therefore, though "God's mercy alone" must finally become the focal point for "both eyes", Calvin does not fail faithfully to warn the souls he is dealing with of the fact that God will one day mount the judgment seat.[45] Calvin was anxious to avoid the

---

[39] *Short Treatise on the Supper of our Lord*, 22, C.Tr., vol. II, p. 175.
[40] *Inst.*, 3:4:3.   [41] C.L., July, 1558.   [42] *Inst.*, 3:4:3.
[43] Letter to Blaurer, C.O., 18:13.   [44] *Inst.*, 3:3:7.
[45] There is a letter written in 1562 to a whole Christian community whose life had become scandalous. It is dominated by the certainty of judgment unless they set their house in order. Cf. "To the Church of..." C.O., 19:609.

use of any kind of psychological pressure or technique in order to enable people to open their hearts and confess. The Roman Church had ruined the confessional by such tyranny and priestcraft. In the reformed Church "those who use it (the confessional) according to their need" should "neither be forced by any rule nor be induced by any trick to recount all their sins" (Calvin believed, in any case, that no one could ever make an adequate confession to another human person even if he tried). True pastors must stoutly defend this principle "if they want to avoid tyranny in their ministry and superstition in the people".[46]

Though we can discern a few general principles in Calvin's approach to the cure of souls, there is spontaneity in how he responds to quite different people in quite different situations. He certainly observed the people around him and knew human nature. "I know the disposition and character of each one of you",[47] he said on his deathbed to the Seigneurs of Geneva. But he knew them as individuals and not as typical cases to be analysed, written up, classified, and approached by a worked-out technique. His variation in approach may be noticed in the extraordinary variety of his expressions and counsel in his letters which never became stereotyped. He never played the same record twice. Each soul is new, each situation is new, and God's way must always be found out afresh, as we face each new day with his Word.

Sometimes Calvin used great gentleness and sympathy when he dealt with an erring soul. Sometimes he was blunt but restrained.[48] To bring Legrant back to the faith however, he took an entirely different way: "I should never have expected to find you guilty of such madness as to listen to the falsehoods of Satan, in that cursed school which sets at naught all religion, and tempts men to licentiousness, making a mock of God and whatever is holy. Experience shows what fine things you have learned there — to scatter jests about like deadly poison, and so scandalise the poor and already distracted church. Reflect on the words — 'Woe to him through whom offences come.' I spare you not, that God may spare you. I will let you feel the wretchedness. ... Return to

[46] *Inst.*, 3:4:12.   [47] C.Tr., vol. I, p. xcii.   [48] Cf. pp. 183f.

the fold of Christ, and be assured that all who loved you in former times will be filled with joy to be able to love you again more than ever."[49] Calvin knew his man and there was some hope.

He does not appear to have been so hopeful when at the King of Navarre's own request he wrote that monarch to tell him what people were saying about him. He tried to be honest in a tactful way that would show some respect for whatever dignity remained with the poor king: "What is whispered about is that some foolish amours prevent you from doing your duty. ... If you are angry, Sire, that they should entertain such an opinion of you, I pray you reflect on the number of young girls that give occasion for it ... I entreat you, then, Sire, to rouse yourself up in good earnest."[50]

Pastoral Sympathy

Ernst Pfisterer, seeking to explain why people in their thousands were drawn to Geneva from all over Europe, and why Calvin's own congregation after years of resistance finally gave in to him, attributed his influence to both his tireless pastoral fidelity, and the power of the Word of God.[51]

We must recognise the strength of both these factors. Calvin himself would no doubt have attributed the success of his ministry primarily to what he himself described as "the Spirit of God which resonated through the voice so as to work with mighty energy",[52] and he would himself have explained that the Spirit of God works in spite of the frailty and sinfulness of the human instrument.

But important though his preaching was, his genius and work as a pastor have to be taken full notice of. The documents of the time bear witness to the extraordinary effectiveness of this aspect of his ministry. One of his closest colleagues over the years in Geneva described in some detail how Calvin dealt with people: "No words of mine can declare

[49] C.L. to Augustin Legrant, February 23, 1559.
[50] C.L. to the King of Navarre, May, 1561.
[51] Quoted from E. Pfisterer, *Calvin's Wirken in Genf.*, 1940, p. 18 in W. Kolfaus, *Die Seelsorge Johannes Calvins*, 1941, pp. 9-10.
[52] C.L. to Somerset, October 22, 1548.

the fidelity and prudence with which he gave counsel. The kindness with which he received all who came to him, the clearness and promptitude with which he replied to those who asked his opinion on the most important questions, and the ability with which he disentangled the difficulties and problems which were laid before him. Nor can I express the gentleness with which he could comfort the afflicted and raise the fallen and the distressed."[53]

Those who sought his counsel found in him, not only wisdom, but the strength that God often communicates to people through a trusted pastor. A letter from Anton Laborier, one of the martyrs of the Reformed faith, to his wife illustrates the genuine devotion people had for him:

> Anna, my good sister, you know that you are still young, and are about to be separated from my society. If such be God's good will for us, comfort yourself in Him, and with the thought that Jesus Christ is your father and your husband ... Pray to Him without ceasing for His holy word. Seek ... the counsel of our right-minded friends, especially that of M. Calvin. He will not let you come to harm if you act according to his wish; and you know that he is led by the Holy Ghost. If you marry again, and I advise you to do so, I beg you, hearken to his opinion, and to do nothing without him.[54]

In our final evaluation of Calvin we will take note of how often and artificially he forced himself to adopt a "public" character.[55] He seemed in his pastoral work to be able at times to throw this off entirely to reveal a quality which helped people to find themselves comforted, encouraged and enlightened by his intimate conversation as he came very close to people in sympathy. This attracted people to him. The Marchioness of Rothelin journeyed to Geneva especially to counsel with the Reformer to derive "consolation ... and some accession of courage for the time to come".[56] Laurent

---

[53] Des Gallars to Crespin, C.O. 36, Preface to *Comm. on Isaiah*.
[54] Crespin, *Histoire des Martyrs*, vol. II, Toulouse, 1887, p. 232.
[55] Cf. Ch. 17.
[56] C.L. to Farel, September 14, 1557.

de Normandie's wife on her deathbed felt herself so close to him that she was able to seize his hand and give thanks to God "by whose hand she had been brought to that place where she could die in peace".[57]

He seemed able to communicate the same encouragement and strength to people through his personal pastoral letters. Two of the martyrs awaiting death in prison in Lyons received a joint letter. One of them, Louis de Marsac, wrote back to Calvin "Sir and brother, ... I cannot express to you the great comfort I have received ... from the letter which you have sent to my brother Denis Peloquin, who found means to deliver it to one of our brethren who was in a vaulted cell above me, and read it to me aloud, as I could not read it myself, being unable to see anything in my dungeon. I entreat of you, theefore, to persevere in helping us with similar consolation, for it invites us to weep and to pray."[58] Obviously in the writing of the letter Calvin had tried to put himself and his sympathy into its very style and content, seeking even while he was writing to share in his own emotions what he believed they were suffering.

"My dear and beloved brother," he once wrote to one facing possible martyrdom, "if, free from fear and anxiety, I should animate you and your brethren in office to endure the strife which awaits you, my language would rightly be considered cold, and even disagreeable. Distressed, however, as I am on account of your danger, and trembling as I do while exhorting you to perseverance and trust, this letter, which is a living image of my heart, and shows all its inward emotions, will speak to you no less clearly than I could myself were I present, and a partaker in your troubles. And certainly, if the worst should happen, it would be my wish to be united with you in death rather than to survive you."[59]

If we were to select one quality more than another which made him especially helpful we would refer to perpetual sense he had of his own inherent personal weakness.

Of Gregory the Great, Jean Leclercq observes: "Gregory's

[57] Cf. *Concerning Scandals*, Dedicatory Epistle, p. 2.
[58] Crespin, *Histoire des Martyrs*, vol. I, 1885, p. 730.
[59] Letter to Macarius, May, 1558, C.O., 17:91.

poor health is one of the great events in the history of spirituality, since to some degree it determines his doctrine. It gives it those qualities of humanity and discretion and the ring of conviction which explain his influence." There is no doubt that Calvin's constantly recurring bouts of intense pain and the physical weakness he had always to live with gave him too the same "strong sense of human suffering, of the effects of original sin and also the value of human weakness and temptation for spiritual progress".[60] Moreover the shattering blow he received through the death of his own wife, who for a few years had brought immense joy to his life, helped him greatly to be of comfort to the bereaved.

In the many more ordinary and less dramatic cases he had to deal with — of habitual moral weakness or sudden lapsing, of human questioning, loss of spiritual vision, warmth, and life, he was helped to minister because he knew so personally that any strength he possessed came entirely from God. He felt always that he was a weak man able to be strong by the grace of God, and only able to help others simply because he knew himself helped out of exactly the weakness he found so prevalent around him. His own experience of himself, therefore, always enters what he has to say, and it makes him able to convey hope. When he writes to Renée the Duchess of Ferrara to rebuke her for a serious lapse and to try to help her to recover, he approaches the subject with fine tact: "I shrewdly suspect that you have been obliged to swerve from the strict path in order to comply with the world." And then he includes himself in the next few sentences: ". . . and indeed the devil has so triumphed over us that we have been constrained to groan over it, hold down our heads, and make no further inquiries". And now he can converse with her simply as one as weak as herself on her own level — a sinner trying to help a fellow sinner — and he shows her how he himself has always found it: "As our heavenly father is ever ready to admit us to his mercy, and where we have fallen

[60] Jean Jacques Leclercq, *The Love of learning and the desire for God*, New York, 1961, p. 36. Possibly the fact that after so many serious spells of illness Calvin managed to recover his buoyancy of heart and spirit, helped him to retain in his teaching his healthy New Testament stress on the resurrection power which also comes here and now to those who bear the cross.

holds out his hands to us that our falls prove not mortal, I entreat you to take courage."[61] Even in the midst of a deservedly harsher rebuke to the King of Navarre, he pleads with him to "trample underfoot the vanities that very soon lead us astray without our being aware of it".[62]

[61] C.L. to Duchess of Ferrara, February 2, 1555.
[62] C.L. to King of Navarre, May, 1561.

CHAPTER 13

GUIDANCE FOR THE CHRISTIAN LIFE

A "Calvinistic" Way of Life?

THE breadth of Calvin's sphere of influence in succeeding generations can be deduced from the variety of meanings which have been attached to the word "Calvinism". In England in the seventeenth century the term was often used simply to refer to a form of Church government in which ordinary laymen could figure too prominently to suit the tastes either of the nobility or the landed gentry or some of the clergy. In the discussion of historical theology the term has been used, in a more carefully defined way, to denote the body of theological tradition which characterised those churches or groups of congregations which in the course of the Reformation seemed to come most strongly under the influence of Calvin's teaching. It has also been often used to denote a way of life, a way to face its problems and challenges and to take its pleasures and sufferings in the midst of the great changes that were taking place in their world. The people around Calvin in Geneva required not only spiritual comfort and assurance, they also required guidance as to how each individual in the practice of daily living should respond to the grace of God through a life of faith and obedience. Calvin responded to this need and gave people ethical and devotional guidance on a personal level. There is no doubt that his teaching in this respect gave a characteristic stamp to the ethos and culture of the communities which were most directly influenced by his work and writing. Troeltsch, indeed, has affirmed that Calvin's influence produced a "type of humanity" which "even today affects the whole of

European civilisation", even people who are not aware of the fact.[1]

Within this Calvinistic tradition of Church government, theology, ethics and culture there have appeared many features which did not truly reflect the mind and attitude of Calvin himself. The use of a personal name to describe the appearance of certain views and attitudes at a given period can be highly confusing, and can give a distorted view of how things work out historically. We have to avoid thinking of Calvinism as something that Calvin through his particular personal and intellectual influence produced in Geneva and also managed to inject as a life-force within the stream of history. Possibly we are nearer the truth when we think of Calvinism as having always been a valid and possible attitude in a life-style within the Christian tradition. Though it had earlier expression, it nevertheless appeared on a larger scale and in a more recognisable form in the sixteenth and seventeenth centuries when in a remarkable way it was felt to be suitable especially for this age. During this period it appeared first in Geneva. It appeared as a way of life arising out of a certain vision of life that was a response to the Word of God under the conditions then prevailing.

Hilaire Belloc therefore exaggerates when he writes "No Calvin, No Cromwell". Cromwell would have been very much the kind of leader he was because he had the Bible to teach and inspire him, and he read it. He, too, lived in an age when the preaching of the Word of God especially was a powerful force in directing men's lives and moulding their characters, and the problems he faced were similar to those Calvin faced. What Calvin did was to clarify the practical issues and theological problems. He helped people to get to the heart of things, and to see life and the Gospel in its wholeness.

"The Golden Book of the Christian Life"

From the beginning of his ministry, Calvin laid emphasis on the Ten Commandments as a guide to Christian behaviour.

[1] E. Troeltsch, *The Social Teaching of the Christian Churches*, vol. II, E.T., London, 1931, p. 578.

He expounded these in his first edition of the *Institutes*, and in the little catechism which he wrote for the young in Geneva in 1537 entitled *Instruction in the Faith*. They had to be kept not simply according to the letter, but according to the Spirit, as Jesus had taught in the Sermon on the Mount.

In his exile in Strasbourg he must have realised, however, the need for further instruction on this matter. He therefore selected some important texts, mostly from the New Testament, and he ventured to draw a picture of the kind of person he expected Christians in his day to become.

The new 1539 edition of the *Institutes* which he wrote in Strasbourg therefore contains a section on "The Life of the Christian Man" in which, with some detail, he described the response by which he believed the people of his day could best express their devotion to God and obey the call of Christ to take up their cross and follow. He placed this section at the very end of this edition. He did not alter its wording in his two later revisions of his work though he divided it into five chapters and placed it differently. He valued it enough to have it printed separately at one time. People found it especially helpful. It was the first section of the *Institutes* to be translated into English and it was then given the title: *The Golden Book of the Christian Life*.

In the final edition of the *Institutes* we have this description of the Christian life included in Calvin's discussion on Repentance. Obviously he thought of the Christian as always called upon to live a life of true repentance. He admitted that the words "sanctification" or "regeneration" could replace "repentance", but he preferred his chosen term.

He explained that there are important differences between the life of faith and evangelical repentance which was to be expected from a Christian, and the artificial life of penance and good works which was standard practice within the Roman Church of his day.[2] He felt it was important to bring out these differences carefully since some of the old attitudes and forms of response had to be avoided. Moreover he showed that the evangelical way of life which he tried to recover from the New Testament, was based on quite

[2] *Inst.*, 3:4:1ff.

different pre-suppositions from the way of life worked out as the noble ideal by the ancient philosophers and the modern humanists,[3] and, of course, he continually contrasted the Christian way with that of the contemporary libertarians.

After a short introduction to these important chapters, Calvin defines the Christian life as having four central features, each feature being given one chapter to itself. These are: "Self-denial", "Bearing the Cross", "Meditation on the Future [i.e. Heavenly] Life", and "The Use and Enjoyment of this Present Life".

The Christian is thus asked to regard himself as always in this life placed like the disciples in the Gospels. He is called to follow Jesus on the way to the Cross. But he must remember, as he listens, that this Jesus who is present here to lead him through this world, is also the Ascended Lord who belongs to the new, future, and heavenly world beyond. The call to come and follow Jesus is therefore a call to him to lift up his mind and heart intently towards the exalted Lord, even as he has to make his difficult way through this present life.

The Christian, therefore, according to Calvin, in following Jesus, now becomes a pilgrim moving between two worlds. As he denies himself and takes up the cross allotted to him by life and by God, he must orient himself all the time to heavenly destiny to be accomplished through his own death and resurrection. Moreover he becomes united to Jesus in body and soul through the Spirit not simply after death but here and now. Here and now, through what Calvin calls a "mystical union",[4] with the exalted Lord who is calling him he is empowered to offer his life for such self-denial and cross-bearing. Moreover he is kept, like a compass, always oriented towards heaven and the life to come while he is enabled to spend himself in faithful earthly service of his fellow men and women.

In his letters Calvin consistently applied his teaching on these matters to people in their life-situations. A study of his correspondence can help to throw light on his teaching and to show how closely it was related to his practice.

[3] *Inst.*, 3:6:3-4.
[4] Cf. e.g., *Inst.*, 3:1:1; 4:17:1, etc.

The Call to "Self-Denial"

Following the tradition of Church fathers like Augustine, of many mystics and saints, especially of the German mediaeval mystics which so greatly influenced Luther, Calvin regards the root of all our sin as being our perverse self-love.[5] Our self-will which always hardens itself in opposition to what is of God, resists the change which the Spirit of God seeks to work within us, and creates a fierce inner conflict, as we seek to follow Christ.[6]

We discover that "our greatest enemy" is not the devil, the persecutor, or even the world but that self-centred principle which Paul called the "flesh".[7] "We are called ... to strive against ourselves and our passions",[8] aware that God is always testing our faith "to know whether in seeking after him, we have been renouncing self".[9] When he was faced by division within a Church he sometimes went to the heart of the matter, and instead of simply exhorting people to begin loving each other, he told them to stop loving themselves. "You know the rule which the Holy Spirit lays down to reconcile us to one another. It is that each should yield and give up his right, that we should seek rather to edify our neighbour in his eternal interests than consult our own selfish desires."[10]

To control this inner selfish perversity, "to yield our right" and to "strive against ourselves" with any hope of success is, however, impossible unless we first adopt a drastic treatment, the kind of radical surgery that was described by Jesus when he spoke of plucking out the eye and cutting off the hand. "There is no other remedy but to tear out of our inward parts this most deadly pestilence of love of strife and love of self, even as it is plucked out by scriptural teaching."[11] This is an

---

[5] Cf. R. S. Wallace, *Calvin's Doctrine of the Christian Life*, Edinburgh, 1959, pp. 61, 119f.

[6] Rom. 7:15ff; Gal. 5:17f.

[7] C.L. to the Brethren of France, November 1559.

[8] C.L. to Church in Paris, September 16, 1557.

[9] C.L. to Madame de la Roche-Posay, June 19, 1549.

[10] C.L. to the French Church in Frankfurt, March 3, 1556.

[11] *Inst.*, 3:7:4; cf. 3:8:5.

important "first step" in which a man "departs from himself" in order to be able to serve God.[12]

Calvin found analogies for the drastic and violent nature of such self-immolation both in circumcision and in the temple sacrifices. It is by the sword of the Spirit that we are enabled thus to slay our "common nature" as a sacrifice of ourselves before God. Nothing must be omitted from the totality of the sacrifice. Every aspect, attitude, love, prize, habit of the old self must be brought to the altar and slain. "It is impossible to employ body and soul with sincerity of heart in the service of God while we make a semblance of agreement with idolators."[14] No honour is ever given to God "while a mortal man dares to appropriate the smallest portion of the glory which God claims for himself".[15] Indeed, Calvin warns, unless the sacrifice is of everything then we are in danger of forfeiting life and salvation.[16]

Even after the sudden death-blow has been given, the struggle continues. The self principle never dies, therefore the whole Christian life is marked by continual self-restraint, alertness and discipline. We begin to be safe only when we have made it the habit of our lives to forget ourselves[17] and have become "long accustomed" to prefer the will of God to our own affections, however virtuous they may be.[18] Yet even at this stage always we have to be watchful: "Let us learn that even although the unruliness of our wayward flesh has been already subdued by the denial of ourselves, to walk in fear and trembling, for unless God restrain us, our hearts will violently boil with a proud and insolent contempt of God."[19]

The single-hearted integrity and sincerity which we are enabled to attain when by the Spirit we are enabled to make this total self offering to God, Calvin regarded as "perfection". The Bible does not define perfection by enumerating great virtues, and by asking us to attain such to

[12] *Inst.*, 3:3:8, 3:3:5.
[14] C.L. to a French Seigneur, October 18, 1548.
[15] *Comm. on Ps.*, 9:1.
[16] C.L. to Monsieur de Budé, June 19, 1547.
[17] C.L. to Mademoiselle de ... January 12, 1549.
[18] C.L. to Marquis de Vico, July 19, 1558.
[19] *Comm. on Ps.*, 19:13.

the highest possible degree. Perfection is simply the opposite of double-heartedness.[20] It is a complete integrity of heart achieved and given when a total response is made to God's grace and God's command. Speaking of Job, Calvin says, "It is stated that he was a perfect man; now this word in scripture is used to represent a character in which there is no fiction or hypocrisy; when a man is the same without as he is within, having no subterfuge in reserve to excuse his turning from God, by employing all his thoughts and affections about Him, and seeking nothing but the entire devotion of himself, of his heart and soul to his service."[21]

It is worth while noting at this point how Calvin in all this teaching is bringing before the ordinary men and women of his day the same call to inward Christian perfection which had too often in the Middle Ages been given only within monastic circles, or specially devout groups. "Through all the Benedictine rule", says Gilson, "one central idea . . . runs: the first duty of anyone who would serve God is to renounce his own will."[22] Gerhard Groote of the Brethren of the Common Life had insisted too that every Christian from pure motives should forsake himelf and be devoted to God.[23] The same teaching is echoed in Tauler and many of the mystics of the time. But it is likely that Calvin's own teaching on such aspects of the Christian life was more directly influenced by Thomas à Kempis' work *On the Imitation of Christ*. There are very close similarities between à Kempis and Calvin when each speaks either of cross-bearing or of self-denial. It is difficult after reading à Kempis' chapter on "A pure and simple resignation" not to conclude that Calvin knew it well.[24]

In the teaching of the mediaeval mystics, however, the self-denial called for was often regarded as a work of human initiative meriting reward and response from God. Calvin,

[20] *Comm. on Jer.*, 29:13.
[21] *Sermon on Job*, 1:1.
[22] E. Gilson, *The Mystical Theology of St. Bernard*, London, 1940, p. 29.
[23] "Turn away thy heart from the creatures, even with violence that thou mayest conquer thyself, and point thy mind continually to God", Gerhard Groote. Cf. C. Ullmann, *Reformers before the Reformation*, vol. II, Edinburgh, 1885, p. 80.
[24] On *The Imitation of Christ*, bk. IV, ch. 37.

however, always regards our sacrifice of self-denial as possible only through the grace of God in Christ. Because Jesus pioneered the way, and first gave, in our name and place, such a self-sacrifice to God, we now, through him and in him, have the power to repeat what he has first done. It is the Holy Spirit who gives us the power to make such a decision before God, and actually reduplicates within us the once-for-all sacrifice which Jesus has made, enabling us to participate in it. Moreover it is only in response to the love of God which we see in the sacrifice he has made for us that we can be inspired with gratitude enough to give our life over to God so completely.

Submission under the Cross

The sacrifice of the whole life must accompany and follow the perfect sacrifice of the whole heart. Luther had insisted that we do not please God by trying to fulfil highly pitched vows within the enclosure of a monastery in order to be superlative saints. True sanctity, rather, consisted in doing our daily task within the earthly vocation to which God has called us, in obedience to his word. Moreover, we need not try to impose on ourselves any kind of self-designed austerity or artificial discipline in order to improve our piety or character. We must let God himself fill our life with the content it requires to make us spiritually healthy. God himself will allow each of us to experience sufficient hardship, disappointment and persecution to sanctify us perfectly. He will thus enable each of us within our calling to make our lives as heroic as he intended them to be without our seeking to overload or divert ourselves so that we can make an extraordinary response to him. "There is no need for any vigils or of special fasts of abstinence, for God gave me a 'Messenger of Satan' (2 Cor. 12:7) together with other difficulties and the crosses of this world, which plague me more than all these things."[25]

Calvin closely followed Luther. For him too, the school in which we are to learn how to work out and express the perfect surrender we have made in heart to God is the school of life

[25] L.W., 5:271.

and not the cloister. Moreover, as we each follow our vocation in this ordinary way of life to which we are called, God himself will measure, shape, and give to each of us with exactly the gentleness or severity which each of us requires, a cross designed to test, perfect us more and more in self-denial, and make us his own. Calvin describes the whole Christian life as a bearing of the Cross.

He was certain that none of us by any kind of evasive action will be able to escape the "harsh and difficult conditions" in which we share Christ's sufferings.[26] Of course we have a duty to remove needless forms of sickness and want whenever we have means to do so at our disposal. He himself tried to remove poverty and sickness from Geneva. But in spite of all our efforts the residual and inevitable burden of suffering will be there for us to make our decision about — disablement of body or mind, poverty, unemployment, unlooked-for disaster, bereavement, boredom, inner and outward frustration, slander — whether we are poor or rich we will "have enough to constitute a cross".

At times our "cross" will have a specially comforting ingredient when persecution, unpopularity, loss and slander are heaped upon us simply because we are making a Christian witness and adopting a Christian attitude.[27] Then we have to count ourselves specially fortunate for we can test the worth of Christ's "beautiful promise" that "we are indeed happy when all the world shall speak ill of us and shall hate us".[28] Yet the "sufferings" and the "cross" that relate us to Jesus Christ and give our life fellowship with him must not in any way be restricted to such special sufferings.[29]

We must "accustom ourselves" to this hard life[30] with "so many and various kinds of evil".[31] When Jesus was sent into the world he was disfigured and "looked upon as execrable and accursed, and afterwards his Gospel was also exposed to

---

[26] *Inst.*, 3:8:1.

[27] *Inst.*, 3:8:7.

[28] C.L. to Madame de Falais, September 1545.

[29] Cf. R. Bultmann, *The Theology of the New Testament*, London, 1952, vol. I, p. 351.

[30] C.L. to Farel, May 24, 1554. We "must by continual training learn to die" C.L. to a Seigneur of Piedmont, February 25, 1554.

[31] *Inst.*, 3:8:1.

every disgrace ... as we see it today".[32] "If Jesus Christ spared not himself for our salvation, it is not reasonable that our life should be deemed more precious than his."[33]

Such cross-bearing will at times seem to us an experience more disturbing, or even shattering, than uplifting. We discover that as Christ increases, we tend to decrease. We have entered a process of sanctification by humiliation, but we are not allowed to regard this even as an ascent into the virtue of humility.[34] As Regin Prenter describes it: It is precisely when the Cross smashes our own perfection to bits, when anxiety strips us of all hope of improvement that sanctification, the right kind of growth downward, making for the growth of Christ in us, takes place.[35]

Therefore we have to renounce any ambition to be great morally or spiritually or to achieve any position of leadership in such matters. We may have to resign ourselves simply to becoming more and more insignificant and penitent — even to be stripped of every semblance of what seems noble. When D'Andelot, in public disgrace, was imprisoned and no doubt harshly judged for his public cowardice, Calvin reminded him that even languishing for such a prolonged time in disgrace and imprisonment and now entirely out of sight of men he could regard himself as fulfilling God's purpose for his sanctification; for not only must we patiently endure to die with our head, but also to be buried with him until he fully restores us again at his coming[36] — a truly comforting moral for one who had indeed reached the depths! As Fenelon said, our self-love makes us prefer injury to oblivion.

Only one virtue really matters in this way of sanctification — obedience — a submissive acceptance of God's will and God's way. "Our sole task is to allow ourselves to be governed by him."[37] By our bearing under the Cross we can give a "genuine proof" that we are able to "renounce the guidance of our own affections and submit ourselves entirely to

---

[32] *The Gospel according to Isaiah: Seven Sermons on Isaiah 53*, trs. Nixon, Grand Rapids, 1953, p. 34.   [33] C.L. to a Seigneur of Piedmont, February 25, 1554.

[34] As in Benedictine circles. Cf. E. Gilson, *op. cit.*, pp. 71-2.

[35] R. Prenter, *The Word and the Spirit*, Minneapolis, 1965, p. 106.

[36] C.L. to D'Andelot, July 1558.

[37] C.L. to the Women detained at Paris, September 1557.

God".[38] Calvin believed that our devotion to God could be more clearly demonstrated by such joyful and passive submission to his will than even through self-initiated acts of gratitude. It is truly a great thing when anyone "has made himself poor as far as depends on himself" and has sold all in order to give to others, but the test of true spiritual poverty demanded finally by God is in whether or not we can patiently endure the loss of worldly goods without any regret when it pleases the heavenly father that we should be despoiled of them.[39] We are always justified in finding support and comfort under the Cross by the knowledge that we are "laying ourselves out for God's service and proving to him our obedience".[40]

Calvin taught that it was impossible to believe in God and still leave any room in the mind for "fate" or "chance" as explanations of our human circumstances. We have to see God's hand either as permitting exactly what comes to us, or as shaping it and bringing it himself. De Sales expresses Calvin's Calvinism at this point, as well as Calvin ever did himself. "Now I say, O Philothea, that we must have patience not only to be ill, but to be ill with the illness which God wills, in the place where he wills, and amongst such persons as he wills; and so of other tribulations."[41] But the hand of God stretched out to us has to be seen as the hand of a heavenly Father. Two letters Calvin wrote to the Duchess of Ferrara in 1555 are worth studying. In the first the stress is on the Fatherhood of God. "God in humbling his children has no wish to cover them with shame for ever." He is the "Heavenly Father, ever ready to admit us to his mercy", and when we fall he "holds out his hand to us that our falls prove not mortal". In the second letter, four months later remembering what he had already written, he adds, "It is certain that God will listen to your groans if you continue to ask him to hold out his hand to you."[42]

[38] I.C.P., p. xxxix. [39] C.L. to De Falais, September 1545.
[40] C.L. to the Brethren at Orbe, March 4, 1554.
[41] *Introduction to the Devout Life*, pt. 3, ch. 3.
[42] C.L. February 2 and June 10, 1555; cf. to Madame de Coligny, September 24, 1561: "Thus, Madame, I pray you, whatever happens, never be weary of employing yourself in the service of so good a Father."

He expressed his disapproval of the stoical attitude which was sometimes adopted by those around him who felt it was surely a sign of human weakness to allow oneself to be emotionally moved by one's personal suffering, and who counselled people under affliction to cultivate an artificial tranquillity of mind, indifference and fortitude — a stiff upper-lip! In a comforting letter to a father whose student son had suddenly died of the plague in Strasbourg, he reminded him that in our grief we are not submitting to blind death or hard fate, but to God, loving, purposeful and sovereign. We are not required to put off that common humanity with which God has endowed us, that being men, we should be turned into "stones". Therefore we can "shed the tears due to nature and fatherly affection".[43]

He occasionally ventures an explanation and even a justification of our human suffering, mentioning sometimes how stubborn we are so that we need correction, of how our sufferings can disengage us from bondage to the world,[44] of how they help us to renounce our own self-love.[45] But at times of greatest desolation when God is slow in raising his arm to remedy things we must believe that he is doing a work that "surpasses our comprehension" and trust that "if there fall not to the ground without his will a single bird, he will never be wanting". He knows and understands our sorrows as he knows and measures our afflictions. "If he sometimes permits the blood of his people to be shed, yet he fails not to treasure up their precious tears as it were in a phial."[46]

The Christian between Two Worlds

Experience of God, as we have it described to us in the Bible, is often linked up with what is sometimes called "mystical experience", i.e. the experience of another world within and yet beyond and alongside the present world.[47] It appears that this other world is here and now opened before us and

---

[43] C.L. to M de Richebourg, April 1541. Cf. *Inst.*, 3:7:9, 1:5:2, for Calvin's view of Stoicism.   [44] C.L. to Marchioness of Rothelin, January 5, 1558.

[45] C.L. to Madame de la Roche-Posay, June 10, 1549.

[46] C.L. to Church in Paris, September 16, 1557.

[47] A. M. Ramsey, *Sacred and Secular*, 1967, pp. 31-2.

inviting exploration. Arthur Weiser in his *Commentary on the Psalms* states his belief that when the people of God went up to the sanctuary at Jerusalem and engaged in the liturgy of the religious festivals which recounted the great past deeds of the God of Israel, they also, at times, experienced God himself as present before them. In this experience, he writes, they found themselves confronted by another world which contrasted with the ordinary world of daily life. "Two different worlds are here deliberately confronted with one another, the one being the world in which man does all that he possibly can do, a world which perhaps may be terrifying but which is transient; the other being the world in which God proves himself a reality, the reality with which the cult community sees itself confronted ... as it remembers the saving deeds of God."[48]

Calvin himself was sensitive to this aspect of Biblical teaching. He noted that when God thrust himself into the experience of people like Jacob, Isaiah, and Ezekiel, he opened up before their vision a whole transcendent realm. Calvin interpreted these visions as being in no way delusive — where God was, another world was — and he affirmed that the souls of those who underwent such experience of God were actually there and then lifted up beyond this world to penetrate this other world of God.[49] In his interpretation of the New Testament he noted that when Jesus invited people to experience God, he described a realm, the Kingdom of God, present both within and above this world which he invited people to enter. Referring to what he believed to be the ordinary level of experience, he often described Christians as those whose minds have been "raised above by a taste of the heavenly life".[50] He found himself especially caught up in this other worldly orientation when he meditated on the love of God, and he invites us to find it so: "If we meditate on the inestimable goodness of our indulgent heavenly father, we shall be base indeed if we are not touched by his love so as to forget and despise whatever belongs to the world, to break all

[48] A. Weiser, *The Psalms*, London, 1962, p. 209.
[49] See Calvin's commentaries in such places and on e.g., Acts 7:56.
[50] *Comm. on Ps.*, 30:4.

the ties which hold us back from him, and disentangle ourselves from every obstacle which dogs our march."[51]

Calvin did not think of his "heaven" as being literally an astronomic reality, an extension of our universe above the sky. A. M. Ramsey, dealing with the problem of the spatial language which has to be used in this discussion, gives an exposition of it which fits in well with Calvin's general catholic stress and viewpoint: "Here in the midst of the world and its processes", he writes, "is the presence of God, and here man must find him. But to be near to God as one receives his reign is to be already in a relationship 'out of the world', and the man or woman who stands childlike in that relationship is already entering an existence beyond the world as well as within it." He continues: " 'the otherness' of the other world is not that of a structure standing out against the world. It is the otherness of man's life with God, invisible, present already, and leading to destiny after death. Just as approach to belief in immortality is through belief in God ... so man knows and approaches the 'other world' through fellowship with God ... some have portrayed it as a *country* or a *city*, others have written only of fellowship with God (1 John 3:13; John 17:3)."[52]

To Calvin, of course, the "other world" is interpreted also as the realm into which Christ has ascended. The "mystical union" with Christ which played such an important part in Calvin's theology, is union with the ascended Christ. When we have such communion with him by the Holy Spirit, Calvin explained, he is not only brought down to us on this earth, but our souls are also raised up to him so that we can participate here and now in his ascended life and glory.[53] Again we must note that this heavenly communion is not a privilege reserved for experts in mystical contemplation. "We tend heavenward", he wrote to all the ordinary members of the Church in Paris, "and have tasted celestial joys."[54]

[51] C.L. to the Brethren of Poitou, September 3, 1554.

[52] A. M. Ramsey, *op. cit.*, p. 11 and pp. 28-9.

[53] Cf. R. S. Wallace, *Calvin's Doctrine of the Word and Sacrament*, pp. 203ff.

[54] C.L. to the Church in Paris, January 28, 1555. In this way Christ restores, by his ascension, the orientation to a future and heavenly life with which Adam was originally created.

The "heavenward" reference was meant not only to give a new perspective to man's earthly life, but to dominate all his earthly activity forcefully. It is meant to exercise such a powerful constraint on us here and now that, detached from this present world we become no longer its settled residents but pilgrims on a journey through it. "Dedicate yourselves wholly to our Lord Jesus Christ", wrote Calvin to the French church in Antwerp, "till you be entirely transformed in his image, in order to be participants of his glory, and always keep in mind that you are to pass through and not to be shut up in it."[55] We must begin to find the centre of gravity of the whole world in which we now live, lifted far above its former level. "Those who are not carried above the heavens by this joy so that they are content with Christ alone and despise the world, boast in vain that they have faith."[56] Calvin advised Admiral Coligny to make his "principal study" ". . . that of doing homage to God, dedicated fully to him, and aspiring after the heavenly life".[57]

Louis Bouyer draws a distinction between two different kinds of "spirituality" which he affirms have at times characterised the lives of some people within the Church. The first is "the spirituality which would fain be interested in God only in so far as he can be of use to this earth of ours". This type of spirituality, he affirms, even though it borrows from Christianity all the elements it likes will never be fundamentally Christian. The second type of spirituality is that which is interested in the earth only in so far as it becomes a means of leading man towards God. Bouyer calls this "Christianity pure and simple" without anything to diminish or adulterate it.[58]

We find Calvin's outlook indicated in Bouyer's "second type". Bouyer found this type of spirituality perfectly embodied in the best forms of monasticism. But it was Calvin's purpose that Christianity "pure and simple" should be expected no longer from monks or special experts only, but from the laity in Geneva and elsewhere. Certainly since

---

[55] C.L. to French Church in Antwerp, December 21, 1556.
[56] *Comm. on 1 Pet.*, 1:8.   [57] C.L. to Coligny, September 4, 1558.
[58] L. Bouyer, *The Meaning of the Monastic Life*, p. 27.

P

Calvin's day there has been a shift in Reformed circles towards a "this worldly" Christianity. In my early ministry when I tried to explain the meaning of the Sabbath day, and why we should observe it, nearly all the books I read, and the training I had been given laid the stress on how much we need a day of rest in order to recuperate our strength to enable us to live well and serve our fellow men well during the other six days of the week when we went back to the important tasks of life. It was the standard teaching of the time. It required some adjustment of thought and of exposition to discover Calvin's view, that the Sabbath was intended by God not to orient us to the other six days' work but really to interrupt it, to spoil it, as it were, to detach us from it, and to lift up our hearts above the world, its work and activity so that we could become more detached in our attitude. Calvin shows where his priority lies by inserting his chapter on the *meditatio futurae vitae* before he deals with the "use and enjoyment of this present world".

The Use and Enjoyment of This Present World

For Calvin the orientation to eternal life did not mean an evasion of our responsibility to serve or enjoy this world. Therefore, as we should expect from a social reformer, before he finishes his exposition of the Christian life, he draws us back solidly to earth with a chapter on "the use of the present life and its helps".

Yet he believed that we will never be able to enjoy the world as we should do, unless we first learn to despise it. When he wrote to Madame de Cany: "I entreat you to exercise yourself in the doctrine of renouncing the world" he was repeating what he had already said with emphasis in his *Institutes*.[59] She did not need much explanation of what he meant. The belief that we must cultivate a "contempt for this world" was current in the teaching of the Roman Church at the time and was held by others too.[60]

[59] C.L. to Madame de Cany, June 8, 1549. Cf. *Inst.*, 3:9:1-12.
[60] E.g., in 1551 Benedetto Palmio wrote to Ignatius that the subjects which "lie close to the hearts of men of perfection" were "contempt of the world, self-denial, the

This "world", Calvin taught, tends to become so much "present" with us that our minds become "fixed" on its splendour, and "overwhelmed" in its delight.[61] Therefore we are diverted from our central purpose in life. Moreover it shows itself with features that are often alien and antagonistic to a life centred on God. Calvin can remind us that the "corrupt enticements and pleasures of the world" can be a "deadly bait luring wretched souls to their everlasting destruction".[62] He wrote a letter to the Duke of Longueville reminding him that the "allurements and delights of the world ... are so many sorceries, so many mortal poisons to draw you to perdition".[63]

Calvin followed Augustine in his belief that the life of the present world around us in contrast to the life of the city of God, was constituted and organised to cater for the love of self. The world outside of us, he reminded Madame de Cany, corresponds to the world such as we carry it within ourselves, before we are made again in his likeness. Because of this she can be free neither from the self nor the world unless both are renounced together.[64]

Calvin warns us also, as we approach the question of the enjoyment of the world, that our hearts and minds are naturally weak. We fail too often to restrain ourselves. Through our "depravity of nature" we have "violent and lawless impulses which war against God's control" and bring us in all our activity into "perpetual disorder and excess".[65] Moreover though God's good gifts are always intended to be like ladders by the use of which we can in gratitude mount up to thankful communion with himself, we, rather, with an innate tendency to drag everything downward to our own level, turn them into sepulchres in which we bury ourselves.[66]

---

cross, death, the love of God, humility ..."; cf. Hugo Rahner, *Saint Ignatius Loyola, Letters to Women*, Edinburgh-London, 1960, p. 461. Describing Richard Baxter, a contemporary writer said: "Self-denial and contempt for the world, were shining graces in him." Cf. John Tulloch, *English Puritanism and its Leaders*, Edinburgh, 1861, p. 389.   [61] *Inst.*, 3:10:3.   [62] *Comm. on Ps.*, 19:8.

[63] C.L. to Duke of Longueville, August 22, 1559.

[64] C.L. to Madame de Cany, June 8, 1549; cf. *Inst.*, 3:19:9.

[65] *Inst.*, 3:3:12; cf. 3:10:3.

[66] Cf. R. S. Wallace, *Calvin's Doctrine of the Christian Life*, pp. 53f, 106, 123, 126.

Thus our relationship with the world becomes the means of our destruction.

Calvin, in face of our weakness, calls on us to engage in the same decisive, violent and sudden inner conversion of heart and mind as was involved in the denial of self.[67] "There is no middle ground", writes Calvin; "either the world must become worthless to us, or hold us as bound by an intemperate love of it."[68] We may also have to deal ruthlessly, too, with the portion of the world allotted to us for our pleasure and enrichment. Dora Greenwell observed with regret that sometimes the "existing perversion and dis-organisation" in life brought about by sin is "so wide and searching that its remedy, to go deep enough to meet and conquer it, must attack the very fountains of life itself". We must sometimes "act as in warfare, carry fire and sword even into a friendly territory, making it bare and desolate, so that the invading enemy when he comes shall find nothing to maintain his forces".[69]

Dora Greenwell speaks of how sad it was to herself that such a painful operation should so often have to take place. She speaks strikingly, and perceptively too, of "a sadness in the history of every deep conversion to Christ — a foreseen pang of detachment, decay and death". But Calvin has another side to plead for. He insists that attaining this contempt for this world becomes almost a natural and easy operation if we can only train ourselves in meditating on the life to come. If heaven is our homeland, what else is the earth but our place of exile?[70] The Christian under those circumstances, as Neville Figgis observes, is "like the child who cannot play the games which commonly delight him, because he is consumed with excitement over the feast to which he is going".[71]

When it comes to instruction on how to enjoy the good things God provides for us Calvin assumes that we have been somehow enabled to detach ourselves and adopt an attitude

---

[67] *Abnegatio sui* and *contemptio mundi* always go together.
[68] *Inst.*, 3:9:2.
[69] Dora Greenwell, *Colloquia Crucis*, London, 1871, p. 36.
[70] *Inst.*, 3:9:4.
[71] J. Neville Figgis, *Civilisation at the Crossroads*, London, 1912, p. 141.

of true faith and gratitude. Under these conditions he allows us breadth and liberty in healthy experience.

He emphasises that God has put many things for us in the earth that have no particular usefulness and about which it must be assumed that they are there only for our enjoyment. "The natural qualities of things themselves demonstrate sufficiently to what end and how far we may enjoy them. Has the Lord adorned the flowers with the great beauty which presents itself to our eyes, the sweet odour which delights the sense of smell, and yet will it be unlawful for us to be moved by that beauty, or affected by this scent? What? Has he not so distinguished colours as to make some more lovely than others? What? Has he not given qualities to gold and silver, ivory and marble, which in our esteem makes them more precious than other metals or stones? Did he not, in short, give many things a value apart from their necessary use?"[72] He thought it necessary to quote only two passages of Scripture to support his argument. One is the verse about God's making every tree "pleasant to the sight and good for food". The other is the Psalmist's verse about "wine that gladdens the heart of man" and "oil that makes his face to shine".[73] In one of his sermons he expands on these texts, pointing out that when God could easily have given man only bread and water treatment, and could have made fruit to grow without any leaves or flowers, He has nevertheless added wine and the other luxuries to comfort and rejoice our hearts and our senses.[74]

Deliberately on this matter he shows more breadth than many of his predecessors. The text about God giving us all things richly to enjoy, Augustine had regarded as applying almost wholly to things eternal: "things eternal for enjoyment, the things temporal for use. Things temporal for travellers, things eternal for inhabitants." Calvin on the same text commented briefly: "His kindness extends far and wide beyond our necessity."[75]

[72] *Inst.*, 3:10:2.
[73] Gen. 2:9 and Ps. 104:15.
[74] *Serm. on Deut.*, 22:9-12, C.O., 28:36.
[75] Cf. Augustine, *Sermons on the New Testament* (Library of the Fathers), Oxford, 1854, vol. I, p. 119 and Calvin's *Comm. on 1 Tim.*, 6:17. While Augustine had

It is noticeable that Calvin gave some encouragement especially to people with opportunities for a high standard of living to enjoy it in a moderate way provided they cared for their poor neighbours. He pictured King Josiah who "ate and drank" and also "did justice and righteousness" as ideally illustrating the use of wealth. By his social righteousness, he showed forth the image of God. His "eating and drinking" meant that at the same time "he lived cheerfully, enjoyed prosperity, spent a peacable life".[76] Calvin therefore recognised that the divine law permitted the man who had wealth to live "more freely and sumptuously by special divine favour". He approved of the banquets that Job's sons and daughters gave for each other. Such good feasting, obviously approved by the Holy Ghost, was a sign of real friendship amongst them and was vastly preferable to the cat and dog fights indulged in by most families. Even in the case of churlish Nabal, the Carmelite, it was a good thing for him to invite his friends to a feast and regale them liberally.[77] People are allowed to live up to the privileges God gives them, each living in his station "slenderly, or moderately or plentifully".[78]

Calvin no doubt realised that in his day the humanistic culture and the commerce which he believed to make an important contribution to the wealth of society depended to a large extent on the liberal use and flow of wealth. The following comment seems directly to link up the old wealthy family with cultural pursuits: "certainly ivory and gold and riches are good creations of God, permitted, indeed destined by divine providence for the use of man. Nor was it ever forbidden to laugh or to be filled, or to add new possessions to old inherited ones, or to delight in music, or to drink wine."[79]

He did not, like many others who have shared his concern for individual sanctity, condemn expensive or even careful

---

conceded that we cannot use some things without a measure of enjoyment, he had nevertheless intended to lay down the rule: the world must be used, not enjoyed. Cf. *On Christian Doctrine*, ch. 4-5.

[76] *Comm. on Jer.*, 22:15.

[77] *Sermon on Job*, 1:2-5, C.O., 33:39f; *Homily on 1 Sam.*, C.O., 30:65-6. Cf. E. Doumergue, "Calvin: Epigone or Creator", in *Calvin and the Reformation*, pp. 48-9.

[78] *Inst.*, 3:19:1.   [79] *Inst.*, 3:19:9.

ornamentation in clothing. When he writes that the purpose of clothing "apart from necessity" is "comeliness and decency",[80] there is some breadth of meaning in the word "comeliness". In his comments on 1 Pet. 3:1-4 he condemned any extreme interpretation of Peter's warning and enlarged on this matter: clothing, he affirmed, can be elegant. The use of gold is not necessarily excluded. It can involve also the use of sumptuous material. After all, skill in making such came from God![81]

If he suspected, however, that ambition, pride, vanity or excess were involved in any kind of luxury or display, Calvin spoke in quite other language. When he heard about the splendour of the Royal Weddings of 1559 he wrote in a warning letter to the Duke of Longueville who had been present: "I am not so austere as to condemn the fêtes of princes, nor the rejoicings with which they celebrate their nuptials. But I am convinced, Monseigneur, that when you enter into reflection with yourself, having recalled your thoughts from the pomp, vanities and excesses by which they may have been led astray for a moment, you will pronounce these things a gulf of ruin and disorder."[82]

Calvin insists that our approach to this world must in no way be combined with, or result in, any ingratitude to God for all the good things with which he has always intended that our life on earth should be full. The fault that prevents us from its legitimate enjoyment lies not essentially in the world but in ourselves and in an evil power that in no way belongs in its nature to this world. We must not regard earthly pleasures

[80] *Inst.*, 3:10:2.

[81] *Comm. on 1 Pet.*, 3:1-4. Wesley, with concern for the poor, condemned "costliness of apparel" as "directly and inevitably destructive of good works". We must not speculate, he argued, on why God puts precious stones in the natural world — why have so many poisons a place in creation? Cf. *Works*, vol. 9, pp. 47-9. Was he directly questioning Calvin's view? But Luther liked the gold and gems which Abraham sent to Rebekah, and approved of the "finery, banquets and merriment, of the feast Laban gave for her. Such things "attract young people to an honourable marriage". LW, 4:275-6.

[82] C.L. to Duke of Longueville, May 26, 1559. In his first sermon on Job 1:2-5, Calvin especially condemns banquets because people hardly ever indulge in them with moderation: "See what banqueting breeds. Inclined as men are to vice, it is impossible to avoid sin." Yet, he adds, that "God can remedy our infirmities", and that "the thing itself is good".

and indulgences as in themselves essentially evil. But we have to face the fact that the world does not present itself to us, nor can we ourselves approach the world, in the way God originally intended.

Calvin was concerned that we should always maintain liberty of conscience in our use and enjoyment of earthly things and pleasures. We do not decide what is right and wrong by simply following the customs of others or of the Church. In this matter we must not be brought back under the bondage of law. Life opens to many of us possibilities for the enjoyment of pursuits and pleasures that are neither commanded nor forbidden. The use and enjoyment of these things falls under the category of what is "indifferent". These things are matters not in themselves either righteous or corrupt, often having to do with man's physical rather than his spiritual life. In the use of such things we have to make our decisions before God, by faith, and often by ourselves.[83] We may sometimes have to compel ourselves deliberately to break through the restrictive and hampering man-made traditions by which the conscience is brought into bondage.[84]

When he engaged in such discussion Calvin nearly always asks us to remember how our behaviour is going to affect our neighbour, especially the weak one for whom Christ has died.[85] We must not revert to our self-love even in the name of our liberty before God. We can sum up his teaching the whole matter in a sentence of his own: 'Pleasure is indeed to be condemned, unless it be combined with the fear of God, and with the common benefit of humanity."[86]

[83] *Inst.*, 2:4:6; 3:19:6.
[84] *Inst.*, 3:19:7.
[85] *Inst.*, 3:19:10.
[86] *Comm. on Gen.*, 4:26.

CHAPTER 14

PASTORAL EXHORTATION AND ASSURANCE

The Call to Watchfulness and Discipline

THOUGH the bonds which unite the believer to Christ are eternal, in God's predestinating grace, Calvin warned people not to break these bonds, not to cast away divine grace, and plunge themselves into eternal ruin. Even though he taught that God's love holds on to us firmly, Madame de Rentigny is warned: "Beware . . . lest God who has retained you hitherto and still retains you, does not give you loose reins."[1]

We must train ourselves to be steadfast in "a hard, laborious, troubled life, a life full of many and various kinds of evils".[2] God tests us through time. "The patience enjoined us is not that of a year or two's duration but . . . we are called upon to keep our affections in suspense." It has to be "the business of our lives to acquiesce in all submissiveness and humility to his good pleasure".[3] Moreover Satan, who finds that often he cannot bring us down at one blow, has it as one of his prime devices to sap and destroy us by long lapse of time.[4] For those who fall through the lusts of youth, there is some hope that they will recover, but "he who through his whole life" has "hardened himself in contempt of God, can hardly ever be healed and be amended by correction".[5]

A friend once described the Reformer as "a bow always taut". He never seems to relax, and he gives warning about the dangers of doing so. "If we should relax ever so short a

---

[1] C.L., April 10, 1558. [2] Inst., 3:8:1.
[3] C.L. to Madame de Coligny, February 27, 1559.
[4] C.L. to the prisoners at Chambery, October 5, 1555.
[5] Comm. on Jer., 3:20.

time, all the knowledge we have acquired soon dwindles away. For we are so full of vanities and evil affections that this will very speedily corrupt the good seed which God has sown in us unless we be constantly intent on cultivating it, plucking up the evil, confirming the good."[6]

We have to engage, therefore, in constant warfare if we are to win through to the end. If God himself is doing battle on our side, then "we are called to combat ..."[7] and arm ourselves. If God offers us comfort and courage we, at the same time, must "take courage and continue resolute and magnanimous."[8] "Our progress is certain provided we keep following however faintly."[9]

It was characteristic of Calvin himself always to be full of burning enthusiasm, and we are not surprised to find him continually warning us against quenching the zeal God has given us and allowing it to grow cool.[10] He lamented that too many people become like Jonah for a time, cold and wet, when like Jeremiah we should have the continually burning heart.[11] He warns especially that if we ever have a good impulse, we must act upon it without a moment's delay or inevitably distractions will make us forget it,[12] or we will grow cold upon our good intention.[13] To those whose ardour has cooled even to a small degree, his advice is: "Let us then rouse the sparks of this fervour and let it inflame us, so that we may faithfully devote ourselves altogether to the service of God ... let us stimulate ourselves and may the power of the Holy Spirit be so revived, that we may to the end pursue the course of our office, and never stand still but assail the whole world."[14]

Calvin stressed the need for self-discipline as much as he did the need for community discipline. He pleads with Madame de Cany to engage herself to the end in the "study of

[6] C.L. to French Church at Antwerp, December 21, 1556.
[7] C.L. to Madame de Rentigny, December 8, 1557.
[8] *Comm. on Ps.*, 20:1.
[9] C.L. to Duchess of Ferrara, June 10, 1555.
[10] C.L. to Madame de Falais, October 14, 1543.
[11] *Comm. on Jer.*, 20:10.
[12] C.L. to a French Seigneur, October 18, 1548.
[13] C.L. to Madame de Budé, 1546.
[14] *Comm. on Jer.*, 20:10.

holiness".[15] This involves regular self-examination and self-correction: "You will find it to be of advantage to call yourself to account day by day, and while acknowledging your faults to groan within yourself and mourn over them before God so that your displeasure against whatsoever is evil may grow more intense."[16] We must control the mind, especially, by orienting it to God. Warning d'Andelot of the many troubles he is going to face, troubles brought by "many temptations from within" as well as by his enemies outside, he gives him this practical advice: "elevating your thoughts, learn to stop your ears against all the blasts of Satan . . . Learn to shut your eyes against all distractions. . . ." Especially in d'Andelot's case, succumbing to flattery was to be his great temptation. Calvin reminds him of how Moses in Egypt, as a young man "hardened himself" against such danger.[17]

We can each help and stimulate the other to this disciplined effort by mutually given encouragement. Calvin, like Martin Bucer, believed that within the Church it would be a good thing that people within groups should meet for mutual examination and strengthening.[18] He believed that people required to be challenged to attain Christian standards as much as they required to be comforted because of their shortcomings and sufferings. His own experience led him to regard our human nature as so weak that we require often to have the stern exhortations and warnings of the Gospel and the New Testament repeated to us over and over again by each other. "We give you the advice", he wrote to the Church in Paris, "by which we ourselves would wish to be modified and restrained under such circumstances."[19]

When he wrote a pastoral letter to the Duke of Longueville, he asked him not to find it strange "that I continue to exhort you several times . . . I trust that my diligence will not be disagreeable to you and that you will feel sufficiently convinced of the need you have of it amidst . . . many

[15] C.L. to Madame de Cany, January 8, 1549.
[16] C.L. to Mademoiselle de . . . , January 12, 1549.
[17] C.L. to D'Andelot, May 10, 1558.
[18] He arranged for the Pastors and Council in Geneva to have such meetings for mutual correction.
[19] C.L. to Church in Paris, September 16, 1557.

temptations. . . . I do not doubt that you desire to be fortified by good and holy admonitions to do your duty."[20]

Life before God

Calvin realised the dangers of a preoccupation with a personal holiness and salvation which was not primarily concerned with God's will and God's glory. When Cardinal Sadoleto wrote to woo the people of Geneva back to the Roman fold he seemed to concentrate too much on offering them personal salvation. Calvin was quick to reply: "It is not very sound theology to confine a man's thoughts so much to himself, and not to set before him, as the prime motive for his existence, zeal to illustrate the glory of God. For we are born first of all for God, and not for ourselves." Any true Christian, Calvin insisted, will see through, and avoid — the kind of piety which "keeps a man devoted to himself" and does not "arouse him to sanctify the name of God".[21]

Yet Calvin also pointed out that the Lord, "the better to recommend the glory of his name" has "united it indissolubly with our salvation". In all his exhortations to the personal discipline of making salvation sure, therefore, the central thrust of his message is always to call us to live before God and to seek, in everything we do, his glory alone. Though reference to our duty to the neighbour comes so often to prominence in Calvin's thought, he seems deliberately to ignore it in this discussion. After all, he points out, only from God alone can we receive health and righteousness, and only before God alone can all our self seeking and pride become broken. We must "resolve to hold our life only from him".[22] Therefore Madame de Rentigny must learn to groan "before God", and D'Andelot must learn to harden himself against the world "before God".

Life will often bring us into situations, Calvin believed, when no one else can be our witness and "God alone appears

[20] C.L. to Duke of Longueville, August 22, 1559.
[21] C.Tr., vol. I, pp. 33-4.
[22] C.L. to Mademoiselle de Longemeau, December 14, 1557. C.L. to Monsieur de Budé, June 19, 1547.

before us". Then there can be "no regard for men", and we must be satisfied with the judgment of God. These are the moments when we are challenged to orient our life entirely to God himself, and thus to discover where our life finds its meaning, and has its roots. "When we continue to cleave to God alone, we are, in a spiritual sense chaste, as he requires us to be; but when we seek our safety from this and that quarter we violate the fidelity we owe to God."[23] In his letters, in order to ensure this constant orientation to God in those he is encouraging, Calvin reverts often to the appeal to "maintain his glory seeing that we belong altogether in him". "Choose rather to irritate everyone against you", he wrote to Madame de Coligny, "in order to be well pleasing to him alone. ... It is but just that we should be dedicated to him who has ransomed us at such a price."[24] We must not think it a hardship to create enemies in order to maintain his glory.[25]

Calvin emphasises our need for the constant and careful study of holy Scripture. We are thus to be "daily taught in the school of Jesus Christ"[26] and receive the "instruction" which will fortify us.[27] Our faith and our power to utter confident prayer can soon wilt, unless we continually hear the Word of God. Diligence to receive, every day, instruction from God, will rekindle our love which otherwise will soon wax cold.[28] "The faithful feel that their hearts soon languish in prayer unless they are constantly stirring themselves up to it by new incitements. ... One must frequently lay on fuel in order to preserve a fire, so the exercise of prayer requires the aid of such help."[29] It is, moreover, especially the promises given to us by God in holy Scripture that are the fuel of prayer. The promises of the Word teach us what to pray for and encourage us to ask. "Let us learn", says Calvin, "that God in his

---

[23] *Comm. on Jer.*, 22:21, for above see *on Jer.*, 22:12.
[24] C.L., September 4, 1558.
[25] C.L. to D'Andelot, May 10, 1555.
[26] C.L., July 20, 1558. The Marchioness of Rothelin also has to become a pupil "in the school of the Son of God", C.L., January 5, 1558. Cf. *Comm. on Ps.*, 18:22.
[27] C.L., January 5, 1558.
[28] C.L. to Marchioness of Rothelin, January 5, 1558.
[29] *Comm. on Ps.*, 25:8.

promises is set before us as if he were a willing debtor." It is not in vain to require him to behave towards us a he has promised.[30] "True and earnest prayer" "proceeds ... from faith in the promises of God."[31]

Prayer proceeds also from a sense of our need.[32] "To seek when we feel the need of God's grace is nothing else but to pray."[33] As if we were like little infants turning to their one source of comfort, Calvin speaks of our "betaking ourselves to the bosom of God".[34] We are surely never meant to live in need of God himself when he has promised to satisfy us: "If you feel in yourself more weakness than is desirable, have recourse to him who has permitted that those who trust him shall be like a tree planted by the rivers."[35] Calvin found that in the book of Psalms prayer was often simply the pouring out of the heart to God with all its feelings expressed, in complaint, questioning, request, thanksgiving.[36] It is an "expression and manifestation of internal feeling before him who is the searcher of the heart".[37] In prayer therefore we "lay open before him our infirmities which we would be ashamed to confess before men".[38]

It is remarkable how often in his letters too, possibly remembering the inarticulate and burdened prayers of Jesus as he approached the grave of Lazarus, he refers to praying as a groaning — a groaning within ourselves, before God, for freedom — a groaning which God undoubtedly will listen to.[39] It is the Holy Spirit, he affirms, who "not only dictates our words, but also creates groanings in our hearts ... directs our hearts, and in a manner prays in us ... we cannot pray to God except he anticipates us by his own Spirit."[40]

---

[30] *Comm. on Ps.*, 119:58, *Sermon on Deut.*, 26:16-19, C.O., 28:292.
[31] I.C.P., p. xxxvii.
[32] *Ibid.*
[33] *Comm. on Jer.*, 29:13.
[34] *Comm. on Ps.*, 21:7.
[35] C.L. to Duchess of Ferrara, July 20, 1558.
[36] Cf. *Ps.*, 42:4, 62:8.
[37] *Inst.*, 3:20:29.
[38] I.C.P., p. xxxviii.
[39] Cf. C.L. to Mademoiselle de ..., January 12, 1549; to Duchess of Ferrara, June 10, 1555; to Melanchthon, June 28, 1545.
[40] *Comm. on Jer.*, 29:12.

It follows therefore that our prayers should have a personal spontaneity which is bound to find expression in their form as well as in their content. Since we ourselves must be open and honest, we have to "learn also that when we present ourselves before God, it is not to be done with the ornaments of artificial eloquence, for the finest rhetoric, the best grace which we can have before him consists in pure simplicity".[41] Calvin believed that as Christians we would always be able to find a true spontaneity and simplicity if we thus used the Psalms to help us to pray. Possibly the reason why Calvin did not write a book on private prayer or leave us a book of such personal prayers was because he believed that the book of Psalms could not be improved on for this purpose. He found that the Psalms always perfectly expressed the prayers, moods and feelings of his own heart. Indeed by using them he was helped to understand and know himself better, and he hoped that for other people they would also constitute the perfect prayer book.

Calvin taught that prayer was the "chief exercise of faith",[42] and that faith opens up the way to prayer. "When ... we approach God, faith goes before to illumine the way, giving us the full impression that he is our Father, then the gate is opened and we may converse freely with him and he with us."[43] This indeed is prayer — a conversation with God in freedom. And yet our prayers are acceptable to God only in so far as Christ sprinkles and sanctifies them with the perfume of his own sacrifice.[44] Jesus himself also prays for us by virtue of his sacrifice, makes our prayers heard, and secures their fulfilment. Calvin affirms that there is nothing inconsistent in our directing ourselves in prayer to the person of the Father, but he goes on to suggest that also "we may pray to Christ in truth and holiness" since he either brings us to the Father, or prepares for our coming to the Father, or can help us by his own might since all things are delivered into his hand.[45]

[41] *Comm. on Ps.*, 17:1.
[42] Cf., title to *Inst.*, 3:20.
[43] *Comm. on Ps.*, 18:6.
[44] *Comm. on Ps.*, 20:3.
[45] C.O., 10a:155-6.

We pray in the faith that our prayers cannot be in vain, "that God is not deceitful, that he does not delude nor beguile us with empty words, and that he does not magnify beyond all measure either his power or his goodness, but that whatever he promises in Word, he will perform in deed".[46] If he rejected our prayers God would, in a way, be denying his own nature. We must believe, therefore, that in some way and at some time, we will have the answer, though it may be not exactly as we had planned it.[47] What matters on our part is to acquire the habit of praying continually. If perseverance is required in any aspect of our life, it is especially desired in prayer. We may be faced with overwhelming discouragements, but the only answer to doubt or questioning can only be — more prayer and more discipline.[48]

If we trust God we will go on praying. If we cease to pray, it is a sure sign that we never had faith at all.[49] Yet we are sure to gain the prize by strenuous exertion, and as we pour out our requests our confidence in gaining them should increase.[50] We can anticipate the answer and give thanks as if it had already come, and the pouring out of our hearts can be a pouring out of thanksgiving.[51]

Though Calvin lays so much stress on prayer as an asking, on our part, for an answer on God's part, the unburdening of our hearts in his presence is essentially a means of fellowship with him. God does not need the information we bring to him. He does not need, even, to be prompted by us,[52] but he loves to have us come before him. The heart and goal of prayer is communion with God.

The Note of Triumphant Assurance

Luther's theology is often described, no doubt correctly, as a theology of the cross. The hiddenness of God's presence and

[46] *Comm. on Ps.*, 12:6.
[47] *Comm. on Ps.*, 65:3; *on 2 Cor.*, 12:8.
[48] C.L. to Mademoiselle de ..., January 12, 1549.
[49] *Comm. on Ps.*, 22:4.
[50] *Comm. on Ps.*, 10:13; I.C.P., p. xxxviii.
[51] *Comm. on Ps.*, 13:5.
[52] *Comm. on Ps.*, 17:9; *on Ps.*, 10:13.

power in our midst, and the often painful inward struggle of the believer as he holds on to assurance under the Word of God, are emphasised. When Dietrich Bonhoeffer described Christ's invitation to discipleship as a call to "come and die", he was certainly close to Luther.

Calvin, however, remaining systematically close to the Bible, often said to people, and with equal emphasis, "Come and live!" His theology is as much a theology of the resurrection as it is of the cross. It is true that the Christian, for him, lives continually under the shadow and power of the death of Jesus which enables him through the Spirit to mortify self-will and to submit to God in suffering as Jesus did. Yet we share Christ's resurrection life no less powerfully than we participate in his death. The evidence of such resurrection power may at times be obscure at present. For its fuller proof we have to wait for the final resurrection at the last day. Nevertheless faith has its proofs and the Christian lives triumphantly.

C. K. Barrett has given an accurate expression to Calvin's view in his exposition of a Pauline passage: "The manifestation of the life of Jesus, though perfect only in the resurrection at the end, is already begun, and shines through the sin and suffering of the present life — it appears even in the context of the flesh. Even our present self-centred, man-centred existence shows signs of the transforming power of the Spirit who brings freedom."[53]

It is in Calvin's work on the book of Psalms, on which he commented so autobiographically, that this aspect of his pastoral counselling is brought out most clearly. Many Psalms are about David's triumph in suffering. Therefore we should be radiant: "It would not be enough for God to take care of us and provide for our necessities unless, on the other hand, he irradiated us with the light of his gracious and reconciled countenance, and made us taste of his goodness. ... It is true and solid happiness to experience ... that we dwell in his presence."[54] When David said, "I shall be

---

[53] *Comm. on 2 Cor.*, London, 1973, p. 141. See R. S. Wallace, *Calvin's Doctrine of the Christian Life*, pp. 78-88.
[54] *Comm. on Ps.*, 21:6.

satisfied when I awake in thy likeness", he was not only thinking of the life to come but "he expected to experience in his heart a blessed joy *until* the life to come". This is not yet perfect but is a radiated peace and joy which can be called satisfaction.[55] He who has God has everything requisite to constitute a happy life.[56] This joy comes to us in "full and overflowing abundance".[57] It transports us. Calvin points out that David was "ravished with admiration" for the goodness which he had experienced, uses "rapturous language", had "marvellous and unexpected deliverances" in a context in which he expects us to be roused up to expect the same.[58]

We have selected only a few of many like citations simply from Calvin's comments on the first book of Psalms. Of course the darkness and the danger is also there too, and the battle is long and hard, but the way to fresh triumph and light is always kept open. "God does not suffer the faith of his servants to faint or fail, nor does he suffer them to desist from praying; but he keeps them near to him by faith and prayer"[59] and "though faith does not gain the victory at the first encounter, but after receiving many blows, and after being exercised by many tossings, she at length comes forth victorious".[60]

The five student martyrs in Lyons as they were facing death after their long ordeal wrote to Calvin and the pastors of Geneva a letter expressing their personal confession of faith. It could have been written by Calvin himself for it is in many ways a perfect utterance of his own personal outlook in his language:

> Very dear brothers in our Lord Jesus Christ, since you have been informed of our captivity and of the fury which drives our enemies to persecute and afflict us, we felt it would be good to let you know of the liberty of our spirit and of the wonderful assistance and consolation which our good Father and Saviour gives us in these dark prison cells, so that you may participate not only in

[55] *Comm. on Ps.*, 17:15.   [56] *Comm. on Ps.*, 16:7.   [57] *Comm. on Ps.*, 9:2.
[58] *Comm. on Ps.*, 31:19.   [59] *Comm. on Ps.*, 10:17.   [60] *Comm. on Ps.*, 22:1.

our affliction of which you have heard, but also in our consolation, as members of the same body who all participate in common both in the good and in the evil which comes to pass. For this reason we want you to know that although our body is confined here between four walls, yet our spirit has never been so free and so comforted, and has never previously contemplated so fully and so vividly as now the great heavenly riches and treasures, and the truth of the promises which God has made to his children; so much so that we seem not only to believe and hope in them but even to see them with our eyes and touch them with our hands, so great and remarkable is the assistance of our God in our bonds and imprisonment. So far, indeed, are we from wishing to regard our affliction as a curse of God, as the world and the flesh wish to regard it, that we regard it rather as the greatest blessing that has ever come upon us, for in it we are made true children of God, brothers and companions of Jesus Christ, the Son of God, and are conformed to his image; and by it the possession of our eternal inheritance is confirmed to us.... We therefore praise God with all our heart and give Him undying thanks that He has been pleased to give us by His grace not only the theory of His Word but also the practice of it, and that He has granted us this honour — which is no small thing for vessels so poor and fragile and mere worms creeping on the earth — by bringing us out before men to be His witnesses and giving us constancy to confess His name and maintain the truth of His holy Word before those who are unwilling to hear it, indeed, who persecute it with all their force — to us, we say, who previously were afraid to confess it even to a poor ignorant labourer who would have heard it eagerly.

We pray you most affectionately to thank our good God with us for granting us so great a blessing, so that many may return thanks to Him, beseeching Him that, as He has commenced this work in us, so He will complete it, to the end that all glory may be given to Him, and that, whether we live or die, all may be to His honour and glory, to the edification of His poor Church, and to the advancement of our salvation. Amen.[61]

These were the heights to which a true "Calvinist" could attain at times, especially under persecution, and this letter helps us to understand the effect and spread of his teaching.

[61] R.C.P., pp. 191-2.

PART III

THE THEOLOGIAN

CHAPTER 15

THE NATURE AND PURSUIT
OF THEOLOGY

AS the Reformation became established, and spread over
Europe, it was in the realm of theology that Calvin made
his most important contribution. Philip Melanchthon, indeed, called him, "the theologian". Of Luther, T. M.
Lindsay remarks that "No great leader ever flung about wild
words in such a reckless way". There was a need, after him,
for Calvin, who, as one of his admirers put it, never in his life
uttered one loose word or sentence.

When he became prominent in the expanding movement
people were bewildered by the sheer profusion of thought
which had arisen within its ranks. Here and there the new
enthusiasm of those who had acquired only a partial
knowledge of Holy Scripture was tending to produce a one-
sided emphasis on what was unessential to the faith and
damaging to the growing Church. Wise, decisive and
moderate leadership was required. What was of essential
importance needed to be distinguished from trivial detail,
what was good from what was bad. Calvin clarified for his
contemporaries the meaning of the movement in which they
had been called by God to take part, the issues that were at
stake, and the importance of their own contribution. At a
committee meeting where people for a long time have been
unable to find the proper formula or phrase or solution,
suddenly someone can come out with the exact word, the
exact expression, the way to take, with such finality and
precision that with total agreement further discussion quickly
ends. He did this kind of thing for perplexed individuals and
groups of people around him time and again. Above all, he
enabled the men and women of his generation, to see within
Scripture what many may have looked at, but had never

recognised. His theology was a theology of the Word of God. It can be argued that his contemporary influence was as much due to the circulation of his *Commentaries* as to the *Institutes*, which after all he regarded simply as a key to help people to know what to look for in the scriptures.[1] His chief aim, therefore, as a theologian was simply to give a faithful and systematic account of what he himself found there.

He held that the revelation given to him through Holy Scripture is the only reliable source of our knowledge of God. Though nature also reveals God, and all men and women have a natural instinct for religion, yet our human perversity prevents us from being able to profit from what nature presents to us.[2] We must therefore turn to the revelation given by God to his prophets and servants in the Old Testament, and to the Apostolic witness to Christ in the New Testament. The Holy Scriptures, he believed, were inspired, indeed dictated by God. Their statements, stories and truths must be regarded as having infallible authority. A theologian, therefore, is, and must always remain, a man before the Bible — the "school of the Holy Spirit".[3] We must not "speak or guess or even seek to know . . . anything except what has been imparted to us by God's word".[4]

Holy Scripture, indeed, challenges us as the burning bush did Moses, to turn aside, ponder and reflect.[5] It demands our interpretation so that its manifold wisdom can be displayed in all its true wealth, beauty and clarity. Calvin believed that the unity and rationality of God himself must inevitably be reflected in the Word he has spoken. We ourselves, therefore, must try to discern and to reveal to others the order and system which lie hidden amidst the profusion of its stories and statements, and the apparent confusion of its truths. He found joy in doing so. "How wonderful it is", he writes, "when we

[1] Cf. *Inst.* — Introduction to the 1559 edition.

[2] *Inst.*, 1:3:1, 1:3:3, 1:5:2, 1:15:14.

[3] *Inst.*, 3:21:3.

[4] *Inst.*, 1:14:4; 3:21:2. This does not mean that the natural can in no way become a source of inspiration to the theologian. There is a suggestion in the *Institutes* that Scripture is like a pair of spectacles which enable those who are old or of weak sight to read distinctly what is written in the volume of nature, and Calvin frequently recommends that we meditate on the glory of the created world; cf. *Inst.*, 1:6:1.

[5] *Comm. on Exod.*, 3:3.

are given confirmation through more intense study, of how admirably the economy of the divine wisdom contained in it is arranged and disposed; how perfectly free the doctrine is from everything that savours of earth; how beautifully it harmonizes in all its parts, how many other qualities give an air of majesty to its composition".[6]

Calvin recognised that at the heart of the revelation about which the Prophets and Apostles wrote, there was, for them, a personal encounter with the Word of God himself, the second person of the Trinity. Even though they may also have been recipients of truths and doctrines, the Biblical witnesses also knew themselves as men who have been encountered by God himself in personal love and majesty.[7]

We ourselves must recognise that the Holy Scripture is given by God to us today not simply to present us with ideas and statements, but also to introduce us to the presence of the living God. It was his own experience and conviction that, as God drew near and revealed himself to those to whom he spoke in Biblical times, so he also draws near to us today when his Word is preached within the Church and the Sacraments are administered. He uses the audible human speech and visible actions which are offered in the service of his name, to veil his presence and communicate his grace — just as he used the symbols and signs of the older dispensation. Thus today God "appears in our midst", "allures us to himself", "displays and unfolds his power to save".[8] For Calvin therefore Holy Scripture, as the Word of God to us, is not only an infallible source of true doctrine but also an instrumental means of God's self-revelation. The theologian today, in his approach to Holy Scripture, must seek to find himself, and must regard himself as one brought into communion and confrontation with the Lord himself.

Calvin was convinced that what hinders the attainment of truth in theology is not the difficulty or obscurity of the given revelation or even of the Bible, but the perversity of the

---

[6] *Inst.*, 1:8:1.
[7] *Inst.*, 1:3:1 (a section entitled in the most recent translation: *Man before God's majesty*).
[8] *Inst.*, 4:1:5.

human mind. Therefore he believed that only as the theologian engages in his work in the presence of the living God himself can he hope to overcome his natural inner bias to falsehood, and thus fulfil his quest for the truth.

One of the "five points" which were listed by the Synod of Dort (1619) as being basic to "Calvinism", was the "total depravity of human nature". Calvin himself did not use this phrase, and it can be applied to his own teaching only if it is interpreted with caution. He did not believe that the fall has deprived mankind of all capacity to do or create anything admirable or worthwhile. As we have seen he was always prepared to recognise and encourage whatever was noble, great, or heroic in the natural life of man. Yet he denied the teaching of some of the Fathers of the Church that the fall merely deprived man of certain "supernatural" abilities, leaving his natural gifts and ability uncorrupted. He insisted that the corruption due to the fall is "diffused in all parts of the soul, and that sin overturns the whole man".[9] It vitiates to some extent even the best of these natural virtues and capacities which give him such nobility in distinction from the animal creation and are signs of his having been made in the image of God. Each man carried within him a smouldering ember of evil, a "concupiscence", a tendency to blind self-love[10] which marks everything he does, and which finds its expression chiefly in pride. Though God's image is not totally destroyed in man, yet it is so corrupted that whatever remains is frightful deformity. His nature has become so perverse that he "cannot be moved, driven or led except to evil".[11] He is under a necessity of sinning. His perversity is continually prompting him to new kinds of evil — "just as a burning furnace gives forth flames and sparks, or water ceaselessly bubbles up from a spring".[12] In place of wisdom, virtue, holiness, truth and justice, man produces "the most filthy plagues, blindness, impotence, impurity, vanity and injustice".[13]

[9] *Inst.*, 2:1:8–9.   [10] *Inst.*, 2:1:8, 2:1:2, 3:3:10.
[11] *Inst.*, 1:15:4, 2:3:5.   [12] *Inst.*, 2:1:8.
[13] *Inst.*, 2:1:5. Calvin in his teaching on original sin follows Augustine closely. Thomas Merton has more recently described what is wrong with us as "a basic

This concupiscence perverts even the religious life and Christian service of the believer, and since it "reigns in the very citadel of the mind',[14] resistant to the intake of truth, it has to be faced and contended with especially by the theologian in the pursuit of his calling. Calvin frequently reminds us that we all have within us a "lust to devise new and strange religions".[15] We tend to seek for what does not exist, and thus fail to find what does exist.[16] Most dangerous of all is our tendency to drag God down to the level of our own minds, and our logic, and to imprison him within our own subjectivity.[17]

How then can the theologian discipline the mind and control this inner perversity so that his theology becomes an expression of truth instead of falsehood? Calvin at this point speaks of the power of communion with the living God himself, and of the possibility that in his presence our minds can be brought to complete subjection to the truth under the influence of the Holy Spirit. When Daniel had the "great vision" of the man clothed in linen, he lost all his own personal strength and self-confidence. Before God himself our mental resistance gives way and our pride and carnal disposition become "reduced to nothing".[18] The knowledge of God which comes to us under these circumstances is a knowledge in which the human mind is passive — a knowledge impressed on it by what is contemplated. He speaks of the mind as being "beamed by the light of the Holy Spirit", of the Spirit as making entry for the Word of God, of the mind as "absorbing the Word", and of becoming "endowed with thought".[19]

Obviously, then, in deciding on his theological method, Calvin tried to focus his mind on the objective content of the revelation facing him. He found that to fulfil such a task

---

antagonism between the self and God, due to an estrangement from him by perverse attachment to a 'self' which is mysterious and illusory". "Even the best men . . . when they return to a frank and undisguised self-awareness, confront themselves as naked, insufficient, disgruntled and malicious beings." *Contemplative Prayer*, London, 1973, pp. 122–3.

[14] *Inst.*, 2:1:9.   [15] *Inst.*, 1:6:3.   [16] *Inst.*, 3:23:2.

[17] Cf. R. S. Wallace, *Calvin's doctrine of Word and Sacrament*, p. 78.

[18] *Common Dan.*, 10:8.   [19] *Inst.*, 3:2:34, 3:2:36.

requires disciplined thought. In the opening chapter of the
Institutes he spoke of how through our experience of the
presence and Word of God we begin to attain a true self-
knowledge, and are inwardly enriched by the impressions
and feelings which are now given to us. He admitted that at
times he found it difficult to disentangle our knowledge of
God from our knowledge of ourselves. Yet from the beginning
he tried to avoid the theological method which would begin
with the analysis of our self-consciousness (or our "God-
consciousness") and would give shape to doctrine as the soul
reflects on its own experience. Indeed he found himself
compelled by the very nature of his experience to look
outward, away from self. He speaks at times of how in the
presence of the living Word of God, our minds are opened
and lifted up to find a new centre of gravity. Luther had
already often given expression to the power of faith in this
connection in unforgettable language: "And this is the reason
why our theology is certain", he wrote, "it snatches us away
from ourselves and places us outside ourselves, so that we do
not depend on our own strength, conscience, experience,
person or works but depend on that which is outside of
ourselves and places us outside of ourselves, that is, on the
promise and truth of God, which cannot deceive".[20] Calvin
echoed the same thing in less dramatic style: He pictures the
mind of man as rising up and going "beyond itself" as it
attains the knowledge given to its faith. We do not possess the
things of our salvation, he affirmed, unless we can "transcend
the reach of our own intellect and raise our perception above
all worldly objects and, in short surpass ourselves".[21]

It is at this point that we can understand most fully what
Calvin meant when he said "All right knowledge of God is
born of obedience".[22] He speaks at times of a compulsive
pressure on the mind as it feels itself under the impact of
revelation. We become "profoundly affected" as "we feel
within ourselves the force of it".[23] He confesses that his mind
is not simply "overwhelmed" but also "conquered". This

[20] L.W., 27:387.
[21] *Inst.*, 3:2:14, 3:2:41.
[22] *Inst.*, 1:6:2.   [23] *Inst.*, 1:5:9.

suggests that the mind is taken under control by its object, as it tries to shape its new thoughts. It follows in its thinking the patterns inherent in the revelation before it. "The pious mind", writes Calvin, "does not dream up for itself any god it pleases, but contemplates the one and only true God. And it does not attach to him whatever it pleases, but is content to hold him as he manifests himself; furthermore the mind always exercises the utmost diligence and care not to wander astray, or rashly and boldly to go beyond his will."[24] As C. C. J. Webb puts it: "The mind is so completely informed by its object that there is as little as possible in the notion we have of the object which belongs to our way of apprehending it and not really to the object itself."

This means that as Calvin in his theological work tried to take account of all the Biblical texts before him, all the historical events and oracles through which God revealed himself and his will, he never forgot that the object of his theology was the one to whom they bore witness. Therefore as he dealt with the texts which occupied his mind and sought to compare one with another, to interrelate the themes they discussed, and to give his thinking direction and coherence, he had to penetrate beyond the words of the writers to the reality to which they witnessed, and to bring his mind under the compelling power which had originally inspired them. He sought to allow his mind to be taken up by faith into the Word itself, with its own shaping power, and to become penetrated by it.[26] It has to be noted that the true knowledge of ourselves, which is given to us along with the knowledge of God, also requires in the course of theological study to be investigated in its due place.[27] Yet when Calvin deals with the self-knowledge given to us through the Word he concen-

---

[24] *Inst.*, 1:2:2.

[25] *Problems in the Relation of God to Man*, London, 1915, p. 45.

[26] On this point see, e.g., T. F. Torrance, *Belief in Science and the Christian Life*, Edinburgh, 1980, pp. 4, 9. *Theology in Reconstruction*, London, 1965, pp. 33, 95–6. Simone Weil in *Waiting upon God*, p. 72 writes of "attention" which she defines as an act of "suspending our thought, leaving it detached, empty, and ready to be penetrated by the object. . . . All our thought should be empty, waiting, not seeking anything but already to receive in its naked truth the object which should penetrate it." [27] Cf. *Inst.*, 1:1:3.

trates on the teaching of Holy Scripture as a guide to our understanding of our own inner experience.

We have to be cautious, therefore, when we apply the word "systematic" to the mind and thought of Calvin. For a thinker to discover definite forms and shapes within what has been a seemingly incoherent mass of inspired thoughts and utterances, and for him to be able to give these new and genuine expressions in a convincing order, does not necessarily imply that Calvin's is a logical and systematising mind forcing its own principles and currents of reasoning on the data before him to give it shape imposed from without. It simply means that he himself tried to live and work before God, and that he had a mind sensitive to the realities of the world of life and thought around him. The "beautiful" order[28] in which Calvin was able to cast his thought was an order which with all the artistry and scientific skill of a good theologian, he found concealed in the revelation which had come to him. He had delight and joy in faithfully preserving it as he brought it to light. Calvin certainly brought precise and exact thinking into the decisions he made and the work he did. But it was thinking done by a man whose mind had been totally "subdued" and "made tractable"[29] under the impact of the Word of God. It has been argued that those who subjected Reformed theology to logical thinking and to the basic principles of their own minds, were the later successors of Calvin and of Luther too, the men especially of the third generation.

If we are to understand Calvin's aim and purpose as a theologian more fully, we must also take account of what can be called a "mystical" element in his description of his own experience under the word of God — an experience which he believed was to be shared by all his fellow Christians since he found it described so often in Holy Scripture. He refers frequently in his writings to the penetrating and comprehensive power of faith, through the Spirit — its ability to soar beyond the reach of human understanding and to contem-

[28] Cf. *Inst.*, 1:8:1.

[29] See Calvin's account of his conversion in his Introduction to his *Commentary on the Psalms*.

plate God himself.[30] Holy Scripture, for Calvin, was not only the means by which God himself seeks to draw near to us so that we can experience his presence and hear his voice, it is also the door through which our minds can become lifted up to be given the same kind of vision which at times characterised the Biblical writers themselves. Faith thus enables us through the Word and Spirit to grasp in vision much more than can be immediately comprehended by the understanding. "What our mind embraces by faith is in every way infinite",[31] he wrote. He spoke of our receiving the eye to contemplate what cannot be reached by normal ways of thought, of a knowledge (*scientia*) which is superior to all understanding (*notitia*), and unreachable by the acuteness of our intellect.[32] The theologian must seek to grapple in his mind with what faith has thus seen. He must expect clarification to follow vision, as Christ demonstrated when he cured the blind man at Bethsaida.[33] His theology can therefore be described as "faith seeking understanding".

Calvin was always aware of the inadequacy of his language and thought as he tried to fulfil his task as a theologian. He knew that he could not do justice to "so great a mystery" as the Gospel presents. He confessed such feelings especially when he tried to grapple with the mystery of the Lord's Supper. "Although my mind can think beyond what my tongue can utter, yet even my mind is conquered and overwhelmed by the magnitude of the thing."[34] He quoted Hilary, confessing that he shrank from submitting to the peril of human speech what ought to have been kept with reverence within the mind.[35] He realised that there were many features in the order and arrangement of his doctrines which even after his best efforts inevitably appeared to contradict human logic. Yet he felt challenged to try both to understand and describe, and he believed he could be of service to the Church by giving himself to such a task. "I will

---

[30] I have gone carefully into this aspect of Calvin's experience in my article on "Calvin's Approach to Theology" in *The Challenge of Evangelical Theology*, ed. Cameron, Rutherford House, Edinburgh, 1987.

[31] *Inst.*, 3:2:14.

[32] *Comm. on Eph.*, 3:18; cf. *Inst.*, 3:2:14, 3:2:34.

[33] Mark 8:22–6.   [34] *Inst.*, 4:17:7.   [35] *Inst.*, 1:13:5.

give a summary of my views" he resolved, "I have no doubt as to its truth. I am confident that it will not meet disapproval from the pious heart." He believed that, like Paul, he would be helped by prayer and the teaching of the Holy Spirit.[36]

Calvin did not approach his task, however, as a solitary scholar of the Bible, with mystical tendencies, concerned to clarify his own vision of God, even for the sake of teaching others. For him theology was Church theology. The Church in his time was faced with temptation to compromise with the truth under pressure, sometimes from the world outside, and sometimes from its own inner movements of thought. He saw too many theologians in his day who tended to keep themselves apart from the everyday struggles of the Church, and he was suspicious that some in his day engaged in theological teaching and discussion simply because they loved to talk and be heard. "It is easy for a man within the shady precincts of the schools to be a ready talker." "Many rush to be teachers", he wrote, "and there is hardly one who is not anxious to be listened to."[37]

In his personal account of his early career, Calvin speaks of his desire, as his student days ended, for a cloistered life. He tried at first to confine himself to library work but his task as a teacher was thrust upon him by those who came around "thirsting for knowledge". He finally found himself importuned by Farel to work in Geneva.[38] A theologian, he believed, must leave, "purposeless . . . speculative study" in order to "labour in the word and doctrine".[39] Labour, he himself, certainly did. In a letter written to Farel during his Strasbourg ministry, Calvin described how a messenger arrived to receive some material for the printer when he was not quite ready for him: "I had about twenty leaves to look through. I had then to lecture and preach, to write four letters, make peace between some persons who had

---

[36] *Inst.*, 4:17:7 and *Comm. on Eph.*, 3:18. Mediaeval mystics were sometimes suspicious that theological "speculation" would lead to loss of the power to appreciate divine things by contemplation. Others believed that intellectural clarification would lead to deeper vision.

[37] *Comm. on Jer.*, 1:6, cf. James 3:1, *Inst.*, 3:12:1.

[38] *Comm. on I Tim.*, 5:17.

[39] *Comm. on Jer.*, 1:6, *Inst.*, 3:12:1; cf. James 3:1.

quarrelled with each other, and answer more than ten people who came to me for advice." Fortunately, he was able to add, it was the worst day of the whole year! He wrote to Farel the same day and asked to be forgiven for his brevity.[40]

He had many more such days, later on in Geneva. When his writing was interrupted by callers pressing him with pastoral and city concerns, his custom was to stop dictating to his secretary and give the interview. It was noticed that after the break he was able to resume where he had left off speaking without any gap in the thread of the discourse. Illness was almost the only thing that diverted him from his work, though he allowed himself to be interrupted by callers more readily than by his sicknesses. It was only when it was impossible for any human being to stand that he submitted to lying down. He once took ill in the pulpit, paused and tried to finish his sermon after they passed up to him a folding chair, but he had to give in and submit to be carried home. "When we think of repose", he wrote, "let us only look up to heaven."

Theology, he believed, had a normative function in Church life. The theologian was a doctor of the Church called into a position of leadership in its thinking, and charged with the pastoral care of the flock as a whole. He must seek to safeguard the "unerring standard both of our speaking and thinking about God" which "must be derived from Scripture".[41] He must seek "by simple and accurate explanation to render Christian doctrine more and more plain and clear to men, and rid their minds of vague causes of discord".[42] It was important therefore, that the theological teachers of the Church always in touch with its thought, and aware of what is being said in the pulpits, should both criticise error and listen to new truth from the Word which might help to reform the accepted faith at different points. There is a need here for love, unity and willingness to reform.

The theologian must also give leadership when the moral and spiritual struggles of the times demanded that the

---

[40] C. L. to Farel, 20 April 1539, and to Prince Porcien May 1563. Calvin's fourth lecture on Jeremiah closed early with the remark: "I wish I could proceed further, but I have business to which I was called even before the lecture."

[41] *Inst.*, 1:6:3. [42] *Inst.*, 4:17:25.

Church should confess its faith in public statement, in order to make its mind and attitude clear on important issues. "How, indeed, can this faith, which lies buried in the heart within, do otherwise than break forth in . . . confession?", Calvin wrote to Luther who himself had written, "A man becomes a theologian by living, by dying and by being damned".[43]

Calvin therefore felt that the theologians of his age whose views deserved to be listened to with greatest respect were those who had proved the truth of their theology by martyrdom. In Crespin's *History of Martyrs* there is a remarkable passage in a letter from him to some believers who, suffering for their faith had written to him asking for his judgment on their creed — whether its theology was correct or required modification. Calvin's reply shows clearly how little he cared about exactitude in an utterance of faith, as long as it was an expression of the boldness and devotion of heart inspired by the Spirit as a living witness to its times. "I do not send you such a confession of faith as our good brother required of me, for God will render that which he enables you to frame, according to the will of the Spirit imparted to you, far more profitable than any which might be suggested to you by others. Even when desired by some of our brethren who shed their blood for the glory of God, to revise and correct the Confession which they had made, I was very glad to see it that I might receive edification therefrom; but I would not add or diminish a single word, thinking that any alteration would have diminished the authority and efficacy, which ought to be attributed to the wisdom and constancy which plainly proceed from the Spirit of God."[44]

For Calvin the first virtue required of a theologian in his day was not learning, or precise doctrinal correctness, but courage and loyalty to the truth. He could not therefore for a moment bear to see or hear it denied or distorted by anyone without going to its defence. "When I see the heavenly doctrine of Christ, of which he has pleased to make me a minister, everywhere contemptuously outraged, how dis-

[43] C. L. to Luther, 21 Jan., 1545; cf. Luther W. A. 5:63:29.
[44] Quoted by P. Henry, *op. cit.*, vol. I, p. 295.

graceful it would be for me to hold my peace."[45] He once in a letter reproached Melanchthon for his slowness to declare his mind and take a side on an important theological issue. "While, however, you dread, as you would some hidden rock, to meddle with this question from the fear of giving offence, you are leaving in perplexity and suspense very many persons who require from you somewhat or a more certain sound, on which they can repose; and besides, as I remember I have sometimes said to you, it is not over-creditable to us, that we refuse to sign, even with ink, that very doctrine which many saints have not hesitated to leave witnessed with their blood."[46]

The zeal with which Calvin always threw himself into whatever task or struggle faced him in the political or church situation of the day was matched by the intense fervour of devotion which marked first of all his inner struggle: to grasp and clarify within his own mind the Word that God was speaking to his generation through Holy Scripture.

Theology for Calvin, was always an affair of the heart. Christianity, he insisted "is a doctrine not of the tongue but of the life and is not apprehended merely by the intellect and memory, like other sciences, but is received only when it possesses the whole soul, and finds its seat and habitation in the innermost recesses of the heart".[47] Even Plato groping in his darkness felt "ravished" by his idea of the beautiful! "How then is it possible", asked Calvin, "to know God and yet be touched with no feelings?" The same Spirit who enlightens our minds when God is known also inspires our hearts with "an affection corresponding to our knowledge".[48]

Moreover, the Word of God which to faith comes so often as a word of promise addressing a "thou" is a challenge to seek more and more, both in friendship and in vision, of what is already given. It therefore evokes on our part ardent

[45] C. L. to the Pastors of Bern, May 1555.
[46] C. L. to Melanchthon, 3 Aug., 1557.
[47] *Inst.*, 3:6:4; cf. 3:2:8.
[48] *Comm. on 1 John*, 2:3. Calvin expected his readers to share the same "zeal for piety" with which he himself was inspired (*Inst.*, 4:17:43). And he continually invites them to share his own inner experience of what he has seen; cf., e.g., *Inst.*, 4:17:4, and 7.

seeking as well as personal trust. "To believe with the whole heart", he wrote", "is not to believe Christ perfectly, but only to embrace him from the heart with a sincere mind, not to be filled with him, but with ardent affection to hunger and thirst and sigh after him."[49] Therefore the theological quest involves the theologian not simply in an effort to know about God but also in a growing desire for union and communion with God himself. Even as we meditate, for example, on the nature of the Trinity we are reminded by Calvin that God offers himself to our faith not only to be heard and trusted, but to be contemplated, and we are urged to "look upon the one God, to unite with him, and to cleave to him".[50] The heart of the theologian, is thus continually lifted above the level of objective study.

The place of "meditation" in the theological task should be noted. "The love of Christ", wrote Calvin, "is held out to us to meditate on day and night and to be wholly immersed in. He who holds to this alone has enough. Beyond it there is nothing solid, nothing useful, nothing, in short, that is right and sound."[51] This "meditation" (which for Calvin was meant to play a part in the life of the ordinary Christian) involved not only dwelling "long, seriously and faithfully" on the subject matter of the faith and "turning it over in our minds"[52] but also at the same time the kindling of the desire for what is before our thought. "We have to pour into the heart what the mind has imbibed, for the Word of God is not received by faith if it merely flutters in the brain."[53] "The intellect", said Calvin, "is the guide and ruler of the soul . . . the will always follows its bidding, and waits for its decision in matters of desire."[54]

The theologian must expect to make progress in this inner quest. "As soon as the least particle of faith is instilled in our minds we begin to contemplate the face of God, peaceful, serene and showing favour towards us. We see him far off indeed, but still so clearly that we know ourselves to be in no way deluded. When the more we advance (and we ought

[49] *Inst.*, 4:14:8; cf. *Comm. on Acts*, 8:3.
[50] *Inst.*, 1:13:2, 1:13:16.   [51] *Comm. on Eph.*, 3:18.
[52] Cf. *Inst.*, 1:14:21.   [53] *Inst.*, 3:2:36.   [54] *Inst.*, 1:15:7.

assiduously to do so) making steady progress, then our view of things becomes closer and more sure, and as it continues he is made even more familiar to us."[55] The prayer which his search after God continually inspires, passes into adoration. He finds that his "mental powers are held in wondering suspense".[56] He finds himself so overwhelmed by the greatness and holiness before him that all thought of investigation ceases and he can only adore.[57]

Blending with his devotional fervour was also the desire for the consummation of those experiences which we have referred to as mystical. These gave Calvin a passion to see and understand more of what he had already been lifted up in heart and mind to contemplate, to taste more of what he had already been given. All this enables us to place Calvin in his theological quest among those who found themselves, as a recent author put it, "gripped by an almost biological hunger for fulfilment — for that beatific vision of God, of which faith is the earthly bait".[58]

After all, for Calvin, the whole of the Christian life was to be lived as "nothing more than a meditation on immortality".[59]

Speaking of the main characteristics of monastic prayer Thomas Merton writes: "The most important need in the Christian world today is this inner truth nourished by the spirit of contemplation: the praise and love of God, the longing for the coming of Christ, the thirst for the manifestation of God's glory, his truth, his justice, his Kingdom in the world. These are all characteristically contemplative and eschatological aspirations of the human heart and the very essence of monastic prayer."[60] He here describes quite precisely the characteristics that mark Calvin as a theologian immersed also in the world of his day.

[55] *Inst.*, 3:2:19.
[56] *Inst.*, 1:5:9.
[57] *Brève Instruction Chrétienne 1537*, 1:3; cf. Leclerq, *op. cit.*, pp. 262–4.
[58] M. D. Chenu, *Is Theology a Science?*, New York, 1964, p. 30.
[59] *Brève Instruction Chrétienne*, 1537, 1:1.
[60] *Op. cit.*, p. 144.

CHAPTER 16

A THEOLOGY: CATHOLIC, REFORMED AND OPEN — CENTRAL ISSUES

(A) The Person of Christ

CALVIN'S ecumenical concern was reflected in the formation of his theological thought. He kept in constant touch with his contemporaries, and not only pled to be listened to, but sought to be guided by their advice,[1] and he did not hesitate to borrow from them. "God has never so blessed his servants that each possessed full and perfect knowledge of their subject",[2] he wrote. In 1653 Thomas Cartwright, the Puritan, wrote in response to an inquiry about the study of Divinity that the writings of other famous men of the age, e.g. Bucer, need not be read if the student confines his attention to Calvin, who "hath in a manner taken that which is fittest in them".[3]

With the same openness he learned from the Church Fathers of whom, like most of his fellow Reformers, he had a massive knowledge. H. Quistorp notes that even in his earliest work *Psychopannychia*, "Calvin's Catholic tendency is clearly reflected in his uncritical acceptance of Church tradition in the form of quotations from the Fathers which are placed in a subordinate position to proof from Scripture".[4] His later work at times abounds in such quotations, especially of course, from Augustine. Even when he does not quote he borrows their thought and language freely. Anyone who becomes intimately acquainted with the *Institutes* and after-

[1] Cf. C. L. to Seigneurs of Bern, 15 Feb. 1555.
[2] Dedicatory Letter to Simon Grynaeus in *Comm on Romans*.
[3] Quoted by A. F. Scott Pearson, *Thomas Cartwright and Elizabethan Puritanism, 1535–1603*, Cambridge, 1925, p. 226.
[4] *Calvin's Doctrine of the Last Things*, London, 1955, p. 91.

wards studies writers like Athanasius and Irenaeus will find himself already introduced to central and important aspects of their thinking.

Of course he only accepted from his wide reading what was in accordance with Holy Scripture. He found, however, that the earliest Fathers of the first four or five centuries "were so cautious in framing all their economy on the Word of God, the only standard, that it is easy to see that in scarcely any respect they departed from it".[5] There is gold to be found in their writings even though there is also some dross. Strangely their successors in later centuries chose the dross instead of the gold and thus brought corruption into the thought and practice of the Roman Church.[6]

In one of his chapters on the subject of predestination, Calvin remarks: "If I wanted to weave a whole volume from Augustine I could readily show that I need no other language than his."[7] At this point we can draw attention to a characteristic feature in Calvin's theology: his power to absorb everything which came to him, to let it if possible find its relevant place in his mind and to weave it eventually into the patterns formed in his thought. He needed no concordance, for his memory served this purpose perfectly. Gilson, in his discussion of the theology of St. Bernard, observes that while there may not have been much in the way of doctrine that Bernard did not borrow from writers like Ambrose, Augustine, Origen or Bede, yet the order and framework of his thought were entirely his own. "To extract the mystical theology of St Bernard from the heap of scattered data in Scripture or the Fathers we should need the spiritual life and speculative genius of St Bernard himself."[8]

T. F. Torrance in his discussion of the theology of Karl Barth writes: "There arise from time to time, men who tower above their immediate context, not only because they are

---

[5] *Inst.*, 4:4:1.

[6] Cf. Prefatory letter to the King of France in the *Institutes*. On the abuse of the Fathers, Luther likewise commented: "We are like people who look at road signs and never get on the road. The beloved fathers wanted to lead us into Scripture with their writings, but we use them to lead ourselves out of it. *To the Christian Nobility*, L.W. 44:205.

[7] *Inst.*, 3:21:9.

[8] *Op. cit.*, p. 32.

men of genius, but because they are so steeped in the history of thought that they attain a breadth and comprehension reaching out beyond the *Zeitgeist* of any one age. That is very true, for example, of Calvin. In some respects he did not have the brilliant genius of Luther, and yet Calvin was far less a child of his own times than Luther, for all his thinking was carried in a dimension of great historical depth, and his essential teaching, far from being determined by any private inspiration, was moulded in the rigorous school of historial exegesis, and historico-theological dialogue with the Fathers. It is for this reason that one can expound Calvin's theology more truthfully out of itself and with reference to the Scriptures and the Fathers, but with less reference to his immediate historical context, than that of any other of the great modern theologians."[9]

Discussing the fascination which his books have had for the best minds in past centuries and the appeal he has for students today, John T. McNeill mentions the "continual sequence of fresh facts and surprises"[10] with which his readers are rewarded on many subjects. One never fails to be impressed by the wide range of his thought even on what seems at first a restricted topic, and the facility and subtlety which accompany its clear expression. As a student who has tried to keep pace with the modern development of Biblical Theology over the past fifty years I found for example that on such subjects as "realised eschatology", "salvation history", "typology", and the unity of the Old and New Testaments, he seemed to me to explain in clearer language what modern scholars were trying to put accross in more obscure terms.

Calvin's teaching on the Person of Christ is both Catholic and Reformed. We could extract from the *"Institutes"* an excellent account of what is today sometimes called a "classical" or "essential" Christology. He gives the orthodox teaching of the early Church Fathers and Councils concisely, fully, and accurately. In his chapter on the Trinity, after discussing the deity of Christ, he speaks of Christ as residing in and sharing the essence of God,[11] and he criticises Arius,

[9] *Karl Barth — An Introduction to his Early Theology 1910–1931*, London, 1962, p. 29.
[10] *Op. cit.*, p. 202.   [11] *Inst.*, 1:13:16.

Sabellius and, of course, Servetus. Later on he proved that "Christ has assumed the true substance of human flesh",[12] and then he turns to the question of "how the two natures in the mediator make one person",[13] proving, as the Fathers did, that they are together in a mystery of duality and unity, in a hypostatic union, and may not be thought of as either fused or separated. He criticises Nestorius who wanted to pull them apart, and the madness of Eutyches who, in his concern to preserve the unity, destroyed both natures. At the same time he castigated Servetus for regarding Christ simply as a "mixture of some divine and some human elements but not to be reckoned as both God and man".[14]

It was characteristic of Calvin, in his subjection to the Word of God, never to modify one clear aspect of the revealed truth even when the full acknowledgment of it brought it into acute tension with other related aspects of the Word. This can be illustrated especially in his Christology. No one more unhesitatingly stressed the real humanity of Jesus, or underlined more boldly the dread, horror and agony in body and soul which he entered and endured in his passion. No one stressed more firmly that in his person the union of God and man was so complete and intimate that through our own union with the grasp of this humanity we share in and experience the divine life and light of God himself. At the same time as he thus stressed the humanity of Jesus, and the essential nature of his union with God, however, Calvin found he had to do justice to those passages of Scripture which bear witness to the fact that in the midst of all the events involved in the incarnation and death of the Son of God, there could have been no possible diminution of the power, reality and glory of his deity by reason of its union with humanity. "Here is something marvellous: the Son of God descended from heaven in such a way that, without leaving heaven, he willed to be borne in the Virgin's womb, to go about the earth, to hang upon the cross; and yet continuously filled the world even as he had done from the beginning." This is a very clear and bold statement of the fact

---

[12] *Inst.*, Book 2, Ch. 13.
[13] *Inst.*, Book 2, Ch. 14.   [14] *Inst.*, 1:14:5.

that when the word becomes flesh, he did not cease to be wholly himself. The divinity was never "confined within the narrow prison of an earthly body".[15]

It must be noted that in making this affirmation Calvin in no way intended to limit the extent to which God identified himself with our human condition in Jesus. It was meant, rather, to underline the wonder of the fact that it was really the eternal God who became one with us in Jesus.[16]

There is no doubt that Calvin greatly valued the orthodox teaching of the Church on the person of Christ. He regarded it as rising directly from Scripture itself, even though it did not use Scriptural language. Obviously he kept it always in mind as a kind of formula which helped him, for example, to interpret the Gospel narratives, for the acts and words of Christ seem at one time to reveal the limitations and frailties of his humanity, and at another time to be attributable only to one who had also the powers and wisdom of God himself. It also helped him in his understanding of the Sacraments. There is little doubt that when he tried to think about the mystery of the relation between God's own gracious presence and action within all the earthly sacramental activity of the Church, he had constantly in mind the Chalcedonian statement about the mystery of the hypostatic union in the

---

[15] *Inst.*, 2:13:14. This doctrine as stated by Calvin was called by Lutherans the Calvinist "extra" or the *extra calvinisticum*. For a penetrating discussion on the importance of Calvin's emphasis, see T. F. Torrance, *Space, Time and Incarnation*, London, 1969, pp. vi, 14f, 18, 24, 31.

[16] Yet it is at this point that Calvin has been accused of Nestorianism (i.e. of holding the divinity and humanity too much apart and of diminishing the influence of the one upon the other). A recent criticism of this aspect of Calvin's theology by W. Fred Graham in *The Constructive Revolutionary*, Richmond, 1971, pp. 179f) has linked this aspect of Calvin's teaching with his suggestion that the deity was quiescent during the passion, and has accused Calvin of denying that the humiliation of Christ was that of God himself. Graham suggests that this apparent belief, on Calvin's part, that God was withdrawn from complete self-identification with Christ in his passion, was given its expression in a "lack of rapport with sinful man" which he detected in Calvin's Geneva. Karl Barth, concerned to show that in Jesus Christ God's deity does not exclude but includes his humanity, has expressed a wish that "Calvin had energetically pushed ahead on this point in his Christology, his doctrine of God, his teaching about predestination, and then logically also in his ethics!" (*The Humanity of God*, London, 1961, p. 49.) For a discussion of Calvin's suspected inclination towards Nestorianism see Kilian McDonnell, *John Calvin, the Church, and the Eucharist*, Princeton, 1967, pp. 10f, 86–91, 212–13, 245.

God-man.[17] Moreover he saw that we can understand the Atonement properly if we understand that both natures in the God-man must play their full part as they operate together the mystery of their hypostatic relationship to fulfil their own work.

He was convinced, however, that it was necessary also to have a more Biblical understanding of who Christ is. He believed that Melanchthon was correct in his affirmation that to know Christ is to know his benefits. His concern was to present a Christ "clothed in his Gospel".[18] It was one of his severest criticisms of the Roman Church and of his early theological training that it was so stuck fast in orthodox teaching that it had refused to come back to the Bible. The Papists, he affirmed, had "nothing but an esoteric Christ, for all their care had been to apprehend his naked essence. His Kingdom, which is his power to save, they have neglected." "Faith," he adds, "should not cling only to the essence of Christ, but should pay heed to his power and office."[19]

Calvin therefore asks us to look at Christ in terms of the function he fulfils rather than in terms of the essence which his humanity seems to conceal. He thus brings us close to the writers of the New Testament who themselves are concerned to show us who he is in terms of what he does for us, and who show first of all how he is associated with his Father in the functions of creation, revelation and redemption.[20] He allows his discussion of the classical doctrine of the Person of Christ, therefore, to come to its climax in a chapter entitled: "To know for what purpose Christ was sent by the Father, and what he accomplished for us, three things above all are to be looked at in him: his offices of Prophet, Priest and King." In the Bible the relations between God and his people are given and controlled by the Covenant God enters with them, under which he binds them personally to himself, and binds himself personally to them. Man in his sin constantly breaks the

[17] Cf. R. S. Wallace, *op. cit.*, p. 167f.
[18] *Inst.*, 3:2:6.
[19] *Comm. on John*, 1:49.
[20] I.e. the N.T. Writers have a "functional" rather than an "essential" Christology; cf. J. F. Jansen, *Calvin's Doctrine of the Work of Christ*, London, 1956, p. 13, and D. E. H. Whiteley, *The Theology of St Paul*, Oxford, 1964, p. 123.

Covenant on his side, and his sin is seen in its full seriousness in such unfaithfulness. Calvin saw that in the Bible the person and work of Christ are understood in the light of the broken Covenant. The Prophets, Priests and Kings in Israel are mediators of the Covenant and are there to proclaim, maintain and repair the broken relationship with God. Christ is to be understood as the one ultimate and effectual Mediator of the Covenant who restores it, and makes it new.

Other theologians before Calvin had spoken of Christ as having in himself the threefold dignity or three graces of Prophet, Priest and King. These included Eusebius, Chrysostom, St. Augustine and Aquinas. Before Calvin, however, as J. Bosc points out, the doctrine is not developed with any approach to consistency or fullness.[21] Calvin he claims breaks new ground in making the offices of Christ different points of departure for considering Christ's work, which, when they have been fully explored, allow the work to be comprehended in its fullness. Calvin's example in using the conception of the threefold office as a means of exploring and expounding the meaning of Christ's work was followed almost universally by theologians of the Reformed tradition. It became an accepted approach in Lutheranism and has been used seriously and fruitfully by theologians of all persuasions.

(B) The Work of Christ

The Catholicity and breadth of Calvin's theology nowhere comes out more clearly than in his teaching on the work of Christ. R. S. Franks in his exhaustive study of the history of this doctrine notes that Calvin "presents the fundamental outlines of the patristic doctrine, especially as we find it in Athanasius, Ambrose and Hilary. He hands on therefore the tradition of the Ancient Church to the Church of the Reformation. In particular, the idea of satisfaction here taught is at once patristic and protestant. The medieval or

---

[21] Cf. *Inst.*, 2:15:1, J. Bosc, *The Kingly Office of the Lord Jesus Christ*, Edinburgh, 1959, pp. 5–6; J. F. Jansen in *Calvin's Doctrine of the Work of Christ*, argues that Calvin throughout all his writing more often stresses only the twofold character of Christ's work — the regal and priestly.

Anselmic mode of stating the question is quite passed over, and Calvin goes back for his connections immediately to the Fathers."[22] This point becomes most obvious in his chapter entitled: "Christ had to become man in order to fulfil the office of the Mediator".[23] The patristic writers stressed that we required to be saved from our physical corruption and death as well as from the guilt of our sin. God, therefore, became incarnate so that by uniting himself with us he might take upon himself our corruption and death, and enable us to share his life and immortality. Moreover, a second Adam had to come and reverse the disobedience of the first Adam. Recalling this teaching, Calvin shows that in becoming flesh, God comes close to us in such a way that "his divinity and our human nature might by mutual connection grow together". In this "holy brotherhood" with us God can therefore "swallow up death and replace it with life, conquer sin and replace it with righteousness".[24]

In discussing how the atonement was accomplished Calvin often tries to draw our attention to what happened in and through the humanity of Jesus. He refers to this in his comment on the verse in Isaiah 53:11: "By his knowledge shall my righteous servant justify many". "Christ justifies us not only as he is God, but also as he is man; for in our flesh he procured righteousness for us. He does not say "The Son" but "my servant" that we may not view him as God, but may contemplate his human nature in which he performed the obedience by which we are acquitted before God".[25]

Calvin emphasises that Christ as man worked to bring about our salvation "throughout the whole course of his

---

[22] *History of the Doctrine of the Work of Christ*, London, n.d., vol. 1, p. 429.

[23] *Inst.*, Book 2, Ch. 12. [24] *Inst.*, 2:12:1–2.

[25] *Comm. on Isa.*, 53:11. McLeod Campbell the great Scottish nineteenth-century theologian who was more sympathetic in his day to Luther than to Calvin admitted "a defect" in Luther's theology. Luther, he said, "keeps before the mind God, as He is revealed to be trusted in . . . rather than the contemplated life of Christ in us in the conscious experience of which we are to grow day by day in the assurance of faith and the free life of sonship". There is profound truth in this assertion; McLeod Campbell himself unfortunately showed little interest in Calvin's theology, but it is at exactly this point, especially in his stress on the work of Christ as man responding in our place and as a pattern to God that Calvin brings into Reformed theology everything that Campbell found lacking in Luther.

obedience ... from the moment when he assumed the form of a servant".[26] He does not think of Christ's death as a saving event apart from Christ's life. The phrase "the blood of Christ" includes for him all parts of redemption in a single word. The "blood" which atones is simply the whole life of Jesus poured out in death.[27] Calvin does not bring up Anselm's argument that the obedient response of Christ's life would be inadequate to atone for sin since this is simply the debt that every rational creature owes to God. He, rather, stresses the fact that Christ's whole life of obedience acquires merit. His obedience is regarded as something that He offers to God as part of His High Priestly Ministry, and it is his obedience that alone gives virtue to His death. "Truly," says Calvin, "even in death itself his willing obedience is the important thing because a sacrifice not offered voluntarily would not have furthered righteousness."[28]

Calvin dwells often on the "exchange" which Christ made with us in and through his human nature. He became incarnate, indeed, in order that he might be able to receive from us what belongs to us and transfer to us what belongs to him. "This is the wondrous exchange which, out of his boundless goodness, he has made with us. Having become Son of Man with us, he had made us with himself Sons of God. By his own descent to earth, he has prepared our ascent to heaven. Having received our mortality, he has conferred his immortality upon us. Having taken our weakness, he has strengthened us by his power. Having submitted to our poverty, he has transferred his wealth to us. Having taken up himself the burden of impurity with which we were oppressed, he has clothed us with his righteousness."[29] Calvin dwells constantly, always in an arresting way, on the paradoxes involved in this exchange, whereby we find "acquittal in Christ's condemnation and blessing in His curse". It is especially in his preaching that Calvin vividly forces the meaning of the atonement on to the minds of his

---

[26] *Inst.*, 2:16:5.
[27] *Comm. on Rom.* 3:14, *Inst.*, 2:16:5.
[28] *Inst.*, 2:16:5, 2:17:3.
[29] *Inst.*, 4:17:2; cf. 2:16:6, 2:2:2.

hearers by dwelling on the contrast between what Christ receives from us what we receive from Him. "The fountain of life goes down to death, he who sustains the universe dies in weakness, he who delivers us from fear dies in horror. He was willing to be disfigured, wounded, whipped blow after blow — this is the medicine by which we are healed! He is imprisoned, we are delivered, he is condemned and we are absolved. He is exposed to all outrages and we are established in honour. He has descended to the depths of Hell, and the Kingdom of Heaven is opened to us."[30]

This exchange, it is to be noted, is not thought of simply as an exchange in outward conditions effected by the decree of One who is above human life. It is a transfer also effected on the level of human life by the initiative and power of the man. Jesus. Our sins are thought of as not only imputed by God to Jesus but as transferred to him. Moreover Jesus is regarded as "transferring to himself" our guilt and sin, and as "taking upon himself" our shame and the reproach of our iniquities.[31] Moreover as he follows the course of his life, the man Jesus is regarded by Calvin as having within himself the source of a new life and grace which can replace what he takes from those with whom he enters into close fellowship. "There are two things to be considered not only in the Person of Christ but even in his human nature. The one is that he was the unspotted lamb of God, full of blessing and grace. The other is that he took our place and thus became a sinner and subject to the curse, not in himself, indeed, but in us." The son of God, though spotlessly pure, took upon him the disgrace and reproach of our iniquities, and in return clothed us with his purity.[32]

To indicate his thought on how this exchange was made, Calvin uses the analogy of how the touching of the innocent animal being laid on the altar in the temple of sacrifice enables the offerer to transfer his own guilt to the victim. When the priests offered the animal to be immolated they laid

[30] Cf. *Serm on Isa.*, 53:4–6, C.O., 35:621, 628, *on Matt.*, 26:36–9, C.O., 46:83, *on Isa.*, 53:9–10, C.O., 35:653.

[31] *Inst.*, 2:16:5–6.

[32] *Comm. on Gal.*, 3:13, *Inst.*, 2:16:6.

their hands on it "as if they threw on the sacrifice the sins of the whole nation". When a private individual offered his sacrifice "he also laid his hand upon it as if he threw upon it his own sin". Thus when Christ came in the midst of human life to become our sacrifice there was such a close and organic relation between Himself and His brothers for whom He was to die, that our sins were really transferred to Him. "As the curse of the individual was of old cast upon the victim, so Christ's condemnation was our absolution and with his stripes we are healed."[33]

At times Calvin, following Luther, allows for the loving sympathy in the man Jesus, to be a factor in effecting this exchange. The suggestion is that Christ through his organic union with our race, and his compassion for individuals around him, was able to absorb into his own mind, heart and Person something of the inner suffering and shame of those around him and to replace with outgoing love and strength what he took from them. His discussion of the healing of the leper is illuminating in this connection. He asks us to note the fact that Jesus, the Son of God, was "so far from disdaining to talk to the leper that he even stretched out his hand to touch that uncleanness". The touch of the hand was full of significance. It was "a token of infinite grace and goodness". It was a sign that in his incarnation he had become united to our humanity in one body that we might be "flesh of his flesh". It was also a sign that within such a close union with us "retaining his innocence", he "took away all our impurities and sprinkled us with his holiness". It was also an expression "of the feeling of compassion".[34] This transference of our burdens to his heart was an act of love. "He was not compelled by violence or necessity, but was induced purely by his love for us and by his mercy to submit to it".[35]

[33] *Comm. on Isa.*, 53:10, *on 2 Cor.*, 5:21; cf. *Inst.*, 2:12:2–3. It is a defect in Paul Van Buren's book — *Christ in our Place*, Edinburgh, 1957, that he does not see how important this aspect of the atonement is for Calvin.   [34] *Comm. on Mt.*, 8:3.

[35] *Inst.*, 2:16:2. Referring to Matthew's comment that Christ when he exercised healing also "carried out sicknesses", Calvin adds the thought that "this refers not simply to the miracles, but to what he did to souls". The implication here is that even during his earthly life he was engaged in actually bearing our iniquities. "It is of our spiritual diseases that the prophet intends to speak." *Comm. on Isa.*, 53:5.

In considering the part played by the humanity of Jesus in effecting the atonement Calvin stresses the place of Christ's intercession. As our priest he prayed to God for us, and it was through his prayer as well as through his self-offering that he obtained access to God for us. Calvin speaks both of our being justified and of God's being reconciled to us "through the intercession of Christ's righteousness".[36] He regards Christ's prayer as arising out of the agony which he entered through his coming close to us, and at the end of his life it arose out of his final passion "when he prayed like a sinner not to be swallowed up in death".[37] Calvin invites us to dwell with imagination and sympathy on this last agony. The physical pain and the fear of the grave are not the worst elements in his suffering. He had a "harsher and more difficult struggle than with common death". He suffered in his soul "the terrible torments of a condemned and forsaken man". This "inward fear of conscience which made Him so afraid as to sweat blood when He presented himself at the Judgment seat of God caused Him greater horror and distress than all the torments of the flesh."[38] The agony in Gethsemane was the beginning of his "descent into Hell". Calvin, following Luther, believed that this disputed phrase in the Apostles' Creed referred to his suffering, on the Cross itself, the full extent of the wrath of God against human sin.[39]

Though it appeared that his agonising prayer was for himself it was nevertheless for us. Jesus never at any time had any thought for himself as a priority in his mind, and especially during his last agony he was representing and presenting us to God.

We are to regard this prayer of Christ as being eternal. Christ's intercession at the right hand of God for ever, is, as it were, the pleading before the Father of the efficacy of his own sacrifice. Just as the Cross was a unique event decisively altering the whole course of history, and introducing new possibilities into history for men in every moment of time, so the Cross inaugurates an eternal intercession through the

---

[36] *Inst.*, 2:15:6, 3:11:23, 3:14:9.   [37] *Inst.*, 2:16:11.
[38] *Inst.*, 2:16:10–11, *Comm. on Acts*, 2:24.
[39] *Inst.*, 2:12:12, 2:16:10.

pleading of which we obtain favour before God even today. Calvin can speak of the blood of Christ as constantly being distilled before the Father. It is through his prayer that we ourselves can pray.[40]

It was his insistence on the full co-operation of both natures in the mystery of the one work that led Calvin to lay so much stress on the part which the human obedience of Jesus, and indeed his prayer life too, plays in the atonement. Calvin avoids reducing the mystery of the atonement so that it becomes simply a work of God himself using the humanity of Christ merely in an instrumental way. He insists that the humanity of Jesus is not merely the instrument of salvation but is the "material cause" of it.[41]

Calvin, of course, explored all the Biblical and traditional ways of expressing what happened in the atonement. At times, he refers to the so-called "classical" doctrine, i.e. that it was a subtle way of outwitting and overcoming the devil by tempting him to think that he could gain a great victory over Christ, and thus luring him to release mankind and enter a struggle which would involve his own destruction. "There is no tribunal so magnificent," writes Calvin "no throne so stately, no show of triumph so distinguished, no chariot so elevated, as the gibbet on which Christ subdued death, and the devil the prince of death."[42] In his deathly agony he was "wrestling hand in hand with the devil's power. He let himself be swallowed up by death, as it were, not to be engulfed in its abyss, but, later to annihilate it."[43] While he re-echoes such aspects of Patristic teaching Calvin more often, refers to Augustine, stressing the fact that in the atonement God deals with the penalty of our sin and guilt.[44]

In his attempt to be true to the Biblical statements which point to the penal aspect of the atonement, Calvin tries to

[40] *Inst.*, 2:15:6.
[41] *Inst.*, 3:11:7, 3:14:17, 21. See in *Essay in Christology for Karl Barth*, ed. T. H. L. Parker, London, 1956, pp. 158ff, the criticism by J. B. Torrance of Gustav Aulen's view of the Atonement as accomplished by the Logos through the manhood as His instrument.
[42] *Comm. on John*, 13:32, on *Col.*, 2:15.
[43] *Inst.*, 2:16:11, 2:16:7.
[44] See R. S. Wallace, *The Atoning Death of Christ*, London, 1981, pp. 81-2.

explain as honestly as possible the apparent contradictions which he finds in what is said. The first aspect of the Cross, Calvin believed, which must strike our terrified minds, if we are ever to understand it with a true appreciation of its glory, is that God has to be reconciled to man. He speaks often and freely of the Father as having to be "rendered propitious", of the wrath of God as having to be "appeased". He speaks of Christ as our high priest obtaining "favour and access to God". He attributes to Christ's sacrifice the power of "expiating, appeasing and satisfying God". Christ is a "propitiatory victim interposing between us and God's anger to satisfy his righteous judgment".[45]

. This view of what happened, however, must "appear to contradict with what is said elsewhere, that we were loved by him before the foundation of the world . . . and that his love for us was the reason why he expiated our sins in Christ". Christ's coming "had its source in the overflowing love of God for us". "By his love, God the father goes before, and anticipates our reconciliation in Christ. . . . It is because he first loves us that he afterwards reconciles unto himself."[46] When we see and grasp such love we refuse to think of God in other terms: "As if the Son reconciled us to him, that he might now begin to love those whom he had hated!"[47]

Today many scholars regard Calvin as being mistaken in his interpretation of the New Testament texts which he read as suggesting that God requires to be propitiated. They stress the fact that, even in the Old Testament, cult sacrifices were regarded not as propitiating an angry God but rather as expiating or wiping out sin. We note that in the New Testament the word "reconcile" is not used of God's being reconciled to us, but of our being reconciled to God. We emphasise that where the thoughts of God being propitiated by man are explicit in the Old Testament, these are of early date, and the predominant later view can be taken to cancel out the earlier view. Calvin, however, rightly or wrongly, felt the tension strongly. It greatly illuminates his thought on an important theological problem to note how he dealt with it.

[45] *Inst.*, 2:15:5–6, 2:16:6, 2:17:4, *Comm. on Rom.*, 3:24.
[46] *Comm. on 2 Cor.*, 5:19; cf. Eph. 1:14; *Inst.*, 2:16:3.   [47] *Inst.*, 2:16:4.

Of course, struggling with the apparent contradictions he holds on most firmly to the love of God. The atonement declares unequivocally that God "was moved by pure gratuitous love to receive us into his favour". This was, according to Augustine "incomprehensible and unchangeable".[48] Such statements, Calvin believed, accurately reflect what is ultimate in the message of the Cross. Yet, he affirms paradoxically that before we can hope to grasp the overflowing love of God for us, we must first have been led to hold the truth that God has been propitiated by a mediator. Though the free and pure love of God was always first in time, nevertheless "as regards to us," writes Calvin, "his love has its foundation in the sacrifice of Christ."[49] Calvin here contrasts the order in which things happen in God, and the order in which they happen in our experience. He believed, rightly or wrongly, that we cannot come to have adequate thoughts about the love which flows to us from the Cross unless our minds are first "struck and dismayed by the fear of God's wrath". Holy Scripture therefore teaches us to perceive that apart from Christ "God is in a manner hostile to us, and has his arm raised for our destruction".[50]

We have to note that Calvin uses the phrase "in a manner" or "so to speak" when he refers to God's anger being propitiated in the Cross. Calvin obviously recognised that though scripture itself speaks in this way it is speaking more inadequately when it does so, than is the case elsewhere. Using such phrases and concepts God is not speaking falsely but he is tempering truth to our weakness and accommodating it to our capacity.[51] Such statements indeed, can mislead unless they are supplemented by statements which appear to contradict them. Calvin obviously believed that while the

---

[48] *Inst.*, 2:16:3–4.   [49] *Comm. on Cor.*, 5:19.   [50] *Inst.*, 2:16:2.

[51] *Inst.*, 2:16:2–3. Whatever decision we ourselves make on the statements about propitiation linked up with anger in God, which, it can be argued, are found even in New Testament texts, we must appreciate the fact that the Cross effects something important on the Godward side of the relation between God and man, and this indeed alters radically the objective conditions under which God now deals with man. Though we might not use Calvin's language, who of us, on the basis of Holy Scripture, can deny that, even as his love overflowed towards us, God had also to deal with something in himself?

whole of Scripture is true and necessary, certain aspects of it at least reflect ultimate truth with more immediate clarity than others. Calvin believed he was on the side of the ultimate truth when he affirmed that our salvation was brought about by a "decree" of pure and incomprehensible love.[52]

It is to be noted that in his discussion of the meaning of the death of Christ, no external conditions are laid down which God had to fulfil in order to be able to forgive us. No "tidy system of punishment" is outlined in order to give us a key to the plan of salvation followed by God. God was not compelled to act nor prohibited from acting by any circumstance or law outside of himself. "If the necessity to be inquired into, it was not what is commonly called simple or absolute, but flowed from the divine decree, on which the salvation of man depended. What was best for us, our heavenly Father determined." When faced with the question why the death of Christ was of value and merit in the sight of God, Calvin's first answer is that God "appointed this method of reconciliation in Christ". The merit of Christ depends entirely on the good pleasure and grace of God.[53]

Yet the cross was not an irrational act. "God appoints nothing at random," says Calvin, "hence it follows that his death was lawful."[54] In all its details it is full of meaning. It speaks. It reveals principles and ways which we must recognise as being characteristic of God's wisdom, justice and

[52] *Inst.*, 2:12:1, 2:16:1. Suggestions are sometimes made that this decree was limited in its scope, i.e. that Christ was given to die only for the elect. We may ask why did Calvin, at the very point where the discussion of such a decree is relevant, not mention it? And when, later in his *Institutes*, he discusses the reprobate and their reprobation why does he not say that Christ did not die for them? The suggestion in *Inst.*, 2:16:1 is that the effect of God's love can indeed be limited only by the inadequacy of our minds to grasp it in its fullness. Calvin never shirks from repeating frequently the Scripture testimonies that Christ is sent to die for, to suffer for, and to save the world. Moreover when he finds the New Testament referring to Christ's death as being for "many" he indicates that the "many" means the whole human race. Cf. *Comm. on Rom.*, 5:10, *on John*, 3:16-17, *on Gal.*, 5:12, *Serm. on Isaiah*, 53; C.O., 35:627, *Serm. on 2 Tim*, 2:3-5, C.O., 53:149, 159-60, *Comm. on Matt.*, 20:8. It must be added that there are occasional statements in which Calvin does not give a clear voice on this matter. For a fuller discussion of this topic see e.g. Brian Armstrong, *John Calvin and the Amyraut Heresy*, Madison, Wisconsin, 1969; A. N. S. Lane, The Quest for the Historical Calvin, *Evangelical Quarterly*, 1983, p. 101.

[53] *Inst.*, 2:12:1, 2:17:1-2.   [54] *Comm. on Isa.*, 53:10.

love. We can find its meaning, however, not from principles which our minds can lay down beforehand but only from what God actually did in the event. We learn from the Atonement itself why it was needed and how it could fulfil this need. The Gospel must be allowed to cast its own light on the subject.

In our review of his teaching on the atonement we have tried to indicate something of the fruitful way in which he explores a multitude of avenues opened up to thought. It is with reference to this aspect of Calvin's theology that J. F. Jansen writes: "Less than any other man of his generation, or for many generations afterwards, did he attempt to force the rigid formulas of a dogmatic system on the free and living thought of the Bible."[55] The Church's thought on the atonement has developed richly during the past century and a half, as Christ's sufferings have been more and more interpreted in the light of the human suffering that a deeply sensitive and sinless man might undergo in real and tragic life-situations dimly parallel to that of the God-man in our midst. Ideas of identification, vicarious suffering, and vicarious penitence have been more deeply explored in this connection. Christ's personal relationship with the Father throughout His passion has been more and more accurately and imaginatively considered, and more attention has been given to the atonement as a prayer. We have tried to show that the seeds of much that is healthy in this development are there in Calvin's thought already.

(C) The Nature and Attributes of God

Nearly everything Calvin said in his teaching about God takes us to the heart of the Gospel and gives assurance. Had this not been the case he could not have won the place he did in the Church of his day. His conversion from Rome meant his deliverance from its teaching about a God who was a "stern judge and avenger of iniquity".[56] "God", he wrote, "cannot be known except in Christ."[57]

---

[55] *Op. cit.*, p. 59.   [56] C.Tr., Vol. 1, p. 62.   [57] *Comm. on 1 Peter*, 1:20.

In his discussion on the nature and attributes of God in the *Institutes* he rejected the introduction into our thought about God, of ideas borrowed from pagan philosophy. One of his chief criticisms of Rome was that his theological training had involved him in a mere "toying with idle speculation"[58] about the "essence of God". Yet over against the ancient pantheistic ideas which were current in his day, and the "stupid imaginings". of others who believed that God had a body he set the philosophical ideas of God which he claimed to find in the Bible itself. He spoke of God's "immeasurable and spiritual essence".[59] Moreover he had no doubt about the personality of the God who had intimate control over every event in the life of each individual.

He believed that God's own personal name twice uttered in his own self-proclamation when Moses was in the cleft of the rock,[60] "Yahweh, Yahweh" (as we would translate it today), announced his "eternity and self-existence". To designate the remainder of the adjectives used or implied on this self-proclamation ("merciful and gracious, longsuffering and abundant in goodness and truth, keeping mercy for thousands, forgiving iniquity and transgression and sin; visiting the iniquity of the fathers upon the children and upon the children's children . . ."),[61] Calvin used in this connection the word *virtutes* which can be translated as "powers". Elsewhere he speaks of God's "perfections" or "excellencies" where we could use the word "attributes". "Whenever God becomes known his powers cannot but display themselves, his might, goodness, wisdom, justice, mercy and truth." When we discern these in his creation or in our experience of his providence we should be filled with wonder and praise.[62]

God, in his activity, never exercises any one of his powers without also in some way displaying the others. When Jeremiah gave a more concise statement of God's exercise of

[58] *Inst.*, 1:2:2.
[59] *Inst.*, 1:13:1.   [60] *Inst.*, 1:10:2.
[61] In *The School of Faith*, London, 1959, p. lxxii. T. F. Torrance suggests that Calvin does not use the word "attributes" because he believed so firmly that such qualities are really possessed by God and are not merely attributed to him by us.
[62] *Inst.*, 3:20:41; cf. 1:5:10, 1:14:2. It has been pointed out that Calvin does not use the phrase "the sovereignty of God" in discussing the attributes.

his "judgment, mercy, and righteousness" on the earth, he was not excluding God's truth, power, holiness and goodness as being displayed at the same time for "how can God's mercy judgment and righteousness be known if not founded on this inviolable truth? And how can he govern the earth with righteousness without assuming his mighty power?"[63] We are to notice that in his discussion of the attributes of God Calvin does not mention as scholastic theologians have tended to do that God is "without passion".[64] Commenting on the passage in which God compares himself to a mother who carries a child in her womb, he criticises those commentators who objected to the suggestion of motherhood in God, and stated their preference for the title "Father". "No figure of speech," he affirmed, "can describe God's extraordinary affection towards us for it is infinite and various: so that, if all that can be said or imagined about love were brought together in one, yet it would be surpassed by the greatness of the love of God." Feeling and emotion, and a desire to impart himself to men are all features of this kind of love.[65]

As Calvin tries to stress the intensity of God's love he uses the Biblical illustration of God's being married to His people, and it is against this background that he finds himself able to speak of God's jealousy. "God very frequently takes on the character of a husband towards us. Indeed, the union by which he joins us to himself when he receives us into the bosom of the Church is like that of holy wedlock, because it is founded on mutual faithfulness. As he performs all the offices of a true and faithful husband, so, in return, he demands love and conjugal chastity. . . . The more holy and chaste a husband is, the more grievous is his wrath when he sees his wife inclining her heart to a rival. So, the Lord who has betrothed us to himself in truth declares that he burns with the hottest jealousy whenever we, neglecting the purity of his holy marriage, defile ourselves with wicked lusts." But even

---

[63] *Inst.*, 1:10:2, Jer. 9:24.

[64] Cf. *Westminster Confession of Faith*, Chapter II:1.

[65] *Comm. on Isa.*, 46:3. Cf. *on Ps.* 103:8. A. Mitchell Hunter, who is by no means uncritical of Calvin's theology in other respects, wrote on this point: "No one has ever spoken or written with more warmth of genuine feeling about the Fatherhood of God and all that it implies of love and care and compassion", *op. cit.*, p. 45.

at a point like this, so anxious is he to safeguard the primacy of love over such jealousy that he can declare that God "is not naturally terrible, but is forced to it by wickedness".[66]

Calvin tries to interpret the more severe Biblical passages about God in the greater light which he feels that the Bible casts upon the love of God. For instance when God is said in Holy Scripture to be angry, this is a "rather harsh" manner of speaking, for God "does not delight himself after the manner of men when he takes vengeance on wickedness". In these anthropomorphisms God is simply "putting on the character of a man" in order to give our minds an appropriate way of thinking about a reality we cannot otherwise understand.[67] But when it comes to the interpretation of the expressions about God that attribute to Him affection and love and compassion, though there is still an element of accommodation to our understanding in this respect too, Calvin is much more firm in insisting that "in human affairs it is impossible to conceive of any sort of kindness or benevolence which he does not immeasurably surpass".[68] Moreover, when the word Father occurs for God there is no suggestion that this is figurative. For Calvin the doctrine of the Trinity implies the affirmation that God is "Father" in His own eternal being. God is Father because "He had a Son in Heaven, from whom and by whom men obtain the sonship. . . . We are now at liberty not only to call God our Father, but boldly to cry Abba Father."[69] The nearer one moves to the heart of God, therefore, one will find a love that attracts and draws, replacing fear. God is being truest to himself when he describes himself in Holy Scripture with the most attractive titles, and the more nearly that a person feels himself drawn to God, the more he has advanced in the knowledge of him.[70]

Calvin tries to do justice to the unique place given in the

----

[66] *Inst.*, 2:8:18; cf. Eph. 5:30, Hos. 2:19, *Comm. on Isa.*, 33:15. In his *Comm. on Ps.*, 145:6, Calvin notes the sudden intrusion of an element of anger and terror into the catalogue of blessings for which praise has been evoked. He comments "some think this is an expression to the same effect. . . . But it seems rather to denote the judgment of God against profane scoffers", i.e. God is "terrible" only when he is provoked to be so".

[67] Cf. *Comm. on Ezek.*, 5:13, 18:32.

[68] *Comm. on Isa.*, 63:9.   [69] *Comm. on Luke*, 1:32.   [70] *Comm. on Ps.*, 145:8.

Bible to the "Glory of God" in his revelation of himself in nature, in all his works and in Christ. Therefore he often gives it special attention by itself and does not enumerate it in his various lists of God's "powers", though at times he links it with God's "majesty". At times he speaks of it as if like his essence it was hidden, incomprehensible and entirely beyond our approach or grasp.[71] Nevertheless, while God keeps his essence reserved and hidden within himself, he stoops to reveal and share his glory with the world and mankind. "Although God is invisible, yet his glory is conspicuous enough. In repect to his essence God undoubtedly dwells in light that is inaccessible, but as he irradiates the whole world by his splendour, that is the garment in which he who is hidden in himself appears, in a manner visible to us."[72] The glory in which God has clothed himself shines in the angelic beings. When man was made in the image of God he, too, was meant to reflect something of the glory of his maker.[73]

A new and more visible manifestation of God's glory has however now broken into the world in Christ. In Christ "the wonderful love of God shines forth which renders this glory visible to us".[74] Calvin emphasises, that the glory of God is seen especially in the humiliation of Jesus. "In all creatures, indeed both high and low, the glory of God shines, but nowhere has it shone more brightly than in the Cross. God so acts here that God's righteousness is veiled under the appearance of what is opposite to it. The humiliation of Christ takes us not only to the heart of the glory of Christ, but of God Himself." Like the thief on the cross faith beholds "life in death, exaltation in ruin, glory in shame, victory in destruction, a kingdom in bondage".[75]

Calvin asserts that the glory of God is so patent, so freely and easily seen, that it is ridiculous of us to try to probe into its

[71] *Comm. on Heb.*, 4:16, *Serm. on Acts*, 1:9–11; cf. R. S. Wallace, *op. cit.*, pp. 1ff.

[72] *Comm. on Ps.*, 104:1–3.

[73] *Comm. on Ps.*, 104:1, *Inst.*, 1:5:1, 1:5:9, 1:14:5.

[74] Cf. *Comm. on John.*, 17:22, *on Isa.*, 42:1f. Note comments on this passage and others by M. P. Hoogland, *Calvin's Perspective on the Exaltation of Christ*, Kampen, 1966, pp. 143–4.

[75] *Comm. on John*, 13:31, 17:1; Cf. Hoogland, *op. cit.*, pp. 138ff. *Comm. on Luke*, 23:42.

essence by speculation.[76] Indeed we believe that it is the glory itself which reveals as much of the hidden essence as we will ever need to know. Such are the chief points which Calvin reiterates time and time again in his teaching about the nature of God. We cannot depart from the subject, however, without consideration of those few difficult passages in his writings which have raised criticism.

Exception has been taken to Calvin's remark that God in revealing his attributes shows himself "not as he is in himself but as he is towards us".[77] This is taken to suggest that alongside what is revealed to us in Holy Scripture, there might also be a hidden area of God's life, possibly a dark area, about which Christ gives us no information and for which we have no guarantee. Confirmation that Calvin had such uncertainty in his mind is found in such passages as that in which he speaks of the "dreadful decree" that involved many people and their offspring in eternal death because it so pleased God".[78] Moreover some of Calvin's statements on the doctrine of providence seem to imply that events all foreordained by God take place exactly according to a pre-determined pattern, no room being left for human freedom or fresh decision by God.[79]

Calvin is therefore accused of seeing God abstractly apart from Christ, of introducing alongside of Christ an unknowable "secret counsel" which can take control of election, and of adopting a "theological determinism which undermines what he himself says about grace".[80]

We will deal in the next chapter with the difficulties which are found in Calvin's doctrine of providence and predestination. It is in place here, however, to ask how far such offending statements in his writings should be construed to cast doubts, on a central aspect of his teaching. It must be pointed out that the occasional statements referred to do not seem in any way to have affected the strength of his reiterated

---

[76] *Comm. on Ps.*, 104:1–3, *on Ps.*, 145:1.

[77] *Inst.*, 1:10:2.

[78] *Inst.*, 3:23:7.   [79] *Inst.*, 1:16:8.

[80] For such accusations see Holmes Rolston, *John Calvin versus the Westminster Confession*, Richmond, 1972, pp. 29–30, W. Fred. Graham, *op. cit.*, p. 178, Paul Van Buren, *op. cit.*, pp. 3–4, A. Mitchell Hunter, *op. cit.*, pp. 48–9.

central conviction. His statement that God revealed himself "not as he is in himself" can be taken simply to imply that there is much in God far more wonderful than the qualities displayed in his revealing acts. Calvin certainly does speak of the "naked majesty of God" which we cannot bear to look at, and which is covered over in Christ, but he insists that it is not darkness but light, which is thus covered over.[81] Revelation, for Calvin, was never a mask put on by God to give himself an appearance different from his real one. It was a veil through which the reality that was covered over might nevertheless really be seen. If it conceals something it does only to reveal what is concealed. As Von Hügel says "The secrets God keeps are as good as those he reveals".[82] Calvin insists that though God certainly renders himself familiar to us, and accommodates himself to our capacity, it is nevertheless *himself* whom he renders familiar to us. "The Lord is always like himself and never laid aside his nature", he affirms. "The sum is this, that God in Himself, that is, in His naked majesty is invisible and that not to the eyes of the body merely, but also to man's understanding, and that He is revealed to us in Christ alone, that we may behold Him as in a mirror. For in Christ He shows us His righteousness, goodness, wisdom, power, in short his entire self."[83]

Calvin had no doubt that in revealing to us the mystery of the Trinity God is inviting us not only to share the knowledge of what he is in himself, but also the fellowship of what he has in himself. Calvin knew that there at the heart of God is the mystery of the love of the Father for the Son through the Holy Spirit. It is for this reason that he comes to speak of this doctrine so soon in his discussion and gives it so much space. Though he used technical terms, and was concerned to be orthodox, there can be no doubt that Calvin as a theologian was trying to do justice to, and to safeguard, the Church's witness to what he himself found revealed at the heart of God in the New Testament: The tender love of the Father for the Son, the complete trust of the Son in the Father.

[81] *Comm. on 1 John*, 2:22.
[82] *Essays and Addresses*, vol. II, London, 1931, p. 218.
[83] *Inst.*, 1:5:9, *Comm. on Isa.*, 14:1, *on Col*, 1:15.

Calvin himself, therefore, did not seriously imagine that in the multitude of such clear statements on this subject his readers would interpret certain other phrases to cast doubt on the sincerity with which he made his basic affirmation of his faith, or rank him in any way with the "schoolmen" whose talk about the "absolute power of God" was to him "a shocking blasphemy".[84] His unshakeable belief was that "God . . . from his very nature is merciful", and that "he has been merciful even from the beginning" so that any appearance to the contrary in our experience or thought does not give us a clue to "his real character".[85]

It may be that in allowing himself to make the statement about God's eternal decree which would inspire "dread" in his readers, Calvin was speaking with the same reserve in his mind as he had when he spoke, as he often did, about God as requiring to be propitiated. Here also was a dreadful truth which, he believed, we have to face in order to be able to grasp the more ultimate truth that God loves us.[86] In our dealing with the God who reveals himself "we are invited first to fear, then to trust" but that which is to be loved and trusted is always more ultimate than that which is to be feared.[87]

The suggestions that certain defects in Calvin's work and attitude in Geneva can be attributed to defects in his doctrine of God[88] should be read with caution. Calvin did not derive his ethics by filtering them through his theology. He, rather, derived both his ethics and his theology directly from Holy Scripture. He himself was of course well aware of the dangers that would ensue if his occasional references to the dreadful aspects of God's self-revelation were given over much weight in his readers' minds, and were allowed to cast a threatening shadow over the light of the Gospel. What had brought about the Reformation was the re-discovery of a gracious God by a people whose most urgent need was to be given a new confidence and liberty in their worship and daily life before

---

[84] *Comm. on Ezek.*, 23:9.
[85] *Comm. on Ps.*, 25:6.
[86] *See* pp. 249f.
[87] *Inst.*, 1:10:2.
[88] As, e.g., in W. Fred. Graham, *op. cit.*, p. 182.

him. It was one of Calvin's basic convictions that where a real knowledge of God exists, "uprightness and moderation" replace cruelty in human life. "Where God is . . . known, kindness to man appears."[89]

[89] *Comm. On Jer.*, 22:17.

CHAPTER 17

THE MAN AND HIS THEOLOGY

(A) Human Deliberation and Divine Providence in Geneva

"FAITH in providence," said H. R. Mackintosh at the beginning of his lectures on the subject, "is another term for personal religion. Absence of it is a sign of personal irreligion." "It is no accident," wrote Barth, "that the Reformation with its re-discovery of the all-sufficiency of the Person and Work of Jesus Christ, and the true divine worship in Him of the sinful man who may cling to the grace of God, and this alone, self-evidently carried with it in all its great representatives, Calvin no less than Zwingli and Zwingli no less than Luther, a kind of rebirth of the Christian belief in providence."[1] Calvin's theological writing on the subject of providence can often be read as a personal testimony to the faith which sustained him in his life's work. He continually finds comfort in the fact that "the Lord has all things in his power, so rules by his wisdom, that nothing can happen that is not ordained . . . so that neither fire, nor water, nor sword can do harm . . . except insofar as God in his good pleasure allows it".[2]

His personal advice on the subject often becomes quite intimate and continually reflects his own rule of life in Geneva: when we are helped by the kindness and support of others around us we are to say to ourselves, "certainly it is the Lord who has inclined their hearts to me"; when, on the other hand we are "unjustly wounded" we are to overlook the wickedness of men and mount up to God who has "permitted and sent" the offence.[3] On the troubles which led to his exile from Geneva he wrote to Farel, "If we know that they cannot

---

[1] Karl Barth, *Church Dogmatics*, vol. III/3, p. 14.
[2] *Inst.*, 1:17:11. [3] *Inst.*, 1:17:7.

calumniate us excepting in so far as God permits, we know also the end God has in view in granting such permission. Let us humble ourselves, therefore, unless we wish to strive with God.[4] Here is a test as to whether our minds are "composed to obedience" — if we allow ourselves to be "ruled by the laws of divine providence",[5] acting in the belief that in the midst of the confusion and opposition caused by sin, by our own personal failure, fear and hesitation, everything is caught up into the working out of God's gracious purpose.

Though Calvin himself does not mention them in this context he obviously regarded in the same light the many illnesses which continually seemed to threaten his usefulness. We could cull much information about sixteenth-century illnesses, and how people tried to cope with them, from his detailed description of his own ailments in his letters. Though he describes them in so much detail he does not complain or fret about them. He seems to accept them as part of the pattern in which God has chosen to weave his affairs.[6]

In the Person of Jesus Christ, Calvin affirms "we have a mirror which represents for us the universal providence of God which extends through the whole world, and yet shines especially in ourselves", who are the members of Christ.[7] We have already noted how Calvin's doctrine of "bearing the Cross" involved the belief that under the providence of God, the Christian can expect to experience the same discipline as Jesus himself experienced throughout His earthly life.[8]

---

[4] C. L. to Farel, Aug. 4, 1538.   [5] *Inst.*, 3:20:51.

[6] An observer could regard it as ironical that it was after his public troubles in Geneva were over that his illness took up more of his life and time. In 1556 they were frequent and persistent. 1558 was another very bad year when he reports himself in his letters as reaching "the acme of suffering" on March 10 with a pain in his side, struck down with fevers and then continual headaches in October, November and December. In February 1559 there is a slight relaxation in this suffering which has already continued for four months and he is given hope of a "return to health". But the relief is of short duration. The sorry catalogue continues, to be varied in 1563 by an experience of excruciating torture when his physician cured him by making him take a horse ride to relieve him of a very painful and large stone, and in the process seriously lacerated him "internally".

[7] *Comm. on Acts*, 2:23.

[8] Cf. pp. 192ff. Calvin therefore finds that God is "especially vigilant in governing the Church to which he shows favour by a closer care" (*Inst.*, 1:17:1; cf. 1:17:6). F. Wendel points out that in Calvin's treatise *Against the Libertines*, 1545, he

Calvin often tried to bring home this message when he was preaching about the Lord's Supper. He pointed out to those who participated in the Supper that their eating and drinking meant that they were indeed members of Christ. They could therefore be sure that God would care for the members of Christ's body as he cared for the Head. Christ himself cannot neglect or desert his own members in the concrete trials of earthly life. It is through Christ, therefore, that we have the assurance that the providence of God will especially "shine" on our affairs.[9]

Though he himself writes with such certainty on the subject, Calvin does not suggest that it will be easy for us either to lay hold of or to maintain faith in providence as he describes it for us. We will be tempted to perplexity "when the sky is overcast by dense clouds". We will have to suspend our judgment. We must hold ourselves under control that we do not compel God to render an account to us, but so revere his hidden judgments as to account his will the just cause of all things. In taking such a way we will be helped to see through what causes our perplexity "provided our eyes are pure".[10] Even though we still lie under the power of death, struggle under the bondage of sin, are surrounded by endless miseries, and fight a good warfare, it is good "to transfer our thoughts to Christ, that in him, as in a mirror we may see . . . the immeasurable greatness of that power which has not yet been manifested in us".[11] His own personal experience was often to find the Church in Geneva "tossed about by as many opposing currents as Noah's ark was during the deluge".[12] At critical times "good men from every quarter poured their complaint" in his ears but none was "able to apply a remedy". At such times he found his own courage failing and he poured out his heart on paper to his friends revealing himself as almost in despair of being able to hold on to the

---

distinguishes between (1) a universal order of nature, (2) a special providence having more particular reference to men, and (3) God's government of believers by the Spirit. (*Calvin*, London, 1955, p. 179.)

[9] *Inst.*, 1:16:7.   [10] *Inst.*, 1:17:1.
[11] *Comm. on Eph.*, 1:20.
[12] C. L. to Bullinger, Feb. 23, 1554.

Genevan Church, and wondering how much more deeply it is going to please God to humiliate him.[13] But he held on to the belief that God was there actively engaged in controlling public opinion, the final outcome of every ballot, the opinions of every important councillor, and the decisions of every committee. He recorded his faith that God is especially present to help when we ourselves have no other help but him, and "our eyes are fixed, therefore on him alone".[14]

Yet "the providence of God as rightly expounded does not bind our hands", writes Calvin. He points to the paradoxical element in the experience of those who feel called by God into his service. Even though "the pious man comprehends that he is constituted an instrument of divine providence . . . he girds himself with alacrity, because he is persuaded that his pains are not airily thrown at chance. Indeed, even though "the issue of all things is hidden from us, each ought to apply himself to his office, as though nothing were determined about any part".[15] Even though we know that the outcome, and the final responsibility for achieving it is in the mind and hands of God we ourselves feel as constrained and as deeply involved in the venture as if we too were responsible for success or failure.

Our part, of course, must at times be mainly to wait on God, even when everything is thrown into disorder, and we see "the gulf daily opening before our eyes".[16] Though God sets boundaries to curb evil, he sometimes allows it to grow to titanic proportions, even urging his own enemies on by his hidden power so that the ultimate triumph of his people might be the more wonderful.[17] Therefore we find ourselves constantly overtaken by events that we cannot understand or control. "It is truly the office of God to lead us on like poor blind persons, when we are brought to a stop with all our

---

[13] C. L. to Viret, Dec. 14, 1547. "My influence is gone . . . unless God stretch forth his hand." This letter describes a dramatic incident in which Calvin risked his life when he pushed himself into the centre of a street quarrel between two factions who had drawn their swords, and though seriously manhandled managed to prevent bloodshed.   [14] C. L. to Bullinger, May 7, 1549.

[15] *On the Eternal Predestination of God*, trs J. K. S. Reid, London, 1961, X:8, p. 171.

[16] C. L. to Marchioness of Rothelin, Jan. 5, 1558.

[17] *Comm. on Jer.*, 6:4–15, *Serm. on Job*, 36:6–14.

human means, and to devise expedients which we should never have thought of, enabling us to surmount every obstacle though all the while we see not a whit. It is at the same time our office to pray to him to be pleased to open our eyes; that as soon as he gives us some sign we may immediately follow it."[18]

The implication of this and other autobiographical passages in Calvin's letters suggests that he found that at certain times God opened up special opportunities for human initiative, and on such occasions laid the onus of responsibility more acutely than at other times on the human agent. Thus even, when he sought guidance from God often it had to be waited for till "the critical moment". In a comment on one of the Psalms we find him undoubtedly reflecting on his Genevan experience: "The Lord . . . promises 'the spirit of counsel' but he does not always give it to men at the very beginning of any matter in which they are interested, but suffers them for a time to be embarrassed by long deliberation without coming to determinate decisions, and to be perplexed as if they were entangled among thorns, not knowing whither to turn or what course to take."[19]

In facing the elect with their need to make decisions God seems to invest them with his own freedom and he leaves on them the onus of using every means they can lay hold of to achieve their aim. Providence excuses no man from being prudent. "God's providence does not always meet us in its naked form, but God in a sense clothes it with the means employed."[20] Yet we "must not neglect the aids which it is lawful to employ", he wrote. "Though we are unconquerable, we must omit nothing by which we may oppose and frustrate the crafty devices of our enemy."[21] He realised therefore that in his attempt to win through in Geneva he would require to be as wise as a serpent while he tried at the same time to be as harmless as a dove.

In making our decisions we must seek first of all the wisdom

[18] C. L. to Duchess of Ferrara, June 10, 1555.
[19] *Comm. on Ps.*, 13:2.
[20] *Inst.*, 1:17:4.
[21] C. L. to Bullinger, May 7, 1549, to Farel, Feb. 5, 1542.

which is from above. He warns the Church at Angers not to use any kind of "worldly wisdom" which can involve crookedness, but under the guidance of Christ to act with the "prudence of the Holy Spirit" which is "conjoined with simplicity".[22] Yet he also recommended the exercise of human shrewdness. He reminds his readers in the *Institutes* that in order to preserve our own lives we have been endowed naturally with the "arts of deliberation and caution" which are to be employed in the service of God's providence. The Christian may well therefore bring such "human deliberation" into agreement with "divine providence".[23] There is no doubt that an important factor in his success in Geneva was due to his shrewd ability to manage difficult situations, to influence people and take them with him. Certainly he showed no care or tact in order to win over to his cause those whom he counted as unrepentant and impossible enemies of the Gospel. Indeed his deliberate policy was ruthlessly to offend such, but his tactfulness and wisdom in dealing with the people he knew he must win and hold, are remarkable, and the wisdom he sought to instil in others through his letters can teach us much about the art of successful leadership.

He was wise enough to learn quickly from his early and rash mistakes in Geneva. On his return to the city immediately after his exile he deliberately sealed his lips about the past, taking care to "bring no accusation on anyone", and he avoided all the cheap celebration and idle chatter that makes such an occasion a temptation to those who like superficiality. On the very first Sunday when his sermon began he took up his exposition at the place in Scripture at which it had been interrupted three years before, and entirely ignoring what had happened he proceeded to preach on the text before him. He expressed his disgust for those in history who have tried to rule their subjects chiefly by instilling fear (as he felt the Libertines wanted to do in Geneva). Only the most despised of men could adopt such a conception of government. Fear would lead to a hatred of the ruler, and no ruler should court hatred.[24] Anyone in

---

[22] C. L. to The Brethren at Angers, Sept. 9, 1555.
[23] *Inst.*, 1:17:4.   [24] C. L. to Viret, Sept. 9, 1555.

leadership must be gentle, open-minded, and always moderate. Any trace of impatience, harshness, or violence would rightly expose him to ridicule and destroy his influence. His writings, especially his letters, describe the stance to be taken in dealing with the difficult people around. It is important he thought, that we should try to win those who oppose us, and this cannot be done if we adopt an attitude of open warfare. "If we wish to be useful" we must be prepared to swallow "many annoyances and indignities".[25] "Nothing more exasperates or whets men on to resistance than the belief that their sentiments are being challenged."[26]

Calvin therefore tried to disarm the perverseness of others by "patient suffering and meekness",[27] yet maintaining a front of "inflexible firmness". "We must not by any means appear to be timid."[28] When he faced his opponents publicly he did not fail to show his courage. On one occasion he thrust himself between opposing Councillors' weapons when a riot was beginning in the courtyard of the City Hall, and challenged them either to put up their swords or begin with himself!

It is when Calvin begins to explain the nature and effect of our freedom and responsibility before God that we find ourselves at a point of difficulty in his teaching. He was concerned not to leave more room than Holy Scripture itself gives to such human freedom. He condemned, for example, the idea that the universe could be subject to a "confused and

---

[25] *Comm. on II Tim.*, 4:2   [26] C. L. to Perucel, Aug. 27, 1554.
[27] C. L. to Charles du Moulin, July 29, 1554.
[28] C. L. to Bullinger, March 28, 1554, to Du Moulin, July 29, 1554. We find an exact parallel of how Calvin on a human level went about affairs in Geneva, in J. S. Mills' account, in his Autobiography, of how he himself succeeded in his job in the East India Company: "I could not issue an order or express an opinion without satisfying various persons very unlike myself that the thing was fit to be done. I was thus in a good position for finding out by practice the mode of putting a thought which gives it easiest admittance into minds not prepared for it by habit; while I became practically conversant with the difficulties of moving bodies of men, the necessities of compromise, the art of sacrificing the non-essential to preserving the essential. I learned how to obtain the best I could when I could not obtain everything; instead of being indignant or dispirited because I could not have entirely my own way, to be pleased and encouraged when I could have the smallest part of it; and when even that could not be, to bear with complete equanimity the being overruled altogether."

promiscuous government" in which God was regarded as determining and starting off the general motion which drove the whole system, but did not specifically direct the action of each individual creature, man having the ability to "turn himself hither and thither by the free choice of his will". He disliked the idea of a universe in which affairs have to be carefully proportioned between God and man, God seeing to his plan and part, and man being inspired with a movement by which he can act in accordance with his own nature. He also repudiated the doctrine that God simply watches and fore-knows, or permits, events which he does not determine. God's providence, he insists, is not merely His fore-knowledge, it "pertains no less to his hands than to his eyes".[29] Scripture, he insisted, speaks often and clearly about God's directing the malice of men, of His hardening their hearts, of His actively using the deeds of the wicked for his purposes. The language is so explicit that the idea of permission is not adequate to describe God's part — even though we can never tolerate the suggestion that God is the author of evil.

In rejecting any doctrine that might involve the domination of affairs by a possibly erratic power or motion within the creatures, Calvin chose to speak of a "secret plan" in the mind of God and an "eternal command" from which events flow.[30] In his discussion he frequently uses the word "determination" in a context that seems to imply pre-determination. He finally summed up his stance in a statement which seems to deprive human beings of having any significant decisions about shaping either the course of history or their own salvation. "We hold God to be the disposer and governor of all things who from the remotest eternity decreed what he was going to do, and now by his power carries out what he has decreed. Hence we maintain that by his providence not only heaven and earth and inanimate creatures, but also the plans and wills of men are so governed as to move exactly in the course which he has destined."[31]

Calvin had little difficulty in justifying this statement as

[29] *Inst.*, 1:16:4.
[30] *Inst.*, 1:16:6, 1:16:4.   [31] *Inst.*, 1:16:8.

it relates to the responsibility of the wicked for their sin.
Certainly all men sin necessarily. Being what they are they
cannot help it. Yet even in such sinning the power of will is
not destroyed. It is only the power to will the right that is
destroyed. Therefore though all men sin necessarily they sin
voluntarily. Their will determines itself by itself. They are not
compelled to sin, they choose to sin. In Niebuhr's words,
though they sin inevitably, they sin responsibly. Necessity is
therefore no excuse for sinning. When a man acts wickedly
he acts by will and not by compulsion.[32] Calvin repeated
Augustine's illustration of the putrefying corpse. It is stirred
up by the sun's rays, but the stench comes not from the rays
but from the corpse.[33] The wicked are thus responsible and to
blame for their wickedness over which God continually has
control. The behaviour which God bends to His purpose
in spite of their intention cannot be called obedience, for
obedience depends on knowledge, and all wicked deeds are
judged by the end at which they are aimed. When Caiaphas,
in the council which decided that Jesus must die, said "it is
expedient that one man should die for the people", he was
vomiting out an ungodly and cruel plan. But God turned his
tongue to a different purpose "so that under ambiguous
words he at the same time proclaimed a prophecy".[34] God
can thus accomplish through wickedness and even through
Satan, what He has decreed by His secret judgment, and yet
never declines from His own nature. Even though He uses
evil, and though he can be said even to send evil spirits to
serve him, he never contracts defilement from evil.[35]

When we try to square Calvin's statement however, with
his own assertion that Jesus Christ is the "mirror of
providence", and with his own confessed experience in
relation to, and under the grace of Christ, we certainly have
difficulty with it. Surely the decision and freedom of Jesus in
the obedience which he offered to God was as important in
what was accomplished by him as the inviolable decree from
remote eternity — and we too are enabled to share this
responsible freedom when we deal with him! It seems that

---

[32] *Inst.*, 2:2:7, 3:23:9.
[33] *Inst.*, 1:17:5.
[34] *Comm. on Acts.*, 2:23, *on John*, 11:49.
[35] *Inst.*, 1:17:5, 1:18:2, 2:4:5.

Calvin at this point transgresses a rule he followed so faithfully at other points in his theology, and closes a gap which should be left open.[36] Possibly he was too afraid that if he made concessions to man's free-will, God would be left sitting idle in heaven.[37]

At this point we must listen seriously to the criticism of Karl Barth that the Reformers "were pointing us to the dark" when they spoke about the decree of God fulfilled in creaturely events, and that they courted the danger of producing either a Stoic or grudging form of Christian obedience. Barth insists that in exerting his providence, God must be regarded as ruling over a world of freedom, not as a tyrant but as Lord of the Covenant of Grace, leaving room for autonomous activity on the part of the creature, surrounding the activity of creature by his own activity in such a way that though the free creature does go of itself, it can and does go only the same way as the free God.[38]

(B) Predestination and its Problems

Even a minimal account of Calvin's theology cannot avoid the discussion of this subject. It provided the answer he found through Christ and the Scriptures to some of the most pressing questions which arose during his life and ministry. Why did he find himself given a place among the elect people of God within the Church, on the side of justice instead of unrighteousness, with his mind inclined to truth instead of error, with his heart concerned for the glory and kingdom of God? Why did the gospel not find the same reception among those to whom it was preached? Why was it that where some were being amazingly converted, others remained indifferent

---

[36] Is Calvin not perhaps thinking here from a long-term viewpoint looking backwards rather than forward? — a viewpoint in which the external pressures shaping our life-history seem to dominate all else? Lord Haldane, the humanist philosopher and statesman, was once asked whether with the aid of such knowledge as experience had brought, he would like to begin his life anew. He replied in the negative. "For," he added, "we are apt greatly to underrate the part which accident and good luck had really played in shaping our careers." Richard Burdon Haldane, *An Autobiography*, London, 1929, p. 353.

[37] *Comm. on Acts.*, 2:23.

[38] *Church Dogmatics*, Vol. III/3, Edinburgh, pp. 92–4, 115–16.

and some were hardened into a more determined opposition to the truth and to the ways of God?[39] Why was it that "among a hundred to whom the same discourse is delivered, twenty, perhaps, receive it with obedience and faith: the others set no value upon it"? The diversity he argued, was not "due to the malice and perversity of the latter . . . for the same wickedness would possess the mind of the former, did not God in his goodness correct it".[40] Moreover, he observed that the covenant of life was not "equally preached to all". He asked therefore, "Why did not God will the Gospel to be preached to all indiscriminately from the beginning of the world. Why did He allow so many peoples for so many centuries to wander in the darkness of death?"[41] He found himself forced to answer: "Can any reason be asserted why God should not call all alike, except that in his sovereign election he distinguishes some from the others?"[42]

"We are near to God," he affirmed, "not as having anticipated his grace, and come to him of ourselves, but because in his condescension he has stretched out his hand as far as hell itself to reach us." "God", he wrote, "does not go beyond himself" to find the cause of his mercy. When he chooses or favours one rather than another the cause can lie only in his own pity or good pleasure.[43] He believed that the only way in which he could adequately meet the pastoral care needs of many anxious people around him was to dwell on the theme of God's grace in our predestination. "We shall never be persuaded as we ought to be, that our salvation flows from the fountain of the mercy of God, till we are made acquainted with his eternal election." He was aware that the doctrine could cause obscurity and dread if misapprehended by trembling souls, and that for those who loved to engage in theological discussion with "carefree assurance" it could mean entry into "a labyrinth with no exit". But it is precisely at the points where such frightening darkness threatens that we can find strength and comfort in the truth.[44] The

---

[39] *Inst.*, 3:21:1.   [40] *Inst.*, 3:24:12.
[41] *Inst.*, 3:21:1, *On the Eternal Predestination of God*, IX:5, p. 149.
[42] *Comm. on Ps.*, 64:5.
[43] *Comm. on Ps.*, 65:4; *Inst.*, 3:22:6.   [44] *Inst.*, 3:21:1.

doctrine, he believed, could be taught in such a way that it gave the trembling soul the assurance that the love of God goes out to each particular individual. It was an aspect of the Gospel of which everyone had a right to hear and a duty to think about.[45]

He believed that we must presuppose that if God elects some rather than others, he has by making this very choice also rejected those who are not chosen. He wrote to Melanchthon, "The doctrine of the gratuitous mercy of God is entirely destroyed unless we hold that the faithful whom God has thought fit to choose out for salvation, are distinguished from the reprobate by the mere good pleasure of God."[46] Wherever God interposes actively in his grace in a situation in which two men become separated one from another by the strange gulf between salvation and damnation, the grace of God seems to exert a pressure in both directions across the gulf. Attempts to save God's reputation by denying any kind of condemnation to those who are passed by, may be well intentioned, but according to Calvin, they are ignorant and childish. "There could be no election without its opposite reprobation."[47]

With the same stress on God's initiative in, and control of, all earthly events as he gave in his thought on providence, Calvin, therefore, consistently refused to admit any theory on the subject which would make God a spectator rather than an agent in what was happening in the world. Some of the fathers had tried to avoid what they felt to be harsh implications of the more blunt statements of the doctrine. God's predestination, they affirmed, means simply that he knows unerringly what men are going to do. Therefore for him to decree anything beforehand means that he is prepared

[45] *Inst.*, 3:21:1, 3.

[46] C. L. to Melanchthon, Aug. 27, 1554,

[47] *Inst.*, 3:23:1, Karl Barth in his attempt to reconstruct a doctrine of predestination more Biblical than that of Calvin agrees that up to this point, Calvin is on the right side: "To an opposing world the election must of the same force become non-election or rejection, because there exists a sphere of damnation ordained and determined by God as the negation of the divine affirmation and the work of the almighty non-willing which accompanies God's willing." *Church Dogmatics*, 11/2, p. 27.

always to act in the light of what He knows men are going to do. In reply to this interpretation Calvin quotes Augustine: "God does not find but makes men elect".[48] The reason why God foreknows a thing is that he himself has already determined it. When the Apostle Peter understood this, he spoke of the Cross as happening "according to the predeterminate counsel and foreknowledge of God". He made God's "counsel" precede His foreknowledge. Nothing would be more absurd than to imagine God "looking down from on high to see whence salvation was to come to mankind".[49] If foreknowledge determined predestination it would only be a foreknowledge of merit, and the Bible excludes merit.[50] Other theologians with the same aim of mitigating the harshness of the full Scriptural teaching asserted that for God to predestinate something implies nothing more than that God permits it to take place. Calvin, in reply to this theory, emphasises that there is a clear difference between doing and permitting to be done. When the Scripture says "God hardened Pharaoh's heart", it means what it says and is concerned to make the power of God conspicuous.[51]

As he saw in Christ a "mirror of divine providence" so he also saw Christ closely related to predestination. For him the man Jesus himself was the elect man, was made the Christ and given merit solely by the grace of God. "He did not become the Son of God by living righteously but was freely presented with this great honour, that he might afterwards make all others partakers of his gifts."[52] Calvin describes Christ, in the words of Augustine, as the "bright mirror of free election", for by no virtue of his own but purely by God's good pleasure "even in the very womb he became head of angels, the only begotten Son of God, and the image and glory of the Father".[53]

Christ is not only "the bright mirror of the eternal and hidden election of God". He is also the One in whom and

---

[48] *Inst.*, 3:22:8.
[49] *Comm. on Acts*, 2:23.
[50] *Inst.*, 3:22:5.
[51] *Comm. on Exod.*, 4:21; 14:17.
[52] *Inst.*, 2:17:1–2; *Inst.*, 3:22:1.
[53] *Inst.*, 3:21:1; cf. *On the Eternal Predestination of God*, X:6, p. 127.

with whom each of us finds himself elected. "Those whom
God has adopted as sons, he is said to have elected not in
themselves but in Christ Jesus, because he could love them
only in him." Moreover, men are elected not only *after the
pattern* of Christ, and *in* Christ, but also *by* Christ. Christ
"claims the right of electing in common with the Father",
and "makes himself the author of election".[54]

Election, however, would remain hidden if it were not
somehow manifested or conveyed to men during their earthly
lives by some kind of calling. "Calling is the proof of secret
election."[55] Moreover, "the enjoyment of election is
in some measure communicated" to those who are called.
Calling, however, for Calvin was always a calling by Christ.
It normally takes place as a deep and firm inward conviction
which possesses the believer when he hears the Gospel
preached and addressed to him. In the Gospel he hears the
voice of Christ spontaneously offering Himself as our
Shepherd, and declaring that we are of the number of His
sheep.[56] This experience obviates all doubt and is the sure
proof of election. This does not automatically take place
simply through the hearing of the outward word. Our hearts
must at the same time be inwardly illuminated by the Spirit
and united to Christ. "For since it is into his body that the
Father has decreed to ingraft those whom from eternity he
wishes to be his, if we are in communion with Christ, we have
proof sufficiently clear and strong that we are written in the
Book of Life."[57] Calvin thus indicates at the same time the
help to assurance that we can find through our participation
in the Church and its sacraments.

Throughout the history of Protestantism men have sometimes been advised to find the proof of their election in certain
inward experiences, and much has been written about
Calvin's supposed teaching that earthly prosperity and the
ability to do good works are of some importance as additional
signs of election. It is significant that in his chapter on
Predestination Calvin more clearly than anywhere else,
ignores such approaches to the problem of assurance, and

---

[54] *Inst.*, 3:24:5, 3:22:7.   [55] *Comm. on 1 Tim.*, 2:4.
[56] *Inst.*, 3:24:1, 6.   [57] *Inst.*, 3:24:4–5.

appeals to his readers to make their election stand in Christ alone and in the relationship they find to Him through the Word and Sacrament within the Church. For Calvin Christ is the only mirror in which we ought to "contemplate our election". "If we seek for the paternal mercy and favour of God, we must turn our eyes to Christ in whom alone the Father is well pleased. . . . If we are elected in him, we cannot find the certainty of our election in ourselves; and not even in God the Father, if we look at him apart from the Son."[58]

Undoubtedly for Calvin himself, his sense of eternal election was closely linked up with his conviction of having been called also to his earthly task in Geneva, and helped to inspire him in its fulfilment. He noted as he read the Psalms, that King David often found strength in the certainty that he had not thrust himself into the office of King of his own accord, and would otherwise have been "contented to have remained humble and obscure".[59] Neither had he himself in Geneva ever tried to thrust himself into where he was, nor had he chosen his task: "If our calling is indeed of the Lord, as we firmly believe it is," he wrote to Farel, "the Lord himself will bestow his blessings, although the whole universe may be opposed to us."[60]

Calvin gave a warning early in his discussion of Predestination that it could become a confusing, even dangerous, doctrine if we do not discuss it with great caution.[61] Obviously, as far as his own personal faith was concerned, he would have been content to give the doctrine a modest but basic place among his other theological statements developed only as far as it would be helpful to edify and strengthen the Church. But attacks were made on his position. Almost against his will he was forced to write several works defending himself. We find him also therefore developing and relocating his statement of the doctrine in his various editions of the *Institutes*.

He tried to reconcile the Biblical teaching about man's responsibility with its teaching on the pure sovereignty of God in man's salvation. He asserted that man with his

[58] *Inst.*, 3:24:5.
[60] C. L. to Farel, March 1539.
[59] *Comm. on Ps.*, 18:19.
[61] *Inst.*, 3:21:1.

natural power of willing, always by himself wills wrongly and perversely. His will, however, is made free to choose the good when he is approached by Christ himself in His sovereign and predestinating grace, and as he is challenged to choose. Only in choosing Christ does the will act freely as it was meant by God to act. When a man is saved by faith in Christ, the Spirit therefore breaks the bondage of the will so that he now has his liberty to choose. The Spirit, however, does not confer on man the faculty of willing, but the power to will rightly.[62]

In the midst of such discussion of the problems raised by the doctrine of Predestination Calvin became involved in speculation on matters about which Holy Scripture gives us no clear guidance. He tends in such cases to leave matters open. In answer to the question whether God ordained the fall of Adam, he quotes Augustine with approval: "God . . . so ordained the life of angels and men as to show in it first of all what free will could do, and secondly what the benefit of his grace and his righteous judgment could do." This citation suggests reluctance on the part of Calvin to say without qualification that God planned the fall of man. Calvin himself had already insisted that Adam was created with freewill. This seems to imply that he wanted the free decision of Adam to be seen to play some part in the entry of evil into the world. Yet in the midst of such qualifications he raises the question whether God could possibly have "created the noblest of his creatures to an uncertain end", and he affirms that "no one can deny that God foreknew what end man was to have before he created him, and consequently foreknew because he so ordained by his decree.[63]

A further problem which arose acutely in connection with the doctrine of predestination was in connection with the universal preaching of the Gospel. Does it not seem to involve play-acting to invite people to believe and respond, if it is already ordained that they should reject the invitation? On this question Calvin again seems to speak with two voices. He insists that "God does not bind himself by a fixed obligation

---

[62] *Comm. on Ezek.*, 11:19–20; cf. *Inst.*, 2:2:27.

[63] *Inst.*, 3:23:7. On this point I am indebted to a conversation I once had with Professor Stanley Russell.

to call all men equally". He interprets the Biblical statements that God wills "all men to be saved", and desires to "have mercy on all", in such a way that they do not contradict an inviolable decree of reprobation. Moreover, he dwells on the significance of the fact that God has not arranged that the Gospel be preached everywhere geographically.[64]

Often, however, we find him firmly insisting that the outgoing of our preaching, prayer, evangelism and love must be universal. The doctrine of reprobation is something that must be kept in mind, but it is not to be acted upon. Nor is it to be preached. "Were anyone to address people thus: If you do not believe, the reason is because God has already doomed you to destruction, he would not only encourage sloth, but also give countenance to wickedness." Even though we may believe that all will not be saved we are to preach to all. "Because we do not know who belongs to the number of the predestinated or does not belong, our desire ought to be that all may be saved."[65] Love, according to Calvin, must always go out to all men, even though it might at times, especially centre on those who believe, and "when we pray, we ought according to the rule of charity to include all, for we cannot fix on those whom God has chosen or whom he has rejected."[66]

Calvin finds justification for any contradiction which he appears to show in this matter, in the doctrine of an apparent double will in God. We must accept that God's will will appear to us as twofold. The will of God which he sets forth in his Word is the will that the Gospel should be universally preached and that all should be saved. In appearing to us to will this God "clothes himself with human affection" and "descends beneath his proper majesty". We must not, therefore, dispute with subtlety about his incomprehensible plans, and must act in accordance with his will as it challenges us to act in this particular way. Yet this does not prevent God from decreeing before the foundation of the world what he will do with every individual. This is his hidden secret will by which he elects some and rejects others,

---

[64] *Inst.*, 3:22:10; 3:24:15–17; *comm. on 1 Tim.*, 2:4.
[65] *Inst.*, 3:23:14.   [66] *Comm. on Jer.*, 15:1–2; *on Col.*, 1:4.

and governs all things to their destined end.[67] Though Calvin can ask us to think in terms of a double will in God he is always anxious to remind us that God's will in itself is simple and one. "If anyone objects that it is absurd to split God's will, I answer that this is exactly our belief, that his will is one and undivided — but because our minds cannot plumb the profound depths of his secret election, to suit our infirmity the will of God is set before us as double." This is one of these matters in which at present we "see through a glass darkly and must be content with the measure of our own intelligence".[68]

Calvin does venture to find some reasons why the Gospel should be preached indiscriminately in a situation where some are irrevocably on the way to damnation. The external word renders the wicked inexcusable, and is an evidence of the grace by which God reconciles men to Himself. It reveals the full extent of the perversity of those who damn themselves in rejecting the Gospel as they are seen to harden their hearts and deafen their ears. There is moreover always sufficient light even in the merely external word to convince the consciences of the ungodly.[69] For believers, on the other hand, the preaching of the Gospel to the ungodly proves that "the way of salvation is not shut against any order of men", and "the consciences of the righteous . . . rest more secure when they understand that there is no difference between sinners, provided they have faith".[70]

It is a valid criticism of Calvin's teaching that he tends to balance reprobation against election in a way that is not Biblical. There is no doubt that in Holy Scripture reprobation is always incidental and subordinate to election, and is not meant to have the prominence in our theological thought which we should give to the doctrine of election. God has pleasure in the election of his people but he has no pleasure in the death of the wicked.[71] "It is not suggested", says Pierre Maury, "that the hardening of Pharaoh's heart is in the same

---

[67] *Inst.*, 3:24:17; 3:20:43; *Comm. on Ezek.*, 18:23; *on 1 Pet.*, 3:9. See Brian Armstrong, *op. cit.*, pp. 186ff.

[68] *Comm. on Matt.*, 23:37, *on Ezek.*, 18:23.

[69] *Inst.*, 3:24:15, 13.　　　　[70] *Inst.*, 3:24:16–17.　　　　[71] Ezek. 18:23.

category as the choosing of Israel by God's amazing grace."[72]
Bearing this in mind, some earlier theologians had tried to
formulate a view of reprobation that did not relate it to God's
will in quite such a positive and direct way as election.
Augustine and Aquinas, for instance, suggested that the
rejected should be regarded as abandoned by God and thus
damned by natural laws rather than by a decree from all
eternity. Others, however, such as Isidore of Seville and
Gottschalk formulated a doctrine that more equally balanced
both sides of predestination, and at the time of the Reformation Zwingli and even Luther tended to follow them.

There is no doubt that in a number of his statements on this
matter Calvin seems to regard both election and predestination as of equal importance to God in His plan for mankind,
and as engaging Him with equal pleasure. He suggests that
hardening is in God's hand and will just as much as mercy is.
He asserts that "there is certainly a mutual relation between
the elect and the reprobate".[73] Moreover we have from him
sentences like: "To the gratuitous love with which the elect
are embraced there corresponds on an equal and common
level a just severity towards the reprobate."[74]

A more serious criticism of Calvin's doctrine of predestination, however, is that he fails consistently to relate every
aspect of the doctrine to Christ. We refer again here to the
"decree which should strike us with awe", which involves
"many peoples with their infant children in eternal death
without remedy". "Here," adds Calvin, "the most

---

[72] P. Maury, *Predestination and other Papers*, London, 1960, p. 59.

[73] *Inst.*, 3:23:1.

[74] *On the Eternal Predestination of God*, V:1, 3; pp. 69, 90. On the other hand, it must
be pointed out that in his discussion of election Calvin stresses the fact that the cause
lies entirely in the grace of God, and thus in God's hidden decree. In his discussion of
reprobation, however, he more often emphasises the proximate cause — man's sin
and rebellion. T. F. Torrance points out that Calvin was always careful to give the
negative results of election (condemnation or reprobation) only incidental mention
in any creed or cetechism to which only the positive affirmations of faith belong. If
Calvin's exegesis is examined it is found that he has no hesitation in stressing the fact
that there is no joy amongst the angels over the death of the wicked, and in one
comment he can write: "When God adopts severity towards men, he indeed does so
willingly, because he is the judge of the world: but he does not do so from the heart,
because he wishes all to be innocent." *Comm. on Lam.*, 3:31–3; cf. *on Isa.*, 1:21.

U

loquacious tongues must be dumb!"[75] We seem here to have
an absolute predestination and reprobation antecedent to the
election of Christ and apparently independent of the electing
Christ himself. Moreover, as Barth points out, God's way of
working here seems to be different from that of the Lord who
in Holy Scripture is "free at every moment to make His
decision, and who marches on from one decision to another,
the Lord of life and death, in whose power it is to elect or
reject, both to raise up and cast down".[76]

We are at this point standing before the same difficulty as
we have found earlier in Calvin's thinking on providence. It is
notable that in this section in which he speaks of the "horrible
decree" he relates it to the wisdom and power of God but has
no mention of His love. To us, as we look at God's action in
Christ, predestination seems to take place in time. It is as men
face Him in historical encounter, that on the side of both God
and man, decisions are made that determine destiny. Within
such decisions God is always Lord and acts as a living power
within history. Barth's complaint is that in Calvin's presenta-
tion of this aspect of the subject, even God has become His
own prisoner, and He appears to be no longer a living power
acting in history.

We have to note the change of place Calvin gave in his
theology to the discussion on Predestination. In the first
edition of the *Institutes* it is discussed briefly in connection with
belief in the Church. In the following editions it is discussed in
connection with providence. In the final edition, however,
Calvin separated these two doctrines from each other. He
placed his discussion of predestination after he had discussed
his doctrine of Christ, and at the climax of his discussion on
"how we receive the grace of Christ". It may be that through
this final arrangement he desired to show the doctrine in a
slightly more central position, to show more clearly its
practical value for living. It shows moreover that he himself
had no desire or inclination to discuss a decree of eternal
election before he had discussed fully the person and work of

---

[75] *Inst.*, 3:23:7, *Decretum quidem horribile fateor.*
[76] *Church Dogmatics*, vol. 11/2, pp. 188ff, p. 64. See M. J. Forelly, *Predestination, Grace and Freewill*, p. 126, for a similar criticism of Duns Scotus.

Christ. Thought on predestination must always be subordinate to thought on Christ.

One significant feature of the place he now gave to the doctrine in the *Institutes*, however, is that it appears next to his chapter on prayer. We remember how he himself admitted that discussing Predestination was like "looking through a glass darkly", and involved the danger of becoming lost in a labyrinth with no exit.[77] In discussing prayer the sense is much clearer, and we are in no danger. Might it not be that Calvin wanted us to remember firmly that it is the God before whom he have become confident, and with whose Fatherly love we have become familiar, in our prayer life, who is the God of the "dreadful decree"? If such a decree seems to cast a shadow, it need only be momentary, if we will look at the whole subject under the full light of the Gospel. Moreover it is in prayer that we find ourselves most free before the living God to ask and to be heard.[78]

(C) A Contrast in Styles

An influential characteristic of "Calvinism" which we undoubtedly find in Calvin himself was a desire for simplicity. In his own life-style he preferred plainness (in the good sense of that word) to any kind of unnecessary elaboration. It is true that we have from his pen a generous admission that God has given us, in the natural objects around us, many things designed to give us pleasure as well as to be of use. Moreover he conceded that for those to whom God has given wealth a certain measure even of luxury in life-style is allowable.[79] Yet he lamented, that too often a departure from simplicity in their way of life proved a tragic snare to the wealthy. His comments on Jeremiah's word to King Jehoiakim on the unrighteousness of his ill-gotten wealth are illuminating. He concentrates his criticism rather on Jehoiakim's use of this wealth in building spacious upper rooms for his palace with cedar panelling and vermilion painting: "Men never go to

[77] *Comm. on Ezek.*, 18:23, *Inst.*, 3:21:1.
[78] For Calvin's affirmation re answers to prayer see R. S. Wallace, *Calvin's Doctrine of the Christian Life*, pp. 290ff. [79] Cf. p. 91 and pp. 203ff.

excess in external things except when the heart is infected with pride, so that they do not regard what is useful, what is becoming, but are carried away with every kind of excess. . . . It was part of luxury to adorn the walls with various paintings as though men wished to change the simple nature of things."[80]

We need not regard this desire for sheer simplicity in life and its background as due to something inherently "puritanical" in his natural makeup or in his cultural inheritance. It was, rather, an attitude and preference which he felt bound deliberately to cultivate in order to conform to the service of the Gospel. For example, he believed that the way of life of a Christian leader who would make his mark in Church or city must be itself simple and thus straightforward. The people whom he wished to win over in Geneva were those who had been enlightened by the Word of God, who would suspect the pomp and artificial dignity which depended on the traditionally elaborate trappings of earthly government and would expect an integrity in which the outward behaviour is a true expression of the heart.

He admired the way in which Moses by his sheer personal openness attracted the respect and trust of those he was sent to teach and lead, and was able to work with them: "There is nothing which so greatly facilitates the transaction of all affairs as the constant course of an upright and innocent life."[81] Such was to be his course in Geneva. He would seek not to rely on any kind of artifice, however well intentioned, he would not "hunt after favour . . . from the desire of pleasing". "A good course requires a good instrument", he wrote to Farel, just as he was preparing to depart from Strasbourg to take up a new ministry. If people are to be made "willing to be taught by us" we must "gain their esteem" by "fairness and moderation".[82] "For the sake of peace and cordial agreement . . . I lay restraint upon myself", he wrote to Myconius six months later.[83] A Christian leader must labour "to obtain credit by his integrity".[84]

---

[80] *Comm. on Jer.*, 22:14.   [81] *Comm. on Exod.*, 4:18.

[82] C. L. to Farel, Sept. 16, 1541.

[83] C. L. to Oswald Myconius, March 14, 1542.   [84] *Comm. on Exod.*, 4:18.

He felt moreover that the service of the Gospel likewise demanded also a style of teaching and writing which conformed to the way taken by God in his own self-revelation. The life-style God had adopted in the incarnation itself was matched by the simple and humble style in which the Gospels were themselves written — a simplicity which arouses contempt among the proud.[85]

Along with this simplicity in literary style he felt he must aim also at lucidity. The clear and plain truth of the Word of God must not be prevented from reaching people by being presented in obscure and indefinite terms or language, and thus have its truth, fullness, and its ability to bring assurance diminished. He likened the teacher who did this to a thief who plays fast and loose with another's property.[86]

On one occasion Calvin wrote Pierre Viret instructions to give to the Dean of his area as to the attitude he should adopt in the discussions that were then taking place over the Sacrament: "Let him fearlessly set aside all unreasonable views, in replying to them and warning them, taking care that he does not weaken the truths in so doing. Nor is it allowable to complicate by ambiguous and obscure language what requires the utmost clearness or perspicuity."[87]

Obviously he believed that the cultivation of ambiguity in style and expression, in face of the clarity of the truth, was often due to the lack of the frankness and boldness in face of the opposition to the truth which was so frequently encountered in the theological discussions of the day. "I study in good faith, and perfect candour", he added, "openly declare what I have to say".[88] "I never, by employing an ambiguous form of expression captiously brought forward anything different from my real sentiment."[89] He certainly achieved his aim. "Men might not like what Calvin said", commented Owen Chadwick, "they could not misunderstand what he meant."[90]

---

[85] *Inst.*, 1:8:11. Cf. *Concerning Scandals*, Edinburgh, 1978, pp. 4 and 15f.
[86] C. L. to du Tillet, Jan. 31, 1538.
[87] C. L. to Viret, Aug. 1542.
[88] C. L. to Bullinger, March 1, 1548.
[89] C. Tr., vol. II, p. 253.
[90] *The Reformation*, London, 1964, p. 92.

He aimed also at brevity. Indeed, he once described his ideal as the attainment of "lucid brevity".[91] Even when he had much to say on any one subject he tried to make his points in brief condensed phrases and sentences, and he moved his discourse on as quickly as possible from one point to the next. In the structure of his sermons he abandoned the mediaeval habit of selecting one theme for one whole discourse, of dividing it into headings thus giving the preacher and opportunity to dally at length on selected topics spending his time in telling the "sweet stories or not unamusing speculations by which the hearers might be kept on the alert", in the midst of the discussion of the "misty questions of the schools".[92] He reverted to the form of the earlier homily in which the preacher selecting a text covering many and varied points could move through the discourse following the order of the text, and soon passing from one point to the next. It is noteworthy that in place of the long winded, illustrative stories which occupied so large a place in mediaeval preaching, he substituted brief epigrammatic or proverbial sayings.

It must be noted that the clarity he sought was such as would in no way lessen or violate the essential mystery that must always remain at the heart of everything, where God is active, present and personal. But it was precisely because of such mystery that clarity was all the more necessary, not in thinking *through* the mystery of the faith, but in thinking *round* it, in showing where it lies, how great it is and must remain, and in opposing the false doctrines that might obscure it. Even the mystery would be weakened and obscured by unrationality and by careless thinking and language.

"Calvin's style", writes Paul Henry, "is not to be regarded as a matter of course, but is illustrative of the practical tendency of his character. It was with him not nature only, but principle to think and write clearly."[93] It is to be

[91] Introductory Letter to *Comm. on Romans*.

[92] C. Tr., vol. I, pp. 40–1. Calvin is here no doubt referring the volumes of mediaeval "exempla" — the often fantastic and lengthy sermon illustrations — used by the friars in preaching.

[93] *Op. cit.*, vol. I, pp. 428–9.

regarded as something he achieved as the result of sheer hard labour so that he could convince the people he wanted to win for the service of the Word of God. "I modify my style",[94] he wrote to Grynaeus. He certainly believed that it would be appreciated by common people and that it could be a weapon which would help to disarm the natural suspicions and hesitancy of those around him who were honestly seeking the truth. He once boasted to Bullinger that "those who charge others with obscurity allow me the merit of perspicuity. . . . My method of instruction is too simple to admit of any unfavourable suspicion, and too detailed to offend on the ground of obscurity." Thomas McCrie, comparing Calvin with John Knox, attributes his success in Geneva precisely to his straightforward wisdom and eloquence backed up by his equally simple life-style. He gives it as his opinion, that Calvin was inferior to Knox in "masculine eloquence and daring courage", but "excelled him in self-command, in prudence and in that species of eloquence which steals into the heart, convinces, without irritating, and governs, without assuming the tone of authority".[95]

Having traced the ideals in style which Calvin set himself and laboured to attain in the theology he wrote in order to build up and strengthen his fellow Christians, we become all the more astonished when we discover the style he actually used in some parts of his more polemical writings. An able student of Calvin has recently expressed the regret that is often felt by his admirers that whereas the Reformer "reserved his elegance of style . . . for orthodox theology, he showed his contempt for all deviating teaching with the language of the farmyard or the circus".[96]

Undoubtedly in his polemical writing he at times shocks our modern sensitivity in such matters. When he attacked the Lutheran Joachim Westphal in 1556, for his views on the Lord's Supper he used such a spate of vituperative and sometimes bitter language that even his hardened opponent

[94] Introductory Letter to *Comm. on Romans.*
[95] *Life of John Knox*, Edinburgh, 1839, p. 364.
[96] Peter Cook, "Understanding Calvin" in *Scottish Journal of Evangelical Theology*, vol. 2, p. 58.

complained that he must have tried hard not to omit any kind of insult. Six hundred times, Westphal affirmed, Calvin had called him "Thou fool!" thus ignoring Christ's dire warnings.[97]

In the use of such a polemical style Calvin may have been simply following a convention of the times which had been established in the Middle Ages.[98] He had an uneasy conscience at times in having to indulge in such writing. In the case of Wesphal Calvin affirmed that it cost him to assume such a harsh role, and that in doing so he was simply deliberately playing his part in the struggle which theological existence involved in his day. He affirmed that he took no pleasure in being "dragged into the contest". In describing how it happened he admits that, "The book was hastily written. What the case required, and occurred spontaneously at the time, I dictated without any lengthened meditation and with a feeling so remote from gall that I afterwards wondered how such harsh terms had fallen from me while I had no bitterness in my heart." Yet he had to make his opponent feel that "the defenders of truth were not without sharp weapons".[99]

Westphal in writings which were being circulated had, he felt, degraded the ascension glory of Jesus Christ, and given public insult to the Lord. The honour of God was at stake. The Church was being threatened. Such attacks demanded a response, and the opposition had to be crushed, even ruthlessly. He believed he was justified in treating the enemy "as if they were savage wild beasts".[100]

One of Calvin's statements in defence of his own attitude

---

[97] C. Tr., vol. II, p. 347.

[98] Jean Leclercq has pointed out that writers like St. Bernard who exhibit such contrasts in style belonged to an age which "had not developed the complex personality, in which every psychological reaction interferes immediately with another which tempers and modifies it", *op. cit.*, pp. 137–8.

[99] C. Tr., vol. II, pp. 252, 349. Calvin admitted in his self-revealing letter to Zerkinden that in such writings he had indulged in "harsh forms of expression" . . . "wrung from me against my will", which he attempted to soften, but which his enemies could easily make a parade of. C. L. to Zerkinden, July 4, 1558.

[100] C. L. to Melanchthon, Aug. 3, 1557. Needless to say his opponents were just as savage in their reaction. "Truth is a good dog", said Coleridge, "but beware of barking too close to the heels of an error, lest you get your brains kicked out."

towards Westphal, draws our attention to the fact that the custom of his day allowed a person, when engaged in public controversy, to adopt an approach and style of writing different from that which could be expected of him acting within his purely private affairs. Westphal, he insisted, had entered the public arena in order to challenge the truth. In such an arena, hitting and blood-letting were inevitable. If lions and bears have no right to complain of the public reaction to their savage attacks why should this "delicate little man" himself expect to be treated like a brother when he had dared to start playing the game of tearing up the truth of God in public? "The whole question turns upon this," wrote Calvin, justifying himself — "Did I attempt to avenge a private injury, or was it in defence of a public cause that I strenuously oppose Westphal?"[101]

This statement, we believe, gives us an important clue to understanding why throughout Calvin's whole public career there are episodes in which his behaviour and even his character in private and in public contrast in a way which today we find difficult to understand. Undoubtedly in those days, more decisively than today, a man acting in a public office felt constrained to adopt a role which made him feel in some measure artificial within himself. John Knox, perhaps wistfully, once told Mary Queen of Scots that if she could only have known him as an ordinary "private person" outside the pulpit she would have found no offence in him.[102] Calvin lived under the same felt constraint.

In one of his sermons he points out the "great difference" between the anger that proceeds from godly zeal, and the anger that one is moved to, either on account of his goods or his honour, or for any self-centred cause. For "he that is angry and displeased through a private passion is in no wise to be excused . . . for we are too blind in our own passions. Howbeit there is one anger that is good, namely that which proceeds from grief we conceive when God is offended. Then if we be inflamed with a good zeal to maintain God's quarrel, if we

[101] C. Tr., vol. II, p. 351.
[102] John Knox, *History of the Reformation in Scotland. Works of John Knox*, Edinburgh, 1895, vol. 2, p. 387.

are angry, we are not to blame for it."[103] Obviously the
distinction between public and private behaviour was of
decisive importance to Calvin in determining his conduct. He
tried conscientiously to ensure that in all his private affairs his
conduct was dictated by the rule of love as laid down in the
teaching of Jesus. When people insult us as private persons,
for example, "Love will give every man his best counsel, and
all disputes that go beyond it, we regard as incontrovertibly
unjust and impious."[104] Even in conducting a private law-
suit a Christian in court "must treat his adversary with the
same love and goodwill as if the business under controversy
were already amicably settled and composed".[105]

Calvin believed firmly that it was the Bible itself which set
different standards for public and private behaviour. When
David, for instance, was dealing with his own personal
enemies he "poured forth tears into his bosom for those who
plotted to take his life". But when he fulfilled his public
vocation as a king, God made him act as the minister of his
vengeance. Under such circumstances, "woe to us if we
pretend to excel in sweetness and humanity; him who is the
fountain of pity and mercy!"[106] He noted that as Jeremiah
set about his work as a prophet he had at times to "divest
himself of sympathy" and "rise above all human feelings"
when he remembered he was set "as a judge over the people,
or a herald to announce the final doom".[107] Because he
himself was so conscious of his own "public character" he felt
he had to force himself to do likewise. He noted with some
approval that "Jeremiah when he came out of prison spoke
more boldly" than before. "Courage", he commented,
"increased when one obtains the victory and he can then
securely insult his enemies."[108]

He believed, moreover, that the prime consideration which
must motivate the servant of God within public office or

[103] Cf. *Serm. on Job*, 32:1–3.
[104] *Inst.*, 4:20:21.   [105] *Inst.*, 4:20:18.
[106] See C. Tr., vol. II, pp. 346ff. *Comm. on Ps.*, 18:47 and C. L. to Duchess of
Ferrara, Jan. 24, 1564, who had accused some pastors of passing too severe a
judgment on the Duke of Guise.
[107] *Comm. on Jer.*, 7:16; cf. C. Tr., vol. II, p. 347. cf. Henry, *op. cit.*, I, pp. 292–4.
[108] *Comm. on Jer.*, 20:3.

conflict was holy zeal for the glory of God. "Godly minds", he writes, "are sometimes carried beyond the consideration of men to fix their gaze on the glory of God and the Kingdom of Christ. For to the extent that the glory of God is more excellent than the salvation of men, it ought to ravish us to a corresponding love and regard. Believers earnestly intent on promoting the glory of God, forget men and the world and would rather that the whole world should perish than that any part of God's glory should be lost."[109] It was on this principle that he justified the death of Servetus in Geneva. The man was publicly defrauding God of all his honour. In such a case in order to act with "implacable severity", and entirely banish from his own mind and heart all other considerations. It is not in vain that God "banishes all the human affections that soften our hearts; that he commands paternal love, and all benevolent feelings between brothers, relatives, friends, to cease; in a word that he almost deprives men of their nature in order that nothing hinder the holy zeal".[110]

(D) The Private Man and the Public Image

So wholehearted was Calvin in his commitment to his calling and so completely did he throw himself into the battle for God's honour in the public arena, that the view we have had of him, so far in this book, has therefore tended to give us a picture of him mainly as a public figure. We have not so far needed to say much about the kind of man he was in himself — apart from a few references to his pastoral work, and his relationships with some of his colleagues. If we wish to make any fair assessment, however, of his whole character and attitude, and of the exegesis and thought which led him to adopt the strangely contrasting stances in private and public life which we have just now discussed, it is important that we should know as much as we can about the "private person" he actually was, at home, behind the scenes.

The best and most accurate source for this information is,

109 *Comm. on Gal.*, 5:12.
110 *Refutatio Errorum Michaelis Serveti*, C.O., 8:476.

of course, his letters. The references to his marriage which we find in them, for example, made in an unconscious and attractive way, reveal a warm and simple humanity, the appeal of which must have reached all his neighbours. One notable service the Reformers did for each other in the unique circumstances of their time was to offer mutual help in the choice of wives. Calvin, in the sly banter that entered such correspondence with his friends gave his recipe for his wife: "Always keep in mind what I seek to find in her; for I am none of these insane lovers who embrace also the vices of those they are in love with, where they are smitten at first sight with a fine figure. This only is the beauty which allures me, if she is chaste, if not too nice or fastidious, if economical, if patient, if there is hope that she will not be uninterested about my health."[111] His friends found her for him after at least one false trail. He married Idelette de Bure in 1540 in Strasbourg.

Her homecoming with him was certainly no substitute for the modern honeymoon. Calvin's household then contained his brother Antoine, a friend Claude, two pupils, and a French refugee-house-keeper who herself had a child, and who seems to have been unable to control her tongue. There was a household scene one day. Antoine walked out vowing never to come back till the woman was removed. The woman herself walked out leaving her son behind whom Calvin confessed himself terrified of offending lest he too would walk out and come to some grief. The strain was so much that Calvin took one of those bouts of illness in which he showed such a series of complex symptoms that it is no wonder that Idelette herself took to bed for over a week with a fever becoming "so exhausted by frequent vomitings and otherwise, that she can with difficulty sit up in bed". Calvin's comment in the letter in which he describes all this is illuminating: "It seemed indeed as if it had been so ordered on purpose that our wedlock might not be over joyous, that we might not exceed all bounds, that the Lord has thwarted our joy by moderating it."[112]

Further references in the letters of the Strasbourg period

[111] C. L. to Farel, May 19, 1539   [112] C. L. to Farel, Oct. 1540.

show him torn night and day with tormenting anxiety about whether she was suffering without his help when there was an outbreak of plague during his absence at Ratisbon.[113]

Idelette died on March 29, 1549. Calvin speaks of an incident late in her only pregnancy. When she heard that Ami Porral, Calvin's staunchest and most influential friend in Geneva was on his death bed, she went to him apparently on her own impulse, feeling that God had given her a word to speak to the sick man. It was a bold thing for a woman, especially in her condition, to do in these times. But Calvin expresses pride that Porral told her to be of good courage whatever might happen, that she ought to consider that she had not been rashly led hither, but "brought by the wonderful counsel of God, that she also might serve in the Gospel".[114] Calvin refers to her confinement, simply expressing his distraction of spirit in case she should die, and his feeling with her in her discomfort and pain. His final grief in the death of the infant son is something of which we find an echo years later. Throughout the years 1545 to 1549 there is a series of references in his letters to her failing health, a rejoicing over her temporary recovery, a poignant note of concern and embarrassment to Viret after Idelette visited his wife at Lausanne to assist in the birth of the Viret's child and instead of helping, herself took ill.[115]

There are two letters written from the depth of his grief over her death describing her pain, the last conversation, his death-bed promise to care for her children by the first marriage, his deep gratitude for her. "And truly mine is no common source of grief — I have been bereaved of the best companion of my life, of one who, had it been so ordered, would not only have been a willing sharer in my indigence, but even of my death. During my life she was a faithful helper in my ministry. From her I never experienced the slightest hindrance. She was never troublesome to me throughout the entire course of her illness."[116]

[113] C. L. to Farel, March 28, 1541.
[114] C. L. to Farel, June 16, 1542.   [115] C. L. to Viret, June 15, 1548.
[116] C. L. to Viret, April 7, 1549, C. L. to Farel, April 11, 1549. These references to Calvin and his wife should be read in the light of a remark by P. Hume Brown that

The same sympathy and gratitude constantly marked Calvin's relations with people. Benedict Textor, the family doctor, who had attended his wife throughout her illnesses, would take no payment. Calvin took the opportunity of thanking him by dedicating to him his commentary on Second Thessalonians, with a letter of acknowledgment: "The memory . . . of my departed wife reminds me each day of how much I owe you."

Calvin attracted friends, made warm hearted and very close relationships with them and depended more than most people on their comfort and advice.[117] He shared his mind and feelings most intimately with Farel and Viret, and he dedicated his *Commentary on Titus* to them. "I think there has never been in ordinary life a circle of friends so heartily bound to each other as we have in our ministry." But as the circle of his friendships widened there was not much apparent diminishing of the obvious warmth of his affection. He could hardly endure not having some friend near at hand. He bombarded them with letters; begged to be written to, lived for the replies that came, was elated to receive them, and deeply upset for days if he found in them signs of reproach and misunderstanding. He tended always to turn official relationships with other theologians into personal ones. His correspondence with Melanchthon is warm and intimate, and when Bullinger disagreed with him seriously on the doctrine of election in the Bolsec affair he wrote of his "severe pain" and grief beyond measure at the misunderstanding.[118]

In many of the letters there is chatter about personal and family affairs and frequent enquiries after wives and children. When he hears that Viret might visit him he writes a letter full

---

"in the case of finest spirits of the sixteenth century, we experience a shock at what seems the brutality of their relations to their wives". (He was referring to the re-marriage of Sir Thomas More to his second wife within a month after the death of the first.) *John Knox*, vol. II, p. 201; cf. H. F. Henderson, *Calvin in His Letters*, London, 1909, p. 92.

[117] Cf. Letter to Farel (March 28, 1541) on the death of a very dear friend Claude, where Calvin speaks of "how much I stood in need of an assured and faithful friend who might help to uphold me . . . of a good counsellor always at my side"; cf. C. L. to Nicholas Duchemin, May 14, 1538.

[118] Cf. C. L. to Nicholas Duchemin, May 14, 1538, C. L. to Farel, Feb. 19, 1541, C. L. to Bullinger, Jan. 1552.

of excitement going over the detailed plans for each day of a week's holiday in the country with him. When he is trying to induce de Falais to come and live in Geneva, he mentions a cask of good wine that he is keeping for him to share on the great day when he comes. In congratulating him on the birth of a son, he writes: "I am sorry that I cannot be with you for at least a half of a day, to laugh with you, while we wait for a smile from the little infant, under the penalty of bearing with his cries and tears. For that is the first note, sounded as the key-note, at the beginning of this life — the earnest of a better, that we may smile from the heart when we shall be about to depart from it." After a long letter to Francis Daniel discussing the progress of his son in Geneva, and his possible prospects, he says he is sending "as a kind of New Year's gift" a gold piece to each of his daughters — something he had long proposed to do. He is constantly trying and offering to do things for people — to find Farel a maidservant, de Falais a house. So anxious was he to find Viret a wife that he offered to put the question to the girl on his behalf.[119]

Thus we obtain many glimpses of him as his close neighbours and friends must have seen him. Those who lived at peace around him had no difficulty in coming to know the kind of human being they had in their midst. The doors of his house seem to have been always open to refugees, lodgers, students and visitors. He could claim in public that he was always in the habit of listening to the meanest and most despised of the common people.[120] After many years he began even to feel at home in Geneva and was accepted by most as one of themselves. In 1563 he wrote: "I feel to desire to return to my country. . . Here . . . they deem me no more a foreigner. It is as if my ancestors could be named as citizens of this place."[121]

Calvin himself was well aware of many of the faults which at times spoiled his public witness, and belonged to him as a private person. He was frank about them, especially to his friends. When on his deathbed in his farewell words to the

---

[119] For above cf. C. L. to De Falais, Aug. 16, 1547, C. L. to F. Daniel, Feb. 13, 1560, C. L. to Viret, July 13 and 15, 1546.

[120] C. L. Zerkinden, July 4, 1558.   [121] *Dedication to Comm. on Jeremiah.*

magistrates of Geneva gathered around him, he spoke of "my vices" which "have always displeased me", he was speaking to people who were well aware of the moral struggle he always had with himself. He once expressed from the pulpit his doubt whether a woman would be happy with him. He admitted, in his early days to "rudeness" and "imprudence". If he managed in some degree to cure himself of these, his irritability kept on breaking out and vexing him. He admits in one letter that he had in him a "ferocious wild beast" which he had not yet succeeded in taming.[122]

The weakness of which he was most conscious was his vehemency in self-expression. He believed it was important that we should feel and express anger at times. "I would rather be transported with rage than never be angry at all", he wrote to Nicolas Zerkinden.[123] But he recognised that there should be some moderation set to such expression and we find him constantly trying to keep himself and others from over indulgence in anger and sorrow — since God has given us so many remedies alleviating such excessive sorrows. "I do what I can to keep myself from being overwhelmed", he wrote to Farel after the death of his wife. But he often failed consciously at this point and his letters reveal clearly how much his emotional nature was a problem to himself, especially the unusual intensity of his feelings when he was hurt or frustrated.

One of the occasions of which he was most ashamed came at the climax of the trouble he was involved in with Pierre Caroli. The latter was a doctor of the Sorbonne who had turned Protestant and had lived in Geneva during its Reformation. He had been censured by Farel and Viret because of his lax way of life. He became minister of Neuchatel and Lausanne. He believed in purgatory and in praying for the dead. When his teaching was challenged he attacked the Genevan Reformers on the matter of their orthodoxy accusing them of Arianism. Though his charges

---

[122] *Serm. on 1 Tim.*, 3:1–4. CO 53:255; C. L. to Farel, Oct. 8, 1539; C. L. to Du Tillet, Jan. 31, 1538; cf. P. T. Fuhrmann, *God-centred Religion*, Grand Rapids, 1942. p. 74.
[123] C. L. to Zerkinden, July 4, 1558.

had no foundation he pressed them so aggressively that a Synod was held. In spite of affirmations from those he accused that they held to the Word of God, he demanded that Calvin sign a written declaration subscribing to the three ancient creeds — the Apostle's, the Nicene, and the Athanasian.

Calvin's conviction was that to give such a declaration, under pressure by an individual, would introduce into the Church the kind of tyranny which would expose everyone to the charge of heresy who would not speak in the words or according to the will of another. Caroli had already made his views public. His name was linked in people's minds with dubious doctrines. Had he won his way over the signing of such creeds, outsiders would have believed he was correct also on his views of purgatory etc. Therefore Calvin and his colleagues refused to be dictated to by one whom Calvin himself believed "had no more faith than a dog or a pig".

When Calvin went to Strasbourg, however, his friends Bucer and Sturm received Caroli, and approached Calvin to see whether he would relent in his attitude. At a private meeting they hinted that even Farel had thought Calvin wrong. Calvin in a subsequent letter to Farel describes how suddenly his angry passions were kindled. He told Farel in his letter that if he had been there he would also have poured out on him the same fury as he poured out on the others. We must say in Calvin's favour that his repentance was as deep as his anger had been great. "There I sinned grievously in not having been able to keep within bounds for so had the bile taken entire possession of my mind that I poured out bitterness on all sides." He describes further how "when I got home I was seized with an extraordinary paroxysm, nor did I find any other solace than in sighs and tears".

He himself wisely recognised that when he allowed himself to become upset he became physically ill. A letter to Viret describes how once when he thought someone had stolen some of his papers he worked himself up into such a pitch of distress that he had to stay in bed the next day. He describes in one letter in great detail the prolonged illness that took place after he became upset over a violent quarrel between his brother and his housekeeper. Emotionally disturbed he forced himself to eat the meal his cook had prepared, because he did not wish to offend him into the bargain, and his attempt to eat when he knew he should have fasted made him all the more miserable.[124]

How apparently different from this "private" man was the Calvin who in the midst of Genevan politics tried to gear his conscience to "the duty of my office",[125] and who felt himself so continually constrained to uphold God's honour! Those whom he has reason to regard as God's enemies during his lifetime were bound to be deeply offended by his deliberately adopted strangeness. Matteo Gribaldi an occasional visitor to Geneva whom Calvin knew as an anti-Trinitarian and could not trust, complained that elsewhere in the world he had been politely received by kings and emperors, and yet Calvin had never extended to him the courtesy of an interview. Having consented to meet the man in the presence of others Calvin refused to shake hands with him on the grounds that it would be an empty gesture.[126] Gribaldi left the meeting in anger and disgust. He was finally expelled from Geneva for spreading heresy. It must be admitted, too, that some who disliked Calvin's teaching and ideals felt they had to leave Geneva out of fear.[127]

Those who were publicly repelled were responsible for the rumours about the character of the Reformer which were so vexatious to him. No one has been any more successful in the attempt to clear Calvin's personal reputation than Calvin himself was in his lifetime. Current assessments about his personal character even in otherwise well-informed circles are often false and misleading,[128] and those who disagree

[124] For above see C. L. to Farel, Oct. 8, 1539; J. D. Benoit, "Calvin the Letter-writer" in *John Calvin*, ed. Duffield, Abingdon, 1966, pp. 73–4.

[125] C. L. to the Pastors of Bern, May 1555.

[126] C. L. to Zerkinden, July 4, 1558.

[127] Cf. *ibid*. The physician George Blandatra, one of the anti-Trinitarians in the Church of Geneva, caused a good deal of trouble in the Italian congregation, yet was tolerated, and appealed to in private conferences with Calvin. There was no move on the part of the authorities, however, against him, and Calvin pledged his safety to him, but ultimately after seeing that one of the Syndics was accompanied by an officer at a meeting he himself attended, his suspicions were aroused and he fled from the city.

[128] Cf. "The Calvin Legend" by Basil Hall, in *Calvin*, ed. G. E. Duffield, Abingdon, 1966.

with Calvin's beliefs and aims tend to accept the worst kind of rumour about him.

Any agreed assessment of Calvin's character is made difficult by the fact that Geneva was a very small place, obviously full of gossip. The accounts we have of what went on there have never meant to become the basis for serious historical study, and they are punctuated by ambiguous phrases which can be easily misinterpreted. Opponents of Calvin tend, too often, to read a sinister meaning into phraseology and incidents which can be quite innocent.[129] Moreover the obvious contradictions, and the artificiality sometimes apparent in Calvin's behaviour have made him an open field for psychological speculation.[130]

It must be admitted that at certain points where we find ourselves out of sympathy with Calvin's behaviour, we can find fault with his case. We find special difficulty in accepting his exegesis of the Old Testament passages in which he found justification for his policy towards those whom he believed to be God's enemies. He interprets the command of God to Jeremiah,[131] for example, to cease praying for Jerusalem, as a command to the prophet actually to harden his heart. "Jeremiah", he affirms, "is bidden to divest himself of sympathy so that he might rise above all human feelings."[132] Jeremiah, on the contrary kept firm hold of his feelings. His nearness to God even under God's threatened anger made

---

[129] E.g., the facts that Calvin allowed himself to be called away for a short time from the death-bed of his wife, that he also went apart to pray before her death, and that before she was buried he immersed himself in his work have been marshalled to prove that "her death did not cause him any excessive grief". Jean Schorer, one of Calvin's recent successors in the ministry in Geneva has revealed that at the time Calvin so severely disciplined Pierre Ameaux (see p. 60) he knew that the latter had been instrumental in raising Calvin's house rent and in forcing his removal. He therefore assumes that Calvin was moved by spite and interprets the details of the case accordingly. Calvin's use of the phrase "I fear . . ." to express his concern about the "heavy price" Gruet (see p. 82) might be going to have to pay for his misdeeds (cf. C. L. to De Falais, July 14, 1547) has been interpreted as an expression of desire, indeed of impatience to see the enemy destroyed, etc., etc.

[130] See, e.g., Oskar R. Pfister, *Christianity and Fear*, London, 1948: Erich Fromm, *Fear of Freedom*, London, 1942. Such writers trace what they believe to be Calvin's tyranny to his alleged psychological warpedness and instability. Such studies of course take no account of the unexplainable yet transforming power of a genuine Christian conversion, or of the Word of God.

[131] Cf. *Jer.*, 14:11.   [132] *Comm. in loc.*

him all the more sympathetic and human, and created an almost intolerable inner tension in his life. The public service of God thus became for him simply a tormenting and perplexing passion.

Calvin seems to have forgotten at this point that considerations of humanity need not always be sacrificed in order to maintain the glory of God.[133] We have to move to the New Testament to understand Jeremiah here. The humanity of Jesus was dedicated entirely to the glory of God. Everything therefore that is conformed to the pattern of Jesus' humanity must serve that glory. It was through Jesus' suffering for the sins of those he served, that God was glorified, and God's name is to be glorified today especially through the human suffering of those who are full of zeal for his cause.

Another passage in which we could question too even his New Testament interpretation is Jesus' warning to the disciples about their desire to call fire down from heaven on the village which refused them shelter. Calvin admired greatly the holy zeal with which David and Elijah acted in God's name when they were moved sometimes to destroy the enemies of their faith. Indeed he had no doubt that such Old Testament characters in all their important public actions were moved entirely by the same Spirit as controlled Jesus himself and which breathes through the New Testament. Therefore, it did not occur to him that Elijah's action in calling down fire from heaven to destroy his opponents could be criticised. He believed that when Jesus forbade his disciples to copy Elijah, he was in no way criticising the prophet. He was simply warning the disciples that they themselves were tending to "rush into vengeance, not by the command of God but by the movement of the flesh".[134] This interpretation seems to savour of the subtlety which Calvin so often, it must be admitted, tried to avoid. Was he fully aware

---

[133] Cf. his touching letter written in April 1541 to grief-stricken Monsieur de Richebourg urging him to "shed those tears which are due to nature". "Nor", he added, "in the school of Christ, do we learn any such philosophy as requires us to put off that common humanity with which God has endowed us, that, being men, we should be turned into stones." Here in his pastoral ministry Calvin has become the "private man" again!

[134] *Comm. on Luke*, 9:54–5.

of the dangers of allowing himself to become so moved by the occasion before him, and by the impulse that came to him? "The heart is deceitful above all things, and desperately corrupt," wrote Jeremiah, himself "who can understand it?[135] Did Calvin ever really know his own heart well enough to be certain of the spirit he was moved by in the case of Servetus?

In making a final judgment about Calvin, however, we have to remember not only the critical situation he faced in Geneva, but the limitations imposed on him by the times in which he lived and the nature of the religious experience which he shared with his contemporaries in the Reformed Church. His theology, we believe, was a theology in transition. He himself was well aware that the theology of the future Church, in the light of God's Word would say more things than were in his *Institutes*, and might find better ways of putting them. Moreover, at the Reformation it was the whole Scripture in its undoubted unity of witness and inspiration which had such a powerful effect on the minds and hearts of those who heard and read it that it was much more difficult for them within the life-time of their generation to become fully aware of how far and at what points exactly the Old Testament must be criticised and its message modified by the New. Calvin himself was a pioneer in this critical work. Though he wrote most acutely and helpfully on the relationship of the Old and New Testaments, however, and tried with great care theoretically to define the differences between them it seems obvious that in his practical application of his principles he at times failed.

We have tried to show in this work that Calvin's mind was open to the whole message of the Word of God, and that in response to it he tried also to preserve every aspect of a truly Catholic tradition in theology, liturgy and ethics. The breadth of his spirituality, his concerns and programmes, coupled with his shrewd wisdom prevented him from ever becoming fanatically enslaved to any one idea, principle, or aspect of the truth. What was negative about him was simply the other side of what was essentially positive, what

[135] *Jer.*, 17:9.

was judgmental was never allowed to obscure what was evangelical and liberating.

Moreover, in spite of his faults, there is a basic and impressive consistency which runs through everything we read about the man, his work and thought. We cannot doubt the genuineness of his religious experience. It could be said of him what was once said of Cromwell: "He was penetrated to the very core of his being by the thought that God was near to him guiding him, and ordering him and the affairs concerning him".[136] He dealt honestly with his conscience and kept it always open before God himself. This is why he could claim for himself "the guileless uprightness and innocence before God" of which he found so much mention in the Psalms, and which he believed every believer should cultivate and hold on to,[137] and this was the reason why he felt himself "approved of God and the angels".[138] He lived as he prayed, to be able to live, and as he always tried to teach others to live.[139] His life was open before other people. He wrote to his avowed worst enemy in the city challenging him to examine his whole life and work, and affirming that such a scrutiny would yield nothing but a proof of his integrity: "You yourself know . . . that I am one, to whom the law of my Heavenly Master is so dear that the cause of no man on earth will induce me to flinch from maintaining it with a pure conscience."[140]

Even at those points at which we are today most prone to censure him, he makes us somewhat uncomfortable in our criticism. Indeed, he reminds us of aspects of the faith, of which, if our desire is to live the Christian life in its fullness, it is difficult to deny our lack. We may question his unwillingness at times to accept compromise, and the readiness with which he divided the people around him into two opposing

---

[136] John Tulloch, *English Puritanism and its Leaders*, Edinburgh, 1861, p. 158. Tulloch insists that in the face of Cromwell's self-testimony in his letters, to suppose that he was a hypocrite "involves a series of suppositions so incredible as to compel every candid student to part with" the suggestion (*ibid.*, p. 156). The same observation holds with Calvin.

[137] *Inst.*, 3:20:10, *Comm. on Ps.*, 31:20; cf. F. Busser, *op. cit.*, pp. 40, 59–60.

[138] C. L. to Farel, Oct. 10, 1555.

[139] C. L. to Zerkinden, July 4, 1556; cf. F. Busser, *op. cit.*, pp. 20–2.

[140] C. L. to Ami Perrin, April, 1546.

camps. But we ourselves in a world in which many of the powerful currents of life are running counter to the Gospel, and where so many are deliberately adopting a life-style alien to what is Christian, have to face the question of how long we can continue to aim at peaceable and friendly co-operation. We may well question his insistence that zeal for the glory of God should be always our first thought and aim, even when the pursuit of it seems to lead us to deny considerations of humanity, but we have to ask ourselves whether with a more modern version of the Gospel we have not drifted into a deadly smugness. That we lack today anything that corresponds to his "holy zeal" may indeed indicate our greatest fault. We must admit that Calvin applied it meticulously to the discipline of his own personal life before he ever sought to allow it to mark his public "character". It may be that today one of our first needs is to discover what "holiness" and "discipline", two of his central ideas, mean as counterparts and aspects of the "love" which we all agree is central to the Gospel. Only a disciplined Church under a disciplined leadership can survive and meet the challenge of our times. Our judgment of him must at least take account of his extraordinary achievements which can only, with fairness, be attributed to divine blessing and providence. Even in 1550 when otherwise circumstances were very adverse, he could write, as Athanasius did in his day, of those "whose wonderful conversion does honour to our gospel". Of "the magnificent triumph of our teaching", of "men who had previously been devoted to intemperance, licentious practices, unchastity, and shows of the world, avarice, and robbery, now converted to sobriety, chastity, unassuming behaviour, and fair dealing".[141]

Calvin died on May 27, 1564. He was buried in the common cemetery, his grave surrounded by crowds of citizens and visitors, but as he had ordered there was no pomp and no gravestone set up. His death proved how little he had cared for wealth, for he left very little. At the end of his *Life of*

---

[141] *Concerning Scandals*, Edinburgh, 1978, p. 88; cf. Athanasius, *On the Incarnation of the Word of God*, trs. C.S.M.V.S.Th., London, 1944, §§51–5.

Calvin, Beza wrote: "Having been a spectator of his conduct for sixteen years . . . I can now declare, that in him all men may see a most beautiful example of the Christian character, an example which it is as easy to slander as it is difficult to imitate."

SUBJECT INDEX

INDEX OF NAMES